Dining Room Detectives

Dining Room Detectives:

Analysing Food in the Novels of Agatha Christie

By

Silvia Baučeková

Cambridge Scholars Publishing

Dining Room Detectives: Analysing Food in the Novels of Agatha Christie

By Silvia Baučeková

This book first published 2015

Cambridge Scholars Publishing

Lady Stephenson Library, Newcastle upon Tyne, NE6 2PA, UK

British Library Cataloguing in Publication Data
A catalogue record for this book is available from the British Library

ISBN (10): 1-4438-7762-X
ISBN (13): 978-1-4438-7762-6

TABLE OF CONTENTS

ACKNOWLEDGEMENTS

Firstly, I would like to thank doc. Mgr. Slávka Tomaščíková, PhD. for giving me the opportunity to complete my doctoral research and to spend a considerable period of my studies abroad; and prof. Nieves Pascual Soler for her invaluable guidance and support, without which I would never have been able to complete the present work. Secondly, I would like to thank my colleagues, especially Mária, Veronika, and Silvia, for always being willing to discuss any problems that came up, give useful feedback, and share tips. I would also like to express my gratitude to my proofreader Mr Gavin Cowper for his excellent and efficient work, as well as to Mr Sam Baker, my editor at Cambridge Scholars Publishing, for his patience and willingness to answer my incessant newbie questions. Finally, I would like to thank my family for their patience and encouragement throughout the whole writing process.

INTRODUCTION

Hercule Poirot was sitting at the breakfast table. At his right hand was a steaming cup of chocolate.

He had always had a sweet tooth. To accompany the chocolate was a brioche. It went agreeably with chocolate.

He nodded his approval. This was from the fourth shop he had tried. It was a Danish patisserie but infinitely superior to the so-called French one near by. That had been nothing less than a fraud.

He was satisfied gastronomically. His stomach was at peace. His mind also was at peace, perhaps somewhat too much so.

[...] The truth of the matter was, he was bored. All this strenuous mental activity in which he had been indulging—there had been too much of it. It had got him into bad habits, it had made him restless.

Vexatious! He shook his head and took another sip of chocolate.

(*Third Girl*, 7-8)

Gerda lifted a teacup and drank.

"It is all so very worrying. Everything is so worrying . . . You see, John always arranged everything and now John is gone . . ." Her voice tailed off. "Now John is gone . . ."

Her gaze, piteous, bewildered, went from one to the other.

[...]

Gerda leaned back in her chair. Her lips were very blue. She said stiffly: "I feel—not very well—if John—John—"

Poirot came round the table to her and eased her sideways down the chair. Her head dropped forward. He bent and lifted her eyelid. Then he straightened up. "An easy and comparatively painless death."

Henrietta stared at him. "Heart? No." Her mind leaped forward. "Something in the tea . . . Something she put there herself. She chose the way out?"

Poirot shook his head gently. "Oh, no, it was meant for you. It was in your teacup." (*The Hollow*, 287-288)

"I was thinking of when my mother died. I was five I think. Five or six. I was having dinner in the nursery, jam roll pudding. I was very fond of jam roll pudding. One of the servants came in and said to my nursery governess, 'Isn't it awful? There's been an accident and Mrs Craddock has been killed.' . . . Whenever I think of my mother's death, d'you know what I see?"

"What?"

> "A plate with jam roll pudding on it, and I'm staring at it. Staring at it and I can see as well now as then, how the jam oozed out of it at one side. I didn't cry or say anything. I remember just sitting there as though I'd been frozen stiff, staring at the pudding. And d'you know, even now if I see in a shop or a restaurant or in anyone's house a portion of jam roll pudding, a whole wave of horror and misery and despair comes over me."
> (*The Mirror Crack'd from Side to Side*, 309)

In order to live, humans need to eat. This need to eat is so self-evident and the everyday presence of meals in our lives is so much taken for granted that it might seem somewhat pointless to discuss whether or not food is important in human life. It is understood as omnipresent and essential. However, a less obvious aspect of the presence of food in life is the role which it plays in literature in general, and in crime fiction and the novels of Agatha Christie in particular. Firstly, it is necessary to ask whether food is in fact present in crime fiction, and, if so, why focus on it? Is it of any importance whatsoever? What function does it serve in the texts in question?

The answer to the first of these questions is most definitely yes, as the introductory examples illustrate. In fact, when reading through the novels, I discovered that Agatha Christie mentioned food multiple times in every single novel. Hercule Poirot, Christie's most famous detective, can frequently be observed sipping his cup of chocolate, and Miss Marple, another of the author's fictional sleuths, performs a great deal of her investigative work over the course of afternoon teas. Christie's minor characters are also often found sitting around the breakfast or dinner table, and regularly throw cocktail parties, visit restaurants, or reminiscence about the foods of their childhood.[1] Furthermore, Christie, who shared her fictional detectives' distaste for aggression, blood and violence, employed fast acting and relatively painless poisons as her criminals' weapon of choice in the overwhelming majority of her stories (Acocella 2010). And with this use of poison, food and drink enter the crime novel once again. After all, where better to conceal a deadly dose of morphine or arsenic than in a nice warm cup of tea or in a piece of cream cake?

Paradoxically, because food is such a basic, unavoidable part of life, it is often overlooked in analyses of fiction, as depictions of characters eating can seem obvious and natural enough. Yet in this book, food and eating are understood as anything but obvious and natural. The book examines how references to various meals and drinks contribute to the effect of the crime novels of Agatha Christie. It aims to show how depictions of food are used to influence or construct characters, plots, or settings and serve as literary devices; it also intends to examine how the author uses them to tackle issues of identity, crime, or memory. In other words, I aim to answer the three questions listed in the first paragraph of this introduction by proving that the presence of food in Christie's novels is not merely a consequence of the characters' need for food. Instead, it is assumed that food plays a more crucial role, and an attempt is made to explain the nature of this role (or these roles). However, it is first necessary to introduce the figure who occupies an equally crucial place in the analysis and that is Agatha Christie herself.

The Protagonist: Dame Agatha Christie

Dame Agatha Christie was born on September 15, 1890 as Agatha Mary Clarissa Miller to Clara and Frederick Miller. Agatha had two elder siblings, Madge and Monty (Akersten 2010, 16). The family lived in Ashfield, a large Victoria villa (Dorn 1997, 50) in the coastal town of Torquay, Devon. Agatha was a solitary child. She was much younger than her two siblings and was home-schooled, an experience which deprived her of the opportunity to meet other children of her age (Acocella 2010). When she was five years old, her father lost his income and, because members of the upper classes such as himself were not prepared for regular employment, he was unable to find a job. He died at the age of fifty-five, leaving Agatha in the care of her mother.

Agatha got married for the first time at the beginning of World War One at the age of twenty-four (Acocella 2010). Her husband, Colonel Archibald Christie (Dorn 1997, 50), was a member of the Royal Flying Corps. During the war he served on the Western Front, while Agatha worked in the dispensary of a war hospital in her hometown. After the war the couple moved to London and had one child together—a daughter called Rosalind. It was during this time in London that Christie first began writing fiction (Acocella 2010). Her "experiences in a World War One dispensary [...] gave her a working knowledge of poisons," which she made use of when constructing her first detective plots (Mills and Waites 2008).

After the death of her mother in 1926, Agatha moved back to her parents' house "to ready it for sale." During this period, her husband informed her of his relationship with an acquaintance, Nancy Neele, and filed for divorce. A couple of months later Agatha disappeared from her home, and was only discovered a number of days later by the police. For the rest of her life, Christie refused to explain both the reason for her disappearance, and the exact circumstances of the event. However, as the event coincided with one of Christie's major professional successes—the publication of *The Murder of Roger Ackroyd* (1926), it led to a great amount of public attention for both Christie and her writing, and helped to establish her as a prominent figure on the British literary scene (Acocella 2010).

In 1930, Christie remarried. Her second husband, Max Mallowan, was an archaeologist (Dorn 1997, 50). Accompanying him to the sites of excavations, Christie undertook a number of journeys to the Middle East and these visits are reflected in the choice of settings for several of her novels (e.g. *Murder in Mesopotamia*; *Appointment with Death*, *Death on the Nile*) (Akersten 2010, 15). However, despite her success as a writer, Christie reminisced in her *An Autobiography* ([1977] 2011) that she never considered herself a professional author. She wrote: "I was a married woman, that was my status, and that was my occupation. As a sideline, I wrote books. I never approached my writing by dubbing it with the grand name of 'career'. I would have thought it ridiculous" (430).

Despite this belief on her part, Christie's writing definitely became a career and she became a best-selling author, publishing over eighty books in her lifetime ("Dame Agatha Christie" 2013); to date, approximately two billion copies of her works have been sold worldwide (Akersten 2010, 15). Indeed, Christie's profits were such that she was able to support her family members, as well as various charities by donating the rights to her stories or theatre plays (Christie [1977] 2011, 512-513). Moreover, as a member and, from 1958, also the president of the Detection Club (Keating n.d.), Christie not only wrote crime stories, but was also actively involved in forming what would later become known as the Golden Age of detective fiction, a literary movement in its own right (see below). At the end of her life, Christie moved to Wallingford, a historic town in the vicinity of Oxford, where she died on January 12, 1976. She is buried at Cholsey (Dorn 1997, 50).

Christie "began publishing detective fiction thirty-three years after [Sir Arthur] Conan Doyle" and to some extent her work draws on Conan Doyle's heritage through themes such as "the small place, the interrogations, [and] the revelation" (Acocella 2010). Her first attempt at composing a detective story dates back to 1915 and was prompted by "a challenge by her sister Madge." The novel was rejected by three publishers before it was finally published in 1921 as *The Mysterious Affair at Styles* (Dorn 1997, 50). Between *The Mysterious Affair at Styles* and *Curtain: Poirot's Last Case*, Christie published over sixty detective novels (Carter and McRae 2001, 368). A number of these form part of one of her three major series: the Poirot mysteries, the Miss Marple mysteries, and the Tommy and Tuppence series. Poirot is by far the most frequently occurring of her detectives, and his crime-solving career spans thirty-three novels and fifty-one short stories ("Zabila som Poirota, vážení!" 2013, 6). Christie's second most popular detective, Miss Marple, appears in twelve novels and twenty short stories (7).

The "dapper, meticulous, diminutive Belgian detective, Hercule Poirot" first entered the scene in Christie's very first novel, *The Mysterious Affair at Styles* (Dorn 1997, 50). Poirot is a former member of the Belgian police force who left his home country as a war refugee (Dorn 1997, 50) and who has now established himself in Britain as a private investigator. He is depicted as a typical eccentric detective, who

> dyes his hair, [...] smokes thin, black Russian cigarettes, often regarded with alarm by those to whom he offers them; he wears pointy patent-leather shoes ill-suited to walking the grounds of the country houses where he must often do his sleuthing. He deplores the English preference for fresh air, thin women, and tea. Poirot says that, in interrogations, he always exaggerates his foreignness. The person being questioned then takes him less seriously, and in consequence tells him more. His Franglais is a treat. "I speak the English very well," he says proudly. (Acocella 2010)

The Poirot series ends with *Curtain*, which is also the last of Christie's novels to be published in her lifetime (Carter and McRae 2001, 368). Both the first and the last novel focus on the motifs pervading the whole series: "the bond between Poirot and Hastings; Poirot's commitment to carrying out justice, sometimes in unconventional ways; and his interest in promoting romance." Although Hastings is not present in all of the Poirot mysteries, he re-emerges time and time again and also plays a part in the very last novel, *Curtain* (Knepper 2005, 75).

Miss Marple was first introduced to readers in a series of short stories which were later published collectively as *The Thirteen Problems* (1932) (Knepper 2005, 78). The first novel in the Marple series, *The Murder at the Vicarage*, was published in 1930 (Dorn 1997, 50). The Marple series is characterised by the frequent employment of the "garden motif," but also by its "emphasis on evil, and the emphasis on illicit love." Christie ties the two together by drawing symbols of evil "from plant and garden lore" (Knepper 2005, 74). Miss Marple is as eccentric and memorable as Poirot, although in a different way: "her benign countenance, fragility, and Victorian attire" (78) are placed in marked opposition to her inborn instinct for discovering evil, "her tendency to think the worst of human nature, and her unshockability. Her nephew Raymond, a city sophisticate, is naïveté itself in comparison to his old aunt who lives quietly in a country village and misses nothing that happens there" (79). Marple is frequently described as "determined," or even "ruthless" (78) and carries out a strict surveillance over the other inhabitants of her home village, St. Mary's Mead. She is not officially allowed to interrogate, as she is neither a policewoman nor a detective; nevertheless, she is always able to gather the information she needs. She blends in perfectly with the environment and can thus observe events unnoticed; moreover she is not averse to being nosy, or even to "snooping" (Acocella 2010).

The third of Christie's series, the Tommy and Tuppence series, differs from the previous two in that it features not one detective, but instead two cooperating investigators, a pair of friends (later husband and wife) Tommy and Tuppence. This series exhibits traits of the adventure novel and thriller genres to a much greater extent than the other two. The first Tommy and Tuppence novel, *The Secret Adversary*, was published in 1922. In this novel the two protagonists meet in London after they have finished service in the war and make plans to "establish themselves economically and find adventures in the postwar world." Their plans, of course, involve solving mysteries, uncovering spies, and catching criminals (Knepper 2005, 76).

> This first Tommy and Tuppence thriller expresses the high spirits of young people in love and combines the talents of the impulsive, brilliant, theatrical Tuppence with the dogged tenaciousness and common sense of Tommy. In the later Tommy and Tuppence spy-chasing novels, their marriage evolves over time. The couple have children; worry about those grown-up children during World War II; and chafe at the perception of their children and the government that they are over the hill, too old to ferret out spies and solve mysteries. As an older couple, they deal with the discomforts of aging and enjoy the satisfying companionship found in a long-term marriage. (76-77)

Another notable recurring character in Christie's works is the crime author Ariadne Oliver, a character who is based to a certain extent on Agatha Christie herself. Mrs Oliver solves crimes together with Poirot, replacing the faithful Captain Hastings in a number of novels. She first appears in *Cards on the Table* (1936), where she was portrayed as the impulsive and energetic opposite of the orderly and passive Poirot. However, Christie also used Oliver to voice some of her ideas about writing detective stories and about the lifestyles of popular authors. The last novel featuring Mrs Oliver is *Elephants Can Remember* (Knepper 2005, 76), published in 1972 (69).

Christie was an extremely productive writer, and throughout her career she wrote over eighty books ("Dame Agatha Christie" 2013). In addition to the detective novel series, Christie wrote numerous stand-alone crime novels (*Why Didn't They Ask Evans?*; *The Pale Horse*), spy novels (*Passenger to Frankfurt*), and thrillers (*They Came to Baghdad*). She also wrote six romance novels under the pen name Mary Westmacott (Akersten 2010, 16).

In addition to fiction, Christie also wrote drama. In her autobiography, she explained her decision to become a playwright as a reaction to unsuccessful co-operations with other authors who wished to adapt her novels for the stage. As an example she mentioned *The Murder of Roger Ackroyd*, which had been turned into a play under the title *Alibi*. She recalled disliking the ideas of the dramatist, who wished to "take about 20 years off Poirot's age, call him Beau Poirot, have lots of girls in love with him and give him a strong love interest" (Christie 2010). The first of Christie's plays was *The Mousetrap*, which was originally broadcast on BBC radio as *Three Blind Mice* (510). The radio play was commissioned as a birthday present for Queen Mary, but it was later prolonged and adapted for stage production. It was performed for the first time on November 25, 1952 at the Ambassadors Theatre (Dorn 1997, 50) with Richard Attenborough and Sheila Sim as the lead actors (Christie 2011, 512). In 1974 the play was moved to St. Martin's Theatre where it is still performed today (Dorn 1997, 50), making it one of the longest-running plays in the history of theatre ("Dame Agatha Christie" 2013). Another of Christie's famous plays is *Witness for The Prosecution* (1948), "which won the New York Drama Critics' Award for Best Foreign Play of 1954" (Dorn 1997, 50).

In 1971 Christie was awarded the title of Dame Commander, Order of the British Empire ("Dame Agatha Christie" 2013) and in 1977 she published her autobiography (Christie 2010, 28). In the meantime, other authors started to write about Christie or produce their own adaptations of her work. A number of her plays were turned into novels by Charles Osborne (e.g. *Black Coffee* in 1998) and many of her works were adapted for television. Poirot has been played by various actors, most notably by David Suchet, who has played the role in adaptations of all but one of the Poirot stories ("Zabila som Poirota, vážení!" 2013, 7).

Books about Christie abound too. A number of authorised, as well as unauthorised biographies emerged, such as *Duchess of Death: The Unauthorized Biography of Agatha Christie* (2009) by Richard Hack or *Agatha Christie's Secret Notebooks: Fifty Years of Mysteries in the Making* (2011) by John Curran. The notebooks contain excerpts from seventy-three of the author's journals with notes, unused material, illustrations and two Poirot stories which were not published during the author's life. However, there is a relative lack of recorded material featuring Christie herself, as the writer "valued her privacy and rarely granted interviews" (Dorn 1997, 50). Two of the rare recordings of the author's voice include "a 1955 interview for the BBC and a 1974 recording for the Imperial War Museum Sound Archive." Because of this reluctance to speak about herself, much of Christie's life remains as mysterious as her plots, attracting the attention and stirring the imagination of fans, and thus further increasing the famous writer's appeal (Mills and Waites 2008).

Christie is frequently nicknamed the "Queen of Crime," and indeed, she remains the most successful of all of the Golden Age crime authors and the most widely read crime author of all time (Carter and McRae 2001, 368). Her novels have been translated into an estimated forty-five languages (Acocella 2010) and, according to the Guinness Book of World Records, only the works of William Shakespeare and the Bible have bested her in terms of the number of copies sold (Knepper 2005, 70). Moreover, Christie's work is accessible even to those who have not read her books in the form of numerous TV adaptations (71).

Christie was a typical Golden Age author, but she also had no qualms about breaking the rules which she had helped to set up—a technique which kept her audience interested and attracted more and more readers. Indeed, one of the factors determining the selection of Christie as the author to be analysed was her huge readership. Christie's overwhelming and lasting popularity invites scholarly interest, as one cannot help but be intrigued by the secret of her success. Another reason which led me to choose to focus on Christie was that she was a female writer. As will be explained later on, the beginning of the twentieth century was characterised by a rapid feminisation of the crime fiction genre: as the audience became predominately female, more and more female authors began to be published, and even the formula of the crime novel itself was changed to reflect the concerns of its female authors and readers (see 1.1.4; 1.2.3). As I concentrated on the place of food, which is traditionally understood as a feminine pursuit (see chapter two), in the detective novel, I found it especially interesting to see how a female crime writer treated such a "feminine" topic in her novels. The following section lists additional information on the choice of specific texts for the analysis, the methods employed, and the hypotheses set up before tackling the analysis itself.

The Analysis: Food in Crime Fiction

The detective story is now a well-established literary genre with a history dating back to the nineteenth century and the writings of Edgar Allan Poe. As such, it has received a considerable amount of critical and academic interest, both from the crime authors themselves (E.A. Poe, Dorothy L. Sayers, G.K. Chesterton, etc.) and from literary critics and scholars. At the beginning of the twentieth century, during what is now known as the Golden Age of detective fiction, more authors began publishing crime stories than ever before, and the genre began to attract the attention of structuralist literary critics, such Tzvetan Todorov or John Cawelti, who pointed out the formulaic nature of popular genre literature (see chapter one). Crime authors themselves claimed to write their stories following strict rules, creating puzzles governed by set principles. Therefore, a structuralist methodology would appear to be highly suitable for the analysis of detective novels, especially those of the Golden Age period, and that is the reason why this approach is also adopted in this book.

Although a number of scholars have already tackled the issue of the detective novel, much less attention has been focused on the issue of food in literature in general, and even less on food in crime fiction.[2] The structuralist understanding of food is that it is socially and culturally significant and not merely a result of necessity and economy (see 2.1), and this belief informs the analysis to a great extent. However, the structuralist approach alone did not prove sufficient to explain the phenomenon of food as a literary device in crime fiction. Therefore this book adopts a more eclectic approach, combining structuralism with other schools of thought such as feminism, phenomenology, or psychoanalytic theory, and incorporating notions of identity, class, and nation as understood in the field of cultural studies, in an attempt to account for the various occurrences and functions of food which can be found in the analysed texts.

In the process of writing this book, I have been frequently asked by colleagues and friends who were familiar with the topic of my research whether there is any connection between food and crime fiction, whether I could find any references to food in these texts, and, in general, what the point of studying food in literature was. Even the most cursory reading of Christie's novels can show without a doubt that there is food in crime fiction, and that there is plenty of it. Characters eat, entertain each other at dinners, and take care of, feed and poison each other with food. However, the question remains of why food is so closely tied up with crime.

Some possible answers to this question are delineated in section 2.4.1. However, at this point I would like to draw attention to two striking parallels between cooking and crime novels. Firstly, my analysis takes as its starting point the structuralist understanding of crime fiction as a formula, i.e. the text as a whole composed of prescribed ingredients according to a set of established rules. It is interesting to note that the same definition applies to the process of cooking a meal according to a recipe: there also is a list of necessary ingredients and certain methods which must be applied in order to create the final dish. Thus the classical detective formula can be understood as a recipe according to which authors, including Agatha Christie, cook up the meals which they serve to their readers: the murder mysteries.

Secondly, crime fiction and food share the paradoxical connection of pleasure and death. This connection is, in fact, the driving force of the crime novel: the reader is entertained and given a pleasant frisson of excitement by reading about murder. In this respect, the act of eating is strikingly similar; when one eats, one can enjoy the delicious tastes and smells of food and the subsequent pleasure of being sated, but at the same time the act of eating necessarily implies death, whether that be the death of the vegetable or animal one is eating, or the potential threat of death as a result of consuming spoilt, poisonous, or infected foods.

Thus, the hypothesis which has been set up on the basis of the above described parallels, and which represents the driving force behind the analysis of the novels, is essentially that food does not appear in Agatha Christie's novels by mere coincidence. On the contrary, it is assumed that Christie deliberately used food as a literary device, employing it in characterisation, as a tool for constructing plots and in depictions of settings. Moreover, food also serves as a means of destabilising the accepted rules and characteristics of the genre of classical detective fiction, as well as of satirising, or even directly questioning, established notions and stereotypes in society as a whole. By choosing food as the primary concern, I intend to focus on the trend of feminisation of the crime formula which took place at the beginning of the twentieth century. Throughout the analysis I argue that the reason why Christie made use of food references and food imagery so frequently was that thanks to its strong association with women, femininity and domesticity, food enabled her to feminise an otherwise inherently masculine form of writing: the detective story.

By conducting this analysis I hope to expand contemporary Christie scholarship and offer a new, alternative way of analysing literary formulas. Throughout the writing of this book, I have discovered that food has for the most part been ignored by academics in the field of humanities in the Central European context. Therefore, this work would like to bring both food in a general sense and also food as a specific method in the study of literature to attention as topics for academic discussion.

For reasons which were outlined above, the scope of this analysis is limited to only one author, Agatha Christie, but this focus is also limited to only one part of her work, her novels. The decision to focus on Christie's novels rather than on her short stories or her plays was made for two reasons. Firstly, a novel typically places much more emphasis on details than shorter texts and thus offers more space for descriptions of habits, background, characters and, consequently, of food. The length of a novel allows the author more opportunities to employ food as a device of characterisation, description, or as a means of social commentary. The second reason for choosing novels over short stories and plays is connected to changes in the format of crime writing which occurred during the Golden Age period. At the end of the nineteenth century, in the time of Sir Arthur Conan Doyle, the short story was the most typical format for murder mysteries. However, as will be explained in 1.2.1, the more intricate plots and murder mysteries which emerged during the Golden Age demanded more space than was granted by the couple of pages typically covered by a short story, and so the novel became the predominate format in crime fiction. The novel form, like a number of other inventions of the Golden Age of crime fiction, remains characteristic of the detective genre to the present day.

The Setting: The Golden Age

The beginning of the twentieth century saw a rapid rise in the popularity of genre fiction. The by then well-established adventure novel now tackled new, contemporary themes, especially that of "world-domination" with its "threat of chaos and disintegration of the world." In addition, new genres started to compete with the adventure novel for readership. The most notable of these was the "mainstay of twentieth-century fiction"—the spy novel, written by authors such as Baroness Orczy (*The Scarlet Pimpernel*, 1905), Erskine Childers (*The Riddle of the Sands*, 1903), John Le Carré (*The Spy Who Came in from the Cold*, 1963), and Ian Fleming, the creator of the notorious James Bond (Carter and McRae 2001, 367).

However, while spy novels, thrillers and adventure stories were certainly popular at the time, no other genre reached such high levels of readership as the detective novel (368), and the era between the two world wars is therefore labelled the Golden Age of crime fiction. Not only professional writers, but also various intellectuals, theologians, and many others, including C. Day-Lewis, T.S. Eliot and S. S. Van Dine, an expert on Nietzsche, tried their hands at writing crime fiction (Acocella 2010). Moreover, in the 1920s and 1930s various technological developments in the fields of publishing and advertising enabled the rapid printing and distribution of a large amount of cheap books to a rapidly growing reading public. New marketing strategies, such as the sale of books through book clubs or the publishing of books with special features (e.g. books with the last chapter sealed, in order not to reveal the mystery) were designed to further increase sales (Panek 1987, 120-121). But while these techniques did lead to an explosion in the readership of detective novels and a consequent dramatic rise in the number of novels written and published, some authors feared that the massive expansion would result in a general decrease in the quality of published stories, and thereby lead to the loss of the middle-brow status that the detective story had hitherto enjoyed (122).

In order to ensure the quality and purity of the genre, a number of influential writers formed a community which set itself the task of establishing rules for writing high-quality detective fiction. Golden Age detective fiction thereby ceased to be merely one of a number of popular fiction genres, but instead developed into a literary movement in its own right, with manifestoes, critics, and its own canon. All of these developments were embodied in the official organisation of Golden Age crime fiction, the Detection Club, founded in 1928 by Anthony Berkeley Cox. The Club united some of the most prominent crime authors of the era, including Agatha Christie, Dorothy L. Sayers, the creator of the aristocratic sleuth Lord Peter Wimsey (*Murder Must Advertise*, 1933; *The Nine Tailors*, 1934), and religious figures-cum-authors such as the Roman Catholic priest Ronald Knox and the theologian G. K. Chesterton (Acocella 2010). These people worked together to establish a specific "code of ethics," which later came to be known as the Ten Commandments of crime fiction. These rules were meant to ensure that all stories written according to them met the standards of a "good" detective novel, but they also sought to guarantee that the author "played fair" with the reader, meaning that she or he provided all of the clues necessary for the reader to uncover the criminal themselves (Akersten 2010, 15).

Nevertheless, the Club did not only strictly enforce rules and determine which works were worthy of the status of a detective novel. On the contrary, the group was characterised by a certain playfulness and spirit of conviviality which is manifest in their collaborative efforts, such as *The Floating Admiral* ([1931] 2011), a novel to which each member contributed one chapter (Panek 1987, 122). In other words, while the Detection Club writers took the detective genre extremely seriously and worked to set up strict rules, trace the history of the genre and protect its status as middlebrow fiction, they also understood the detective novel as a game, a puzzle (123). Furthermore, while these authors take great pains to establish that their works are true to life, filling the novels with references to real crimes and technical information from the field of criminology, the books are also full of allusions to other literary works and references to the writing process and to the fictional nature of the texts. This intermingling of the playful and serious and of the real and imaginary permeates Golden Age detective fiction (Panek 1987, 124, see also section 1.1.1).

It is also important to note that although classical or Golden Age detective fiction sprang from the roots planted by Edgar Allan Poe and Sir Arthur Conan Doyle in the nineteenth century, a number of changes and developments took place in this period. Firstly, classical authors abandoned the short story form in favour of the novel. This development brought about new challenges, and forced authors to look for new ways of revealing clues to the reader whilst concealing the solution over the course of an entire novel. As a response to this challenge, writers began to experiment with narration and point of view, often adopting the techniques of a third-person narrator or multiple narrators, which were first introduced into the crime genre by Wilkie Collins (Panek 1987, 131-132). Authors frequently borrowed elements from suspenseful genres such as the thriller to add pace and interest to their detective stories (135). Finally, another important trend observed during the Golden Age period was that of the rising dominance of women readers and authors, a development which led to a gradual feminisation of the genre and to repeated attempts to introduce a female detective to the genre (Panek 1987, 128, see also section 1.1.4).

Although, as LeRoy Panek put it, the Golden Age eventually ended after World War Two and the spotlight passed to thrillers and novels of suspense featuring "master criminals without sane motives loos[ing] mass destruction on humanity," rather than a "murder at the garden party" (142), some of the developments of the era, such as the use of the novel form or the manipulation of points of view, have featured in crime fiction until the present day. Moreover, even today some authors work in the Golden Age style, creating novels which are now known as "cosy mysteries," i.e. stories where the victim and the criminal are members of a close-knit group of friends or of a family, which suddenly becomes "too cozy for comfort" (Akersten 2010, 15).

The previous paragraphs have attempted to provide a very brief introduction to the topic of Agatha Christie and the Golden Age of detective fiction, and also to suggest the idea of food as a variable in crime fiction. All of these points are elaborated in further detail in the individual chapters. The text is organised into two main sections: the first and second chapter present the theoretical background, introduce main concepts and provide a brief overview of scholarly literature; while chapters three to five constitute the analysis of the novels itself. Lastly, the annex offers brief summaries of the plots of all of Christie's novels and lists publication information.

Chapter one is dedicated to classical detective fiction. The structure of the chapter is based on the structure of the classical detective formula, its individual sections corresponding to individual elements of the formula: the characters, the plot and the setting, respectively. In section 1.1, the focus is placed on the most crucial of all characters of the detective novel: the detective. Some general observations about the nature of the classical detective are made, however, it is emphasised that the Golden Age was also a period of change and development, the most prominent being the gradual feminisation, not only of the detective, but also of the formula as a whole. This process of feminisation is also explored in section 1.2, focusing on how intuition and abductive reasoning replaced rationality and deductive logic in investigation, and how bloody and physical murder replaced corruption or financial fraud as the crime of choice. Finally, in section 1.3, attention is focused on setting, especially on the shift from the urban settings typical of earlier detective stories towards rural and family settings that would later come to dominate the Golden Age period.

Chapter two introduces the relatively new field of food studies and overviews both classic writing on food and more recent contributions to the field. The organization of the chapter aims to reflect the interdisciplinary nature of the field of food studies by concentrating on one of its aspects in each section. Section 2.1 discusses anthropological approaches to food. Some of the first scholars to take up an interest in studying the role of food in society were anthropologists, and section 2.1 takes a look at classic works of authors such as Claude Lévi-Strauss, Marvin Harris and Roland Barthes. This section then goes on to explore the implications of these theories for present-day food anthropology and tries to pin down the main trends which define the discipline today. Section 2.2 takes a look at food history, exploring classic texts such as Louis Bourdeau's *Histoire de l'alimentation* (1894) in contrast with the works of contemporary historians such as Sidney Mintz, Wolfgang Schivelbusch and others.

Section 2.3 attempts to determine the position of food in philosophy, uncovering the bias against the physical and animalistic present in Western thought from the times of Ancient Greece and Rome until today, but also indicating the existence throughout this time of dissident philosophers who advocated non-conformist, hedonistic value systems. Lastly, section 2.4 examines food as a literary device and as a method in literary criticism, and studies the place of culinary writing within the realm of literature. A special section (2.4.1) is dedicated to the relationship between food and crime fiction, covering various topics including food porn, mystery cookbooks, or contemporary culinary detective novels.

The analytical section intends once again to reflect the basic elements of the classical detective formula as defined by Cawelti, namely characters, plot and setting, but this time introduces the element of food into the formula. Chapter three discusses how food serves to highlight various issues of identity in Christie's novels, namely class (3.1 and 3.2), gender (3.3 and 3.4) and nationality (3.5). The chapter concentrates on Christie's use of food to create stereotypical characters, but at the same time to mock or even disrupt established notions of femininity, Englishness, or the division between classes. Chapter four continues the exploration of the tension between the established and expected and the disruptive and transgressive, which permeates all of Christies novels, focusing on how food is employed in plotting and narration. The chapter takes a look at food and domesticity as methods of surveillance and control, rather than of passivity and oppression (4.1), at the role of feeling, senses and hedonism as alternatives to reasoning (4.2), and at the paradoxical relationship between food as a symbol of safety, care, and nourishment on the one hand, and of danger and death on the other (4.3)

The final chapter, chapter five, explores the connection between food and setting. Section 5.1 emphasises the importance of place in the detective novel and explains the interconnection between food and space. It discusses issues such as local foods, tradition, and foodscape. It also focuses on the division of spaces into public and private which dominates Western thought, and shows how this division relates to food; more specifically, how Christie used this division in order to manipulate gender stereotypes and to feminise the detective formula. Section 5.2 deals with food and time, and two concepts are highlighted in this section; firstly the ritualistic nature of eating and its relationship to the ritualistic nature of the crime novel, and, secondly, the connection between food, memory, nostalgia and nationalism in Agatha Christie's writing.

The introduction to this book began with three excerpts from different novels by Agatha Christie. These three excerpts, the first dealing with food as an element defining Poirot's character, the second with food (or drink) as a murder weapon, and the third with food as a means of remembering and fixing events in time, succinctly illustrate the same points which will be dealt with in much more depth in the individual chapters of the analytical part of this book. They prove that food indeed permeates Christie's crime novels on a number of levels, and that it affects all of the elements of the classical detective formula. As such, they also show that this approach can be used to analyse the novels in their entirety from a different and hopefully enriching new perspective.

Notes

[1] such as in *The Secret of Chimneys* (277), *Cat Among the Pigeons* (186, 189), *Lord Edgware Dies* (127), *They Do It With Mirrors* (10)

[2] For a list of authors discussing this topic see the Bibliography or section 2.4.

CHAPTER ONE

THE DETECTIVE FORMULA

The belief that the detective novel is formulaic is a long established one. Tzvetan Todorov ([1966] 2008) maintains that while works of so-called highbrow literature are valued for their innovations and their ability to break with established conventions, popular literature, including detective fiction, is at its best when it most exactly fulfils the norms and requirements of its genre (227). Thomas Leitch (2002) also holds this view, claiming that originality is only valued in popular fiction if it helps to intensify the expected experience without altering it in any substantial way (63-64). P. D. James (2010) even considers the formulaic nature of the crime story to be the main element which differentiates the detective novel from other literary genres, claiming that "[a]lthough the detective story at its highest can also operate on the dangerous edge of things, it is differentiated both from mainstream fiction and from the generality of crime novels by a highly organised structure and recognised conventions" (15).

This chapter presents a discussion of various elements of the classical detective novel, specifically novels which were produced in the period labelled the Golden Age of detective fiction or which were produced by authors who started writing in this period and who remained faithful to the genre even beyond it. Although the above-delineated structuralist approach as advocated by Todorov and John G. Cawelti could be rejected as overly simplistic, it is assumed that this approach is highly appropriate for the study of the classical detective novel, as the appeal of the genre lies precisely in the way in which it restructures and ritualises reality. This simplification allows for the development of the clue-puzzle game which is played by the author and the reader, and also provides a feeling of catharsis which stems from the ritualistic isolation of guilt and its subsequent punishment.

Cawelti understands formula as consisting of the "conventional way of defining and developing a particular kind of situation or situations, a pattern of action or development of this situation, a certain group of characters and the relations between them, and a setting or type of setting appropriate to the characters and the action" (1976, 80). The sections into which this chapter is divided correspond to these elements of a formula. Section 1.1 deals with characters, especially with the character of the detective, who is the main focus of a crime story. Section 1.2 discusses the crime and its investigation, i.e. the central situation and its development. Finally, section 1.3 explains the main functions of time and place in detective novels. The individual sections not only characterise the above elements and describe their development, but also observe and comment upon the two conflicting tendencies at play in each crime novel: the attempt to create a story which is as realistic as possible but which nonetheless respects the necessity of a ritualistic restructuring of reality.

1.1. The Detective

According to Cawelti there are four main groups of characters in a classical detective story: 1) the detective, 2) the criminal (or criminals), 3) the victim (or victims), and 4) the witnesses and/or suspects (1976, 91). However, while the portrayal of minor characters is often superficial and sketchy and their role is usually limited to a couple of pages, the detective's presence is recurrent throughout the story or series of stories, and various nuances of her/his personality are described in great detail, if not always in depth (Giddey 1990, 62). Two other characters besides the detective are crucial to all crime stories—the victim and the criminal. However, despite their significance they can never become the main focus of the story. The character of the victim must not be described in any great depth, otherwise her/his death could arouse feelings of regret and pity and thus distract attention from the real purpose of a detective story: solving the mystery (Cawelti 1976, 91).

Similarly the criminal cannot take centre stage in the story, although for different reasons. If the readers "become too concerned with the motives of the criminal, his guilt is likely to seem increasingly ambiguous and difficult to define" (92). However, in a detective story "there must never be any serious question about either the specific guilt or the evil motive of these characters." The criminal is not permitted to exist as a complex personality with virtues and vices and ambiguous motivations; they "must always be definable as bad" (ibid.). In other words, the only character to be fully delineated in a crime story is the detective, and therefore the focus of the story is placed solely on her/him. For this reason, crime authors take great care to make their own detectives stand out.

The importance of the detectives is such that they frequently assume the role of the author—their names are featured on book covers alongside that of the author, and it is their names, not the author's, which become familiar to the wide public (Giddey 1990, 63). This is also the case of Agatha Christie's two famous detectives, Hercule Poirot and Miss Marple: the books in which they feature are not labelled as Christie Mysteries, but instead as the Poirot Mysteries or the Marple Mysteries respectively, and the two detectives are of much greater interest to the readers than Christie herself. The following paragraphs examine this phenomenon more closely, concentrating on the special status of the detective, the notions of authorship, reality and fiction, the heroisation of the detective, and on morality and immorality in the crime genre. Moreover, they shed light on the gradual feminisation of the detective hero, which took place in the Golden Age of detective fiction.

1.1.1. Detective as Author: Hercule Poirot's Manuscript

In his short study on joint authorship, Joachim Jung (1998) observes that "[t]he classical idea of authorship is that an author expresses his or her personality by producing novels, dramas or poems. The author imprints his style and personal taste on thc phrases he assembles" (Jung 1998, 241). However, Jung contests this notion and argues that the idea of a "self-sufficient author is a mere fiction." He quotes the German writer Reinhard Jahn who claims that an author is always "supported by friends, relatives, companions, publishers, editors" who provide inspiration, feedback, and guidance, and thereby suggests that the function of the author is that of "a mere catalyst who gives form to the numerous ideas, opinions, views, stories, and proposals he had received as material for his plot" (241). Through these insights, Jung wishes to further his thesis that cooperation between pairs (or even teams) of authors on a single literary work does not clash with the notion of creative expression. However, this section argues that the influence on the author does not have to come only from the outside, from real people and events, but also from within—from the writer's work itself. The style and character imprinted on a work of literature is no longer that of the author alone, but it also reflects the nature of the author's characters. The character of the detective occupies a very prominent role in the detective story and often continues this role over a series of connected stories; it is therefore highly likely that the character can become such a force and continuously influence the writing process. Thus in a detective story it is possible to witness a certain merging of two worlds—the real, material world of the author and the fictional world of the characters created by her/him.

In defining a fictional world, Lisa Hager (2012) turns to Roland Barthes and claims it is possible to approach fiction in two ways: either as being passively reconstructed by a reader from clues prepared for her/him by the author, or as being open to a reader's active engagement, allowing for multiple readings, additions to, and reformations of the author's original message. These two types of texts are in Barthes's terminology labelled "readerly" and "writerly," respectively (1974, 4). Writerly texts, allowing infinite possibilities of reading, are the ones which make it possible for fictional characters to gain more dimensions and a wider range of choice in actions and thoughts, and thus become closer to the characters of the real world. Hager claims that Sir Arthur Conan Doyle's Sherlock Holmes mysteries are examples of writerly texts. These stories contain endless amounts of "potential fictional worlds" to which the reader may "desire access": events which are hinted at but not described, past experiences which are not explained and future developments which are not mentioned. These "infinite points of entry into [the] fictional world" (Hager 2012) pave the way for a character to gain independence from the novels on whose pages she/he was born—such characters are no longer limited to what has been written about them. Instead, as a real person, the character now has a past, albeit one which remains unknown within the story itself and experiences not chronicled on the story's pages; by extension, it is also possible to suggest that the character has a future which continues beyond the end of the stories.

Returning to the case of Sherlock Holmes, Conan Doyle's creation is a perfect example of a character who surpassed the popularity of his creator, and at the same time grew independent of him, becoming a real person in the minds of his readers (or rather fans). Cathy Akers-Jordan observes that "[f]or years people called at No. 221B Baker Street, seeking advice from the famous consulting detective, not realizing that the address, like Holmes, was fictional" (1998, 5). Holmes established himself so firmly in the real world that not only readers, but also researchers and academics discuss the character as if he were an independent person. Hager notes that scholarly works on Sherlock Holmes discuss questions such as "Was his addiction to cocaine benign or harmful? Were his feelings for Irene Adler romantic or respectful? Were his origins British or American?" The publications of Holmes researchers collected in *The Baker Street Journal* "become a mix of scholarly articles and what may be termed fan fiction, including stories like 'My First Meeting with Sherlock Holmes' by Ellery Queen and 'Sherlock Holmes in the White House' by Roosevelt" (Hager

2012). In addition, crime authors also approach Holmes in this fashion, and make references to him in their own novels; they use the fictional character of Holmes as a means of confirming the reality of their own stories (Akers-Jordan 1998, 6). The character of Holmes is definitely established in the real world, and can now lend validity to other fictional worlds.

In summary, the character of Sherlock Holmes has gained independence from his author and blurs the borderlines between fiction and reality. However, the mysterious Ellery Queen, an American sleuth-cum-crime-author went one step further and succeeded in usurping the place of the author for himself. The authors of Ellery Queen, American writers Frederic Dannay and Manfred Lee, did not conform to traditional definitions of authorship as were described at the beginning of this chapter. Firstly, they worked as a team, and therefore their novels could not reflect the style or character of a single "genius author" (Jung 1998, 241). Moreover, they did not claim independence from their creation; on the contrary, the central conceit of their books was that the main character was himself the author, and the books were published under his name, itself a pseudonym of the real authors. "For ten years the authors concealed their real identity from the public" (243). Thus, the duo profited from what they considered a typical trait of detective fiction, i.e. that "[p]eople remembered the name of the sleuth but often forgot the name of the author. To give themselves a double shot at being remembered, they used the same name for both. Queen wasn't just an amateur detective, he also was a successful writer of detective stories whose name was on the very book that you had in your hand" (Wheat 2005, 87).

However, Dannay and Lee did not draw the line at making Ellery Queen the author. They further deconstructed the fiction/reality boundary by making Queen an editor, establishing the *Ellery Queen's Mystery Magazine*, in which short stories of other crime authors (belonging to the real world) were collected and published, chosen on the basis of "Ellery Queen's taste" (Wheat 2005, 89). Thus, as with Sherlock Holmes, the fictional detective successfully entered the real world, merged with his authors, and, moreover, exercised influence over this real world by chronicling and evaluating the work of crime authors according to his standards, despite being a fictional character himself.

A similar merging of fiction and reality, as well as a tendency to identify the stories with the detective rather than with the author, can be observed in the work of Agatha Christie. For instance, the character of Ariadne Oliver—an amateur investigator and crime author who appeared in a number of novels such as the *Hallowe'en Party* or *Elephants Can*

Remember—has some affinities with the above-mentioned Ellery Queen. Oliver, like Queen, is involved in solving crimes and then writes about these experiences. Moreover, as Christie admitted herself, Oliver is a semi-autobiographical character, sharing not only personality traits, but also writing techniques and strategies with her creator. Like Christie, Oliver constantly wrote down ideas and made notes for her stories, and they also shared a taste for apples (Craig 2009). The crucial difference, however, lies in the fact that Oliver is only a secondary character in the novels, assisting detective Hercule Poirot in solving the crimes, and therefore she is never in a position to influence the development or outcome of the story.

Unlike Ariadne Oliver, Poirot and Miss Marple occupy such positions in the novels and it would indeed be possible for them to insinuate themselves into the world of reality and even to usurp the author's place. But while they both accomplished the former, neither was able to completely succeed in the latter, although there are some tendencies towards this in the case of Poirot. Christie herself encouraged Poirot and Marple's move to the realm of reality by making her characters older — both have a lot of past experience which could provide material for numerous potential fictional worlds. Readers are invited to speculate on the possible past lives of the two sleuths, and to imagine the cases which Poirot had solved as a member of the Belgian police force or the reasons why Miss Marple had ended up as a lonely old lady. In the case of Marple, Christie also left the possibilities open after the last novel, *Nemesis*, in which Marple inherits a considerable sum of money. This gives her the chance for a future life, which she acknowledges herself: "I'm going to spend it, you know. I'm going to have some fun with it" (*Nemesis* 238). In the case of Poirot, Christie limited the number of possible lives by ending the final novel, *Curtain*, with the death of the main character. However, Poirot's death only served as further proof that he had already become firmly established in the real world; on publication of *Curtain*, *The New York Times* printed a front page obituary announcing his death, which begun: "Hercule Poirot Is Dead: Hercule Poirot, a Belgian detective who became internationally famous, has died in England. His age was unknown. [...]" (*The New York Times*, 6 Aug. 1975, 73).

Christie's fans took the reality of Poirot and Marple for granted, writing letters to them with questions about their lives and background and asking Christie to arrange a meeting between the two sleuths (Mills and Waites 2008). Christie stated that such a meeting was impossible, but not on grounds of the incompatibility of the two central characters belonging to different fictional worlds: instead she pointed out that there would be a personality clash between the two. "I'm sure they would not like meeting at all," she says. "Hercule Poirot, a complete egoist, would not like being taught his business or having suggestions made to him by an elderly spinster lady." It is clear that not only the fans, but also Christie herself ascribed a certain independence to her characters. For example, about inventing Miss Marple she writes: "Miss Marple insinuated herself so quietly into my life, that I think I hardly noticed her arrival." When describing Marple's character, Christie did not say she was inspired by or based on the personality of her grandmother, but rather that the two had some things "in common."[1] The author herself developed feelings towards the characters; despite calling Poirot a "complete egoist" and Marple "[p]uffy and spinsterish," she was "fiercely protective" of them and did not want to "hear [other] people talk about those characters in the way that she did" (Bosman 2008).

It is clear that both of Christie's most famous detectives, Hercule Poirot and Miss Marple, were able to develop lives of their own in the realm of the real world, in which they entered into relationships with fans (rather than readers) and even with the author who created them. But it is Poirot who comes closest to acting both as protagonist and author of his mysteries. In Christie's first novel, *The Mysterious Affair at Styles*, Poirot actually commissions Captain Hastings, his collaborator, to write down the story of the crime and its solution (5), mirroring the practice of public figures commissioning ghost writers to write down their autobiographies. In *Curtain*, Poirot goes one step further and actually writes his own account of the case and its solution in a letter to Hastings, which is presented at the end of the book, introduced by the following paragraph:

> (Note by Captain Arthur Hastings: The following manuscript came into my possession four months after the death of my friend Hercule Poirot. I received a communication from a firm of lawyers asking me to call at their office. There, "in accordance with the instructions of their client, the late M. Hercule Poirot," they handed me a sealed packet. I reproduce its contents here.)
> Manuscript written by Hercule Poirot: (257)

Thus, in his last adventure, Poirot becomes his own chronicler, merging the roles of author and character into one.

It follows from the above that in a piece of crime fiction, the detective, the most central of all the characters, frequently becomes an independent figure, freed from the constraints of their fictional world, and can even surpass or replace the author herself/himself. Christie acknowledged this in an essay published in *The Guardian*, in which she warned aspiring crime fiction authors:

> Hercule Poirot has made quite a place for himself in the world and is regarded perhaps with more affection by outsiders than by his own creator. I would give one piece of advice to young detective writers: be very careful what central character you create—you may have him with you for a very long time! ([1945] 2012)

1.1.2. Detective as Modern Hero

According to G. K. Chesterton ([1901] 1974), a detective story deals in a poetic manner not with nature, but instead with culture, human society, and its symbolism (385). The detective serves the heroic role of guarding the society, which is understood in this context as the human attempt to rebel against nature, and the desire to impose stability and order on an ever-changing environment (386). However, with the declining influence of the traditional authorities of social and moral order—the church and the nobility— at the beginning of the twentieth century, this stability seemed feebler than ever (Cawelti 1976, 101). The sense of external social disintegration was heightened by the perception of concurrent disintegration from within; in the twentieth century the mind ceased to be the shrine of the enlightened and straightforward reason, and instead became a battleground where the "conflict between the reasoning and ordered consciousness and the hidden dynamism and anarchy" of the unconscious took place (102).

These combined factors brought a prevalent sense of guilt to the middle and upper-middle classes of the modern population: guilt over the sexual and aggressive instincts supposedly hidden in the unconscious. Moreover the ethos of the modern period, epitomised by capitalism and democracy ascribed great importance to new values such as freedom, independence, and self-reliance (103). One result of this new style of thought was that people were no longer able to rely on outside judgement. It was suddenly necessary for individuals to become their own moral arbiters and to judge guilt or innocence. The detective story, with its clear-cut divisions between morality and immorality and between victim and criminal represents a rebellion against this new situation. While immersed in the pages of a detective story, the reader can forget the tensions of modern democratic society with its associated need to govern and judge ourselves and can also escape from the ever-present feelings of guilt. The heroic detective acting as the unerring arbiter brings justice and punishment, and for a while the reader is absolved from responsibility (Allen and Chacko 1974, 4-5).

Rebellion or "revolt conditions a large part of golden age detective fiction" (Panek 1987, 124). Crime authors fought against lowbrow literature and working class thrillers, attempting to establish their work as being more culturally valid than popular fiction. More importantly, they were also strongly against what was then considered as "highbrow" literature—modernism, the Avant-garde and everything that it represented: the incomprehensibility and instability of the contemporary condition, of the world and of one's own mind (125). The difference between the detective story and the modernist novel is crucial: "In the detective story, when we arrive at the detective's solution, we have arrived at the truth, the single right perspective and ordering of events." In a modernist novel, however, one point of view "does not claim a higher level of reality or meaning" than the others, on the contrary it "reveals that the events are too complex to be understood from a single unified point of view" (Cawelti 1976, 89). While the detective story's aim is to solve a mystery, the modernist novel "further intensifies the inexhaustible mystery of human relationships" (90). Thus the genre of detective fiction represented a revolt against the prevalent scepticism and pessimism of the modern era, with its belief that human lives are ruled by principles of relativity and coincidence. The detective inhabits a world based on rules of cause and effect in which a fixed moral system allows each individual to be the author of their own fate; and in this world, any transgressions will be punished (Allen and Chacko 1974, 2-3).

In this way, the detective story offers the modern reader a certain sense of relief: it frees the reader from the need to decide their own codes of ethics. The classical detective novel is guided by the principle of "patterns of reassurance." It reassures us of the existence of a fixed morality, of the eventual "triumph of the intellect" and human culture over unpredictable natural forces and of the "restoration of a supposedly rational, ordered, and secure world" (Mullen and O'Beirne 2000, i). It achieves this by presenting us with a restructured, ritualistic image of human society, in which "[l]ife goes along well except for the single point that some crime [...] has been committed" (Aydelotte 1967, quoted in Cawelti 1976, 81). In such a society all problems "are objectively caused by an external circumstance, the murder, which can and will be resolved, whereupon the troubles will disappear.... The mess, confusion, and frustration of life have been reduced to a simple issue between good and evil" (81). The detective, adopting the role of hero, overcomes evil and re-establishes the stability of the social order which has been disrupted by the murder.

By acting in this fashion, the detective provides her/his audience with another source of relief. The world of the detective novel differs from the real world in that there is "no sense of universal culpability" (Grella 1970, 33)—the individual is absolved of guilt and guilt is transferred to a specifically named other. By absolving the individual, who is generally the sympathetic character with whom the reader identifies, and by transferring the guilt onto the "least likely person," i.e. the character who means nothing to us and who is of least importance to the social circle, the detective in effect "absolves the readers themselves" (Cawelti 1976, 90). The detective employs her/his "demonic powers to project the general guilt onto specific and overt acts of particular individuals, thus restoring the serenity of the middle-class social order" (96). The detective story brings readers a feeling of catharsis by condensing the pressures of contemporary society "into manageable form" (Knight 2004, 109). In Leitch's words, detective stories succeed in "purg[ing] postreligious audiences of guilt" (T. Leitch 2002, 55).

However, this purging would not be effective if it was carried out by an ordinary person or someone who is themselves a member of the guilty society. Instead, it is performed through "the miraculous intervention of a genius from outside who removes guilt by giving knowledge of guilt" (Auden 1948, 412). Thus the detective becomes a god-like figure who has the power to confer validity to the social order and to distinguish the guilty from the innocent. P. D. James claims that classical detectives possess the "accepted heroic virtues: intelligence, courage and energy" (2010, 16). Moreover, they are detached from the society and gain independence from it, and are therefore entitled to judge it (Cawelti 1976, 104).

However, before the detective can become a hero they must undergo a series of rituals. These initiation or heroisation rituals are present in most detective stories. Firstly, the detective must prove their special skills (Jackson 2002, 17). For instance, Edgar Allan Poe's C. Auguste Dupin and Arthur Conan Doyle's Holmes prove their special abilities by performing tests of deduction in which they infer detailed information about other characters' lives from a minor piece of information or by "reading" their partner's thoughts and determining their state of mind (Cawelti 1976, 82). Secondly, the detective, i.e. "the seeker," "must name and face the murderer. Sometimes [...] she even has to fight the murderer" (Jackson 2002, 17). Often, the detective is doubted by the other characters. Frequently, Poirot is initially disregarded as a boastful, absurd foreigner incapable of fulfilling his promises of solving the crime; Miss Marple, especially in her last adventure—*Nemesis*—is described as scatty, or even senile. In order to reassert their hero status, the detectives need to solve the mystery and this is a task which they must undertake alone. "The sleuth is the only one with the special knowledge to past the test." Upon completing this task, the detective achieves the status of hero (Jackson 2002, 17).

Once the detective achieves hero status, she/he gains a special position among the characters. Firstly, the detective cannot be harmed or killed, and is blessed with a certain "immunity" (Todorov [1966] 2008, 227). Secondly, the detective is endowed with superhuman powers of intellect and reason. Her/his mind works in such an orderly and organised fashion that she/he can control and alter the chaotic world around her/him through the sheer power of reason alone. "[E]verything external to [the detective] can be made to fit the theoretical, the ideal logic" (Davidson 1957, quoted in Cawelti 1976 100-1). Thus the detective affirms the rule of human mind and of the rational social order over natural chaos. Finally, the detective is allowed to act immorally in order to achieve her/his aim, i.e. to capture the villain (see below). "The detective story inevitably contains elements of the hunt. Under all of the acting and the talk, the criminal stalks his victim and the detective hunts the criminal" (Panek 1987, 135). As George Burton observed, "all detective fiction is based on two murders of which the first, committed by the murderer, is merely the occasion for the second, in which he is the victim of *the pure and unpunishable murderer*, the detective" (quoted in Todorov [1966] 2008, 227, emphasis added). Thus the detective is transformed into an "always reliable hero who help[s] a baffled and threatened populace" (Knight 2004, 67), a figure who solves crimes by imposing "the supreme quality of his mind on the apparent chaos of the outer world" (Cawelti 1976, 100), and brings relief to the readers and characters of the story alike by freeing them from their "latent hubris and guilty desires" (Grella 1970, 33). By the end of the story, the hero-detective "has rearranged human relationships to insure the reintegration and harmony of an entire social order" (45).

As can be seen in section 1.1.1, detective fiction authors endeavour to make their stories feel as realistic as possible. In order to do so, they render their protagonists real by treating them as actual people rather than as characters of a novel and by assigning them place and validity in both the fictional and the real world. This strong sense of reality or verisimilitude is of central importance in a detective story (Allen and Chacko 1974, 1). According to Dorothy L. Sayers ([1929] 1974), stories of horror and crime bring the readers a certain sense of catharsis (351), and the above paragraphs prove that this is indeed true of the classical detective novel. Yet in order to enable this catharsis, it is necessary for the readers to be able to identify with the situation at hand, and to be able to imagine the description of the events as something which is real.

Therefore, as Raymond Chandler (1950) aptly stated, "[f]iction in any form always intended to be realistic." Todorov agrees with this claim, stating that "no author acknowledges [the] imaginary nature" of a detective story ([1966] 2008, 228). The hero must be real before he can save us.

This tendency towards realism in the genre of detective fiction is complicated by the need for a mythical or dreamlike "revelatory structure" (228), which serves the ritualistic function of isolating the reader's guilt. The mystery must then be both, realistic and mythical before it can reward the reader with catharsis. This contradiction is embodied in the character of the detective, who is an extremely realistic figure who is even permitted to free her/himself from the fictional world and enter the world of reality, but who remains a completely unusual personality, an eccentric with superhuman powers of observation and deduction (Allen and Chacko 1974, 1). In a crime novel, the detective becomes a modern equivalent of the medieval knight—a hero larger than life (Sayers [1929] 1974, 354).

1.1.3. An Immoral Detective?

The previous paragraphs highlight the special status of the detective in a crime story. Indeed, the detective seems to possess a hero-like, unerring sense of justice. She/he always knows who is guilty and who is innocent, and can distinguish between who has behaved morally and who has not. Unlike in other genres, the investigator in a detective story can never be both the detective and the criminal simultaneously (Cawelti 1976, 133). The detective is by definition a moral figure who is entitled to judge the morality of others. Thus she/he is turned into an "ideal imago"—a hero who is able to face the day-to-day demands of society "which values intellectual prowess more than, say, spiritual or physical attributes" and who can act morally when all others fail. For the readers, the detective offers a model of behaviour which they wish to emulate (Prchal 1997, 30).

Another element contributing to the importance of morality in the genre of detective fiction is the idea of fair play. This concept was born during the Golden Age of detective fiction when a group of contemporary crime authors such as S. S. Van Dine and Ronald Knox, published rules and regulations according to which a detective story should be constructed. These rules involved the doctrine of being "fair" towards the reader: the detective (or the author) must always show all of the available clues to the reader thereby allowing them an equal chance at figuring out the identity of the criminal (Lehman 2000, 47). When Agatha Christie commented on the work of her fellow author John Dickson Carr, she accused him of violating this fundamental rule:

> The clues to the truth are so slight as to be almost unfair. One little sentence slipped into the middle of a tense situation. A mention of a car radiator on page 30 that does not agree with the same car's radiator on page 180. Do you notice it? Of course not! Your eyes are riveted on a suspicious circumstance which you think only you have spotted. Misdirection again. ([1945] 2012)

However, in the end she conceded that Carr was still acting within the limits of fairness and in admiration of his work named him the "king of the art of misdirection" (Christie [1945] 2012). Ironically, Christie herself had been accused of playing foul with her readers after publishing *The Murder of Roger Ackroyd*. In this novel, the narrator is revealed to have committed the crime with the book acting as his letter of confession (Lehman 2000, 47). In the era of classical detective fiction, playing fair and observing the laws of the genre, or, in some sense, being moral, was a necessity if the author and the detective wished to be accepted by the readers. "The great detective not only had to dazzle [...] with intellectual footwork but also had to display every link in the chain of his reasoning, and every link had to hold up under scrutiny" (Wheat 2005, 89).

While the detective's morality is a necessary requirement of the genre of classical detective fiction, the detective differs from the other characters in that she/he is occasionally permitted to use immoral means to achieve her/his ends (Allen and Chacko 1974, 3). Miss Marple regularly lays traps for her suspects and manipulates her witnesses, while Poirot is often caught lying and is not averse to tricking his suspects into making confessions. If we were to judge Marple and Poirot according to the traditional Kantian concept of morality, as it is laid out in the *Groundwork for the Metaphysic of Morals*, their actions would undoubtedly be found wanting. Immanuel Kant ([1785] 2008) believed that actions could only be considered moral if they were motivated by nothing more than an individual feeling of duty. Furthermore, duty could not stem from feelings, common sense, or bodily impulses, but instead solely from "pure reason" (7). Kant termed this tendency of reason to act morally as "will," and he insisted that for a will to be moral, it must be free, i.e. governed only by laws which reason has imposed on itself, and not by laws imposed by any other authority (40-43). However, although the laws guiding one's own morals are self-imposed, Kant believed them to be universally applicable. Indeed, he claimed that people should be willing to accept only those individual moral laws which could also be universally applicable, prompting the reader to ask always: "Would I be content for my maxim [...] to hold as a universal law, for myself as well as for others?" when judging the morality of an action (12). In addition, he claimed that acting morally should be the goal of every individual, regardless of the possible results of the action. One should always choose the action which reason judges as being universally moral, and the circumstances or possible consequences should not be taken into consideration. This belief is known as the categorical imperative (20). In the pursuit of morality, the individual should also be able to suppress their natural inclinations, tastes, desires, or bodily needs (10, 36), as "[d]uty often implies self-denial" (13).

According to the Kantian concept of morality, the rule of reason, which is concerned with actions rather than results, is morally superior to the rule of the body, which is inherently concerned with achieving the immoral satisfaction of needs. Kant believed in the necessity of transcending one's own body in order to achieve morality. Traditionally, detection is viewed as an analogous process: the "repression of the body" is needed to enable deduction and the unhindered work of reason (Pascual Soler 2009, 7). Philosophers such as Kant often held the belief that indulgence in pleasures, especially in the pleasure of eating, prevented the individual from clear thinking, suggesting "that gluttony stupefied the hunger of the mind" (Pascual Soler 2009, 6). Only an ascetic, a person who deprives her/his body of satisfaction and comfort (in other words, a hungry person) can make full use of their mental capacities (6).

Detectives, however, tend to depart from this strict concept of morality in which the individual is guided by duty and self-denial. George Grella (1970) describes Dorothy Sayers's hero Lord Peter Wimsey as "a full-fledged aristocrat, as well as a fop, a bibliophile, and a gourmet," a comic figure who has as many vices as he has virtues, and who over-indulges in sensationalism and sensual pleasures (37). Stephen Knight (2004) lists a number of various immoral detectives ranging from comic characters who simply display a "foolish manner" to complete anti-heroes such as H. C. Bailey's "vulgar and self-seeking Joshua Clank" (99) or Melville Davisson's Randolph Mason, a detective-cum-attorney who defends his clients by making use of loopholes in the legal system (72-73). Yet other detectives go as far as committing murder themselves, such as Bailey's Mr Fortune, who is prepared to kill in pursuit of justice when he personally "throws a villain to his death out of a window" (98-99).

It can be concluded that a strict sense of morality in Kantian terms does not apply to a number of classical detectives. To differing extents, these detectives fail to adhere to the moral codes according to which they judge others. Agathe Christie's Poirot in particular fails to conform to the stereotype of the detective as a machine of reason, but is instead portrayed as a hedonistic detective who pays attention to both the inclination of his mind and the urges of his body. Paradoxically, the immorality of the detectives renders them more flawed, and thus more human, yet it also heightens their status as superior to all other characters. Behaviour which the reader sees as cunning, positive and, to some degree, moral (given that it is carried out as a means of achieving supreme justice and final truth) would be perceived as vile if exhibited by any other character (Allen and Chacko 1974, 2-3). Thus the detective's ability to switch from immorality to morality gives her/him the status of a figure whose judgement of morality is above everyone else's. She/he is turned into an ultimately superior, God-like figure.

1.1.4. Rise of the Female Detective

The heroisation of the detective reached its peak with the character of Sherlock Holmes. Holmes was the ultimate, infallible and superior hero. The Holmesian formula was soon utilised by a number of detective writers and, eventually, it became so dominant that many authors after Doyle started to seek ways to escape from this paradigm (Sayers [1929] 1974, 356). A new style of detective began to emerge who, while remaining ultimately infallible, was now permitted to make mistakes, thereby allowing readers to identify with her/him more easily. The detective no longer represented an omniscient deus ex machina controlling the entirety of the action; instead, she/he sometimes overlooked a clue, was unable to gather sufficient evidence, or was deceived by the criminal (Giddey 1990, 65). This shifted the detective novel further away from its origins in the gothic mystery with its bleak ambiance and demonic characters, and closer to the comedy of manners, in which the minor roles were occupied by stock personalities and in which the detective acquired the features of a comic protagonist, or even of a clown (Grella 1970, 37).

This change was also fuelled by the growing numbers of women reading novels at the end of the nineteenth century. Women now formed the majority of fiction readers and this led to a corresponding increase in the number of female authors. Through the influence of these authors the crime genre acquired new dimensions. Murder gradually became established as the standard crime in detective novels, with its feminine, bodily, and bloody character being far removed from the bloodless political intrigues and property crimes of the earlier nineteenth century detective novels (Knight 2004, 68). In addition, authors now tried to make their detectives more unique and human in character (Giddey 1990, 66), and they attempted to differentiate them from the cynical "hawk-faced" Sherlock Holmes (Sayers [1929] 1974, 356) or the rational thinking-machines of earlier stories. Doroty Sayer's Peter Wimsey is a picture of "feminised masculinity" (Knight 2004, 99) and Bailey's Fortune is possessed of a "round and cheerful countenance and a perpetual appetite" (98). Christie made her "plump fussy" Hercule Poirot "clearly the reverse of the masculine and English Holmes" (Knight 2004, 90). Indeed, the characterisation of Poirot often verges on ridicule, and Christie makes effective use of the juxtaposition between his comically exaggerated personality and his intellectual genius (Giddey 1990, 66). Christie's Poirot is clearly a response to the new trend of feminising the detective. Besides exhibiting feminine traits in his behaviour, Poirot also conducts his investigation using the method of abduction, employing not only reason but also intuition (Pascual Soler 2009, 7-10), a way of thinking which has traditionally been associated with women. Christie moved even further on the way towards the feminisation of the detective formula with the creation of Miss Marple, an elderly spinster who solves domestic crimes in the homes of provincial England.

Christie was not the first to attempt to introduce a female detective. Detectives had traditionally been men, a reflection of the evolution of the profession from the early forms of police in England such as the so-called thief-takers and the later Bow Street Runners (Knight 2004, 10). However, at the time of Doyle's popularity in the second half of the nineteenth century, a new trend emerged within the English society: the rise of the New Woman, a development made possible partly by the 1870 Education Act, which laid the foundations of elementary schooling for all children, boys and girls alike. Gradually, increasing numbers of women became professionals and took positions formerly reserved for men. It was at this time that the first professional female detectives began to appear in crime novels (Rzepka 2005, 145). Yet none of the early "lady sleuths" could be said to represent an embodiment of feminist values. The depiction of these characters tended to "reinforce rather than challenge the 'conventional sex/gender bias' [...] of their readers" (146). The lady detectives were invariably characterised by their looks, being described as "over thirty," or as possessing "a pretty womanly face," "a winsome figure" or "neat primness"; similarly, their crime solving abilities tended to rely on simple tricks rather than on the power of their intellect (Knight 2004, 78-79). Furthermore, the early lady sleuths did not hesitate to abandon "their jobs for marriage with dismaying enthusiasm whenever the opportunity arose" (Rzepka 2005, 146).

As Sayers remarked in 1929, "the really brilliant woman detective [had] yet to be created" (357). The authors at the end of the nineteenth and beginning of the twentieth century therefore faced a new problem: how to introduce the female sleuth into a genre so heavily reliant on masculinist values of violence, action, individualism, and on the acceptance of patriarchal social order (Knight 2004, 163). It is assumed that Christie chose the approach of desexualisation, firstly rehearsed when creating her distinctly un-masculine Hercule Poirot, and later elaborated in the character of the elderly spinster, Miss Marple. This technique is explored in greater detail in chapter three.

1.2. Crime and Investigation

According to Edgar Allan Poe, one of the pioneers of the genre of clue-puzzle detective fiction, a typical detective story has six phases. In the first phase the detective is introduced and often undergoes a ritualistic test of her/his abilities (see above). Then the crime is committed and clues are presented to the detective. After this, the investigation ensues. In the final part of the story, an explanation of the crime is offered, followed by a denouement, which might take the form of the apprehension of the criminal or of her/his confession. The order of these elements is not fixed, but all of them appear in most detective stories (Cawelti 1976, 82). Thus the story "begins with an unsolved crime and moves toward the elucidation of its mystery" (80).

Of the two elements—the crime and the investigation/elucidation—the second one is of much greater importance (Todorov [1966] 2008, 227-28). The crime is not actually described in the pages of the novel, but is instead referred to only at the beginning and often only briefly. The remaining parts of the novel are dedicated to the action, i.e. the investigation, which may consist either of the uncovering of the identity and motive of the criminal or, if the criminal is known, in finding evidence of her/his crime. The action of a crime novel achieves its climax at the moment of explanation; the identity of the murderer is revealed and the significance of individual clues clarified (Cawelti 1976, 80-81). The following paragraphs aim to characterise the aforementioned main elements of the plot of a detective story.

1.2.1. Murder

The occurrence of a crime is the basic condition for the existence of a detective story—without a crime there can be no investigation. Moreover, in order to sustain a whole detective novel, which since the end of the nineteenth century had gradually replaced the formerly popular short story, the crime must be serious enough to warrant an extensive and complicated investigation, a requirement which accounts for the predominance of murder and political intrigue in detective fiction (Cawelti 1976, 81). During the Golden Age of crime fiction, stories featuring political intrigue were gradually dropped and murder became the single crime present in almost all crime novels. In the detective stories of Agatha Christie murder is rendered even more sinister and menacing as it is a domestic murder, a matter of "major personal betrayal" (Knight 2004, 91). The murder happens in a place of trust among the closest of kin and Christie uses a "formulaic, repeatable mode" to create a sense of "intimate danger" and "personal unease" which "emerges even in—especially in—a world secluded from social and international disorder" (92). Christie's novels convey an atmosphere of general menace in which the characters "cannot trust anyone at all." This type of horrifyingly intimate murder is characteristic of many other works of the Golden Age period (91).

The scene of the fictional murder must always "be surrounded by a number of tangible clues that make it absolutely clear that some agency is responsible for it" (Cawelti 1976, 85); in other words, it must be made clear that a murder rather than an accident or a suicide has been committed. In addition, the murder "must appear to be insoluble" (85). According to Cawelti, a crime fulfilling both of these conditions represents the "ideal paradigm for the detective story crime" (85). For this reason, crime writers have developed a certain "penchant for the tangible" (Grella 1970, 47). Not only are clues and irregularities carefully collected in the text and thoroughly analysed, but the books themselves frequently contain a number of "charts, diagrams, timetables, maps, plans, and other concrete evidence" (47) which the reader can examine with their own eyes. Here again, the element of reality is brought to the forefront: the reader gets a real map or a seating-plan of an airplane as a proof of a fictional crime.

Although the investigation and explanation represent the most important parts of a crime story, the story does not actually end at that point. As mentioned above, each detective story contains at least two murders, and the second one takes place in the denouement and beyond the end of the story. The first act of murder, committed by the criminal, must be punished by a second murder, albeit a judicial one; the detective who accuses the murderer of the crime is in fact sending the guilty party to her/his execution (Grella 1970, 44). Thus the investigator represents a mirror image of the villain and death is punished by death. This complementary relationship between the detective and the murderer is also emphasised in the investigation process, where it is necessary for the detective to be able to identify with the murderer, and to think in the same way as she/he would think, thereby uncovering their guilt (Hodgson 1992, 312). The workings of the villain's and hero's minds are identical, but they are used for a different end. Furthermore, the crime committed by the murderer is often solved by duplication (313). Detectives, for example Miss Marple in a number of her stories (*The Murder at the Vicarage*; *The Body in the Library*; *A Murder is Announced*), frequently reconstruct the circumstances which had prompted the murderer to kill in an attempt to force the murderer to reveal their guilt. They engage in "retaliation by repetition" when "the crime is not merely undone but redone, the criminal not only defeated but victimized by his own devices." This suggests that not only actual murder or punishment, but detection itself can "duplicate a crime" (Hodgson 1992, 316).

It follows from the above that the "typical plan of the detective story" is such that "the detective counters and reverses the actions of the criminal, restoring matters to their proper state, making straight what the criminal has made crooked" (Hodgson 1992, 316), which underlines the detective's role as the criminal's reverse image. However, it is not only the role of the detective which is ambiguous, but also that of the victim. The original victim is often an unsympathetic figure—an unkind mother, a twisted husband, a ruthless businessperson—sometimes even such an evil figure that the murderer is pardoned and allowed to commit suicide in order to escape the trial; in some cases, the killer is even allowed to escape punishment completely (Grella 1970, 44). This is possible because "the detective's major concern lies in establishing the general innocence rather than punishing specific guilt, the actual fate of the criminal matters little, so long as he quits his society" (44). However, even if the detective choses to punish the criminal in the end, this often remains undepicted in the story itself. The suspect(s) "will be revealed by the detective, possibly forced to confess," but their actual execution is not commented upon. Although the detective's murder is an integral part of almost all crime novels, the detective does not acknowledge that "in identifying a murderer he too has sent someone to death" (Knight 2004, 88).

Moreover, despite the fact that murder is a crime with tragic consequences, in detective fiction these repercussions are not allowed to influence the story. The victims are portrayed in such a way that there is no motivation for the readers to consider the tragedy of the crime or to learn more about the event itself; the focus of attention lies solely in the proceedings of the investigator. Indeed, the detective should not be personally involved in the crime solution either; her/his role is to operate as a detached observer whose main objective is to uncover the truth and enjoy the "delight in the game of analysis and deduction" (Cawelti 1976, 81). Agatha Christie's Poirot and Marple often solve crimes for their own entertainment or even out of sheer boredom (e.g. in *A Carribean Mystery* or *Three Act Tragedy*). Thus in the portrayal of crime the detective novel is paradoxical: on the one hand a grave and violent crime of murder is depicted and subsequently another murder is committed, albeit indirectly and legitimately, by the hero of the story; on the other hand, no matter how grave this crime, it can never become so interesting as to overshadow the main element of the detective story—the presentation of clues "followed by the parade of witnesses, suspects, and false solutions, which constitute the investigation as it is presented to the reader" (Cawelti 1976, 85).

1.2.2. Method as Ritual

During the nineteenth century, when the detective clue-puzzle story was yet to gain its immense popularity, there were no rules governing the methods of conducting the criminal investigation. It was possible for the detective to arrive at a solution with the help of a convenient coincidence or by suddenly producing a clue which had been hitherto unknown to the readers (Knight 2004, 81-82). Later on, investigators in crime stories began to be constructed as "intensely scientific detectives;" they were labelled as reasoning or "thinking machines" and the use of scientific, rational, and logical methods became the established model (68). Many stories were based on "scientific or technical solutions to a mystery" and on the use of "mechanical devices" (69).

The popularity of the sub-genre of the scientific detective story, however, slowly began to fade away during the 1920s. In this period, fixed rules for writing crime fiction began to emerge and the concept of "playing fair" with the reader was established, thereby making the solution through coincidence or hidden clue an impossibility (see 1.1.3). In this new system, the only means of solving a mystery left to the detective was the application of strictly deductive methods, in which the investigation relied solely on the conscious rational mind of the detective (Panek 1987, 138).

As a result, ordered and systematic thought became the most highly valued asset of a detective. Her/his method always consisted of a standardised sequence of actions, in which she/he needed to take even the slightest clue or incident into consideration and "suspect [all] the characters in order," making no exceptions (Wells 1913, "Chapter 19: Persons in the Story"). The detective had to be consistent in her/his examination of clues and suspects. The story too needed to be consistent and if a clue appeared in the solution it had to be mentioned, however briefly, at some moment in the story (Panek 1987, 132).

However, Golden Age stories found a different way of facilitating the detective's investigation. The loss of the scientific and technical method was compensated for by the acquisition of a new advantage. As a rule, the Golden Age detective was a member of the upper or upper-middle classes of society, and as such had an advantage over the police and other professional investigators when dealing with crime in the typical Golden Age setting—the upper-middle class or upper class household. As a member of the appropriate class, the non-professional detective became "socially acceptable," moreover, she/he was familiar with "the code of the society he investigate[d]" and was thus able to "question with delicacy, notice 'bad form,' or understand lying like a gentleman to the police; therefore, he always triumph[ed] over the mundane ways of the official forces of law and order" (Grella 1970, 34).

The advantage of the detective's familiarity with the environment, together with her/his superior powers of observation and deduction enable her/him to be the first to arrive at the correct solution to the mystery every time. Cawelti notes that

> [i]n the classical story [...] it seems to be important that the detective solve the crime or at least get on the right track from the beginning. In story after story, when the solution is finally revealed to us, we find that the detective immediately established the right line of investigation by making a correct inference from the conflicting and confusing testimony that had baffled everybody else. (1976, 83)

The detective surprises and awes the readers with the deductions which are revealed suddenly at the end of the story. In order to ensure that the detective retains this position of dominance over the other characters, it is necessary for the author to conceal the detective's thoughts and insights from the reader. This can be done in a number of ways. The more traditional method is to employ the character of helper or companion to relate the story. This method was successfully utilised by Doyle whose Doctor Watson became a prototype of the helper figure (Cawelti 1976, 83;

Panek 1987, 132; etc.). However, it is crucial that the helper can never rival the detective in terms of intellectual and deductive ability. Even if the readers have access to the thoughts of the helper's mind, this should never enable them to interpret the clues correctly; the reader should share the confusion of the naïve helper when presented with clues and evidence (Giddey 1990, 71). The second method of obscuring the detective's thoughts in the story which gradually became more common during the Golden Age was the technique of impersonal narration, in which "[i]nstead of the memoir voice, we find wry commentary of a third person narrator taking over the job" (Panek 1987, 132) or the use of multiple narrators, "each of whom moves a step closer to the solution of the crime" (Cawelti 1976, 84).

The solution represents the climax of a detective story. At this moment the "supremely calm detective" takes over and provides "the frantic narrator," as well as the baffled reader, both of whom are by now "hopelessly lost in the maze of clues and testimony," with the correct answers and the truth about the crime (87). The solution is either revealed through a speech which the detective delivers to the characters, or "by means of a trap that both reveals the criminal and apprehends him at the same moment" (90). Sometimes the criminal decides to or is forced to confess and her/his confession "serves [...] as corroboration of the detective's solution" (91). However, even in this case the superiority of the detective must be maintained, and therefore the presentation and confession of the criminal is typically made "too brief to permit the criminal to upstage the detective" (91). The revelation and explanation of the crime is a double source of pleasure for the reader. Firstly, the reader has been involved vicariously in the investigation process in his/her own attempts to guess the solution to the mystery her/himself and will now find out if she/he had been right after all (88). This is the pleasure of the puzzle, or the game, a pleasure that the readers feel even if they have not been able to solve the mystery correctly, because "the puzzle or riddle aspect of the detective story depends less upon the reader's own ability to solve the mystery than on giving him enough participation in it to enable him better to appreciate the wit of the detective and to understand the new perspective on which the explanation depends" (89).

Nevertheless, the reader also experiences a different kind of pleasure—a sense of catharsis. This sense of catharsis is derived from the detective's gradual and methodological process of imposing order on an environment rendered chaotic by the intrusion of the criminal, a process which is achieved by forming a coherent narrative and a "chronological sequence" (Cawelti 1976, 89) from the various clues which are scattered around the crime scene. Once the clues are organised and the villain is identified, the reader is reassured that the guilt lies neither in the society, nor in her/himself, but instead in a clearly marked and isolated other (see 1.1.1). However, in order to lend the solution trustworthiness and to ensure that it conforms to the reality principle, it is crucial that it does not come as a total surprise—the crime cannot be solved by an absurd or impossible situation. On the contrary, it must strike readers as being totally logical (Cawelti 1976, 88); they should end up asking themselves: Why didn't I think of that before?

The methodological steps taken by the detective during the process of investigation represent a ritualistic treatment both of the event of murder itself and its associated guilt. Indeed, Gillian Mary Hanson claims that ritual is "endemic" to detective fiction (2004, 9) and Cawelti labels crime stories "ritual dramas" (1976, 90). Cristina A. Jackson (2002) describes rituals as "proscribed actions designed to restore order" following traumatic experiences, i.e. ones in which people experience fear, pain, or guilt (7). And as the detective's heroic quest is to restore order in a world thrown into chaos by crime and guilt, it is necessary for her/him to perform her/his investigation in the form of a series of standardised, ritualised steps.

The process begins immediately after the discovery of the murdered corpse. The authorities are summoned, evidence is collected, an autopsy or an inquest, and eventually a funeral, ensue (Jackson 2002, 7). Then the investigation commences and it takes the form of "a ritual hunt to override the original murder" (7). During the hunt for the culprit, the detective is granted a temporary immunity from the moral codes which govern the respective society (see 1.1.3); taboos are broken, and immoral behaviour tolerated (Jackson 2002, 16). The ritual of the hunt is closely connected to the representation of the detective as a hero on a quest, an individual detached from the rest of the society and its norms (see 1.1.1). Another ritual frequently present in crime fiction is the "scapegoat ritual," in which the victim of a murder is uncovered as a vile person, therefore unworthy of life; this allows the murder to be rationalised and the guilt to be relieved (Jackson 2002, 16). "Confession forms another ritual act common to mysteries, not just at the denouement but throughout the narrative" (15). Detective stories, especially those with a first person narrator are closely connected "to the ritual of telling stories, an essential part of harmonizing our lives with reality" (15). Finally, the detective's reconstruction of the murder and her/his position as the mirror image of the criminal (see above) represents yet another ritualised procedure (15-16).

To sum up, the investigation process and the revealing of the solution are both governed by principles of logic, order, and method. The classical detective approaches her/his task in an organised manner, and although all of the clues were laid out before the reader, the detective should always be able to arrive at the conclusion first due to her/his superior powers of deduction. These conventions serve a double purpose in the detective story. Firstly, they give the readers the pleasure of involvement in a game of wits with the detective. Secondly, they generate a cathartic effect which ensues after the detective proceeds through a series of ritualised acts in order to successfully transfer guilt to one selected individual and thus restore order and innocence to the rest of the society.

1.2.3. Transcendental Intuition

In the previous section, an unerring, god-like detective hero was presented as the central character of a crime novel. The detective's method was described as being rigorous, deductive, and ruled by logic. However, as is the case with many aspects of the classical detective novel, the method of investigation underwent a number of changes due to the feminisation of the formula (see 1.1.4). The process of feminisation gave rise to the emergence of detectives employing more intuitive methods, or of a character which we might label as an "erratic" detective—a detective who is sometimes her/himself baffled by the evidence and on occasions follows the wrong track, before finally arriving at the correct solution.

In this sense, both of Christie's most famous sleuths, Miss Marple and Hercule Poirot, can be considered as non-traditional detectives. They are neither the reasoning and observing machines of the early stories, nor are they the rigorously deductive investigators established during the Golden Age. Instead, as John Scaggs (2005) points out, Marple and Poirot rely on the use of common sense and intuition (42). This view of Christie's most famous sleuths is shared by a number of authors. Neil McCaw (2010) describes Marple's process of detection as "intuition developed to genius" (55) and Knight observes that Poirot's style of investigation is not based on "male clerical-style observation, but the types of knowledge that are classically, and stereotypically, female," i.e. common sense, observation of domestic details, and intuition. He argues that "Poirot [...] represents a heightened version of female domestic knowledge as a weapon against fictional disorder" (2004, 91).

The erratic detectives refuse to limit themselves solely to the deduction of certain facts from tangible clues and instead employ elements of the method of abduction such as inspiration, intuition, and creativity. Abduction, as defined by its inventor Charles Sanders Pierce, is a reasoning process complementary to the processes of deduction and induction. While, both deduction and induction concentrate on proving a hypothesis, the aim of abduction is to create or select possible hypotheses to explain a specific set of data. Abduction serves to help an individual make sense of and organise such data which are "surprising or unexpected" and thus is crucial to problem solving (Schvaneveldt and Cohen 2010, 2). However, according to Michael Hoffmann (1999) it is not entirely possible to define abduction as a logical operation (227). As with logical operations, abductive reasoning follows a structured sequence:

> surprising fact C is observed
> but if A were true, C would be a matter of course
> hence, there is reason to suspect that A is true
> (278)

But while the process itself is logical, abduction never results in a definite explanation of a problem, and instead offers a number of "potential solutions" (Schvaneveldt and Cohen 2010, 2). "Abduction is concerned with generating plausible ideas, not proving them" and thus requires us to relax "the requirements of 'rules of logic" (5). While a deductive conclusion must "follow necessarily from the premises," in an abductive analysis there are always numerous possible hypotheses (4). Also, while abduction works to create hypotheses from facts, deduction aims to establish that facts prove that a certain hypothesis is true—the two processes work in opposite directions. Abduction can therefore be understood as the reverse of deduction, or indeed, the reverse of logic (Pascual Soler 2009, 9).

When employing the method of abduction, the question arises of why a person would choose one particular hypothesis from the range of possible hypotheses which a set of data might produce. Pierce maintains that it is human intuition which enables us to find the best explanation; we intuitively choose the hypothesis which explains the problem in its entirety and which is at the same time most economical. This process is by no means strictly logical. Sami Paavola (2005) observes that

> Peirce emphasized that abduction is a weak mode of inference coming close to guessing, or even being the same as guessing. But, despite its weakness, it is of utmost importance because it is the only mode of inference that introduces new ideas. Yet abduction is not supposed to be

> pure guessing, or a procedure based on pure chance operations. This is where Peirce introduces the need for instinct. (4-5)

Pierce maintained that instinct is in fact the central element in the process of abduction. As Paavola explains, "[n]ew ideas could not have been produced by chance operations; there simply has not been enough time for that in human history." Abductive instinct, although by definition fallible, is still much more effective than solutions based on "pure chance" (Paavola 2005, 5).

Thus by engaging in the process of abduction, the detective moves away from pure reason or pure logic, often seen as the virtues of a masculine mind, and instead employs methods based on cognitive operations traditionally seen as more feminine approaches: association and intuition. Nieves Pascual Soler (2009) notes that the process of abduction produces a "feeling of great intensity," and it is indeed this emotional aspect which differentiates it from the logical processes of induction and deduction (9). And feeling is yet another element of the mind-set which is traditionally ascribed to women and which is often despised in men. So on the numerous occasions in which Miss Marple comes across a problem which reminds her of something, or is overcome by a sense of evil, as when she enters a certain manor house in *Nemesis*; or when Poirot has the nagging feeling that something is not right and that he has missed a vital piece of information, which comes back to him in a sudden flash, the two detectives are in fact employing the method of abduction. As Cawelti describes it, the erratic or feminised detective uses her/his "transcendental intuition" to arrive at a solution "while the readers [and other characters] sink into confusion" (1976, 86).

1.3. Setting: Time and Place

It has been observed in the previous sections that most Golden Age detective stories can be considered as formulaic due to the fact that they are constructed according to a set of rules. This formulaic nature is evident not only in the characterisation of the protagonist and in the construction and ordering of action and events in such stories, but also in the depiction of setting, which is the last of the integral parts of a detective story (see 1.1). The setting of crime novels adheres to the rules of unity laid out for tragic drama by Aristotle. In terms of place this means that the action in a classical detective story is typically confined to a "fixed, limited locale" (Panek 1987, 134). Such a "closed setting" is used as a tool to isolate suspects and to allow the game of investigation to proceed. If the setting were open, the number of possible solutions would be practically infinite. However, in an isolated house or a train carriage, the detective is faced with a finite set of suspects, thereby greatly increasing the chance of success. The closed setting "also exists to provide for the audience the security of what Aristotle called the unity of place. Too much travelling, he held, disorients the spectator and destroys the illusion the dramatist is trying to create" (Panek 1987, 134).

Aristotle's concept of the unity of time is also employed by detective fiction authors (Panek 1987, 135). The action generally takes place only over a short period, although this usually consists of a few days rather than the single day proposed by Aristotle. The enclosed space and the sense that the time to investigate is both restricted and is quickly running out help achieve the sense of "psychological claustrophobia" (Panek 1987, 135) necessary to evoke a suspicious mood in the readers. Other functions of the settings are more universal: specific settings are chosen to heighten the sense of reality and to involve the reader more deeply in the story (see 1.1.2). The specific features of the setting can also reflect the actions planned or undertaken by the characters or reveal more information about the characters' psychological states (Hanson 2004, 4). In choosing a setting, the detective story's "penchant for the tangible" comes into play again and the settings are rendered more realistic and literally tangible by including maps of geographical places or floor-plans of houses and flats directly onto the pages of the novels themselves (4).

Finally, setting also serves a symbolic function. Hanson quotes some specific examples, such as the idea that railway stations generally "represent order, a link between places" thereby creating "rituals of space and time" which relieve the characters and the readers from the stressful and chaotic reality of crime through their simplified and highly organised "timetables and maps" (2004, 5). However, the symbolic function which is particularly crucial to the detective story is the opposition between public and private spaces. The contrast between what is public, namely the street, the bar, and the city, and what is private, such as the club, the house or even the dining room, symbolically translates into the opposition between masquerade and reality, and between lies and the truth (5-6). The public sphere is where characters wear masks for the benefit of passers-by and thus conceal their hidden secrets, vices, and motives. On the contrary, in the safety and privacy of the home they are able to show their true faces, to reveal their real natures and to confess the truth about themselves.

In the classical detective novel, a reversal of the symbolism of private/public is often employed to achieve a sense of looming danger and ever-present evil. As H. Douglas Thomson (1978) put it, in order to arrive at a dramatic climax it is necessary that the murder "be committed in the last place in the world you would expect it" (151). Thus it is not the dangerous and chaotic city or the public restaurant filled with unknown and possibly hostile people that serves as the setting for terrible deeds in the detective novel, but rather the family home. This supposedly safe and comfortable location with its intimate circle of relatives and friends becomes a space of lies and masquerades in which danger is imminent. This lends the setting a certain carnivalesque quality and helps introduce "a powerful theme of evil and moral decay, a distortion of truth and human values" (5).

1.3.1. Places of Calmness and Places of Crime

When considering the wide range of locations which have appeared in crime novels, Eva Erdmann (2009) notes that "[o]n the map of the world there are hardly any areas uncharted by crime fiction, hardly any places that have not yet become the setting for a detective novel" (Erdmann 2009, 13). However, despite the apparently unlimited variety of possibilities, the immediate location in a classical detective story remains strictly delimited. Cawelti characterises this location as "isolated" and "clearly marked off from the rest of the world" (1976, 96). Although this enclosed space is always surrounded by the "bustling outside world," most typically by the lively and chaotic city (96-97), the outside influences never seem to penetrate the boundaries of the closed-off area of the detective story's action.

Moreover, the novel is closed off from the outside world not only in terms of space, but also in societal terms. The main characters of the classical crime story almost exclusively inhabit the "luxurious surroundings" of upper-middle class society (Grella 1970, 39). "Professional criminals and members of the working classes play very minor roles and servants are used only as passing suspects." The "social conflict outside the murder scene" is irrelevant to the story (Knight 2004, 87). Thus the Golden Age novel "separates a small, homogeneous, elite group from the rest of the world," typically isolating them in a country house or other analogous locales: "the charity bazaars, men's clubs, card parties, hunting lodges, university common rooms, and snowbound resort hotels" (Grella 1970, 39). The upper-class detective hero can penetrate this close-knit community with an ease which is denied to the professional investigator or the police constable (see 1.2.2).

It follows from the above that while some authors, for instance Chesterton, view the detective story as a genre of the city, or even as a kind of urban poetics (Hanson 2004, 6) and consider the cityscape the perfect setting for the detective hero's hunt (7), in the classical story there is a marked preference for the provincial or the rural (James 2010, 13). Erdmann observes this phenomenon in French crime fiction, noting that formerly

> works of European detective fiction, the cases investigated by Commissioner Maigret and those of Nestor Burma, were directly associated with French metropolitan flair and the Quai d'Orfèvres was known even to those who had never been to Paris. Now, formerly privileged settings for crime such as Paris have given way to the omnipresence of crime and the cities must vie for attention with the provinces. This merely reflects the fact that from the earliest times, village gossip and family histories have been an inexhaustible source of inspiration for storytellers. (2009, 14)

In the classical detective story crime becomes omnipresent and omnipotent, entering the familiar little village communities where everyone knows everyone else and people should feel safe, or even the home itself—the very symbol of peace and security.

The transference of crime from the city to the village had practical advantages for authors, too. The demands of the new longer form of detective fiction—the crime novel—dictated that the plot should be more complicated and the setting more elaborately depicted than was possible in the short story (Panek 1987, 131-32). By confining the characters to an enclosed locale, stories gained an aspect of local colour and began to explore the manners and habits of a certain community, which further served to lend "an air of verisimilitude" to the detective novel (Cawelti 1976, 97-98). In addition, the familiarity of the local community represents "the normally peaceful and serene order of society disrupted by the anomaly of crime and restored when the detective isolates the guilty individual" (98).

The symbolic upsetting of order is emphasised by another element of the detective novel: the opening scene. The first chapter of the novel generally takes place in a peaceful and orderly setting, be it in the "serene and rational order of the detective's apartment or in the pleasant warmth and social graces of the country house before the murder" (97). Suddenly, the fact that a crime has been committed is revealed and the calm of the private place is "disrupted by the chaotic outer world that has penetrated the quiet order and left behind [...] hidden guilt." The sequence follows in a circular pattern and, generally, at the end of the story the detective returns to her/his undisturbed study or home, the crime having been solved and order restored (97).

The device of the opening scene was exploited by a number of crime authors. Both Poe and Doyle set the introductions to their stories in the homes of their detectives; detective Dupin's private library and Sherlock Holmes's extravagant study not only served as calm spaces in opposition to the chaos outside, but were also reflections of the eccentric personalities of the detectives (Cawelti 1976, 82). This kind of introductory scene also "emphasizes the detachment of the detective, his lack of moral or personal involvement in the crime he is called on to investigate. The crime represents a disorder outside the confines of his personal existence, which thrusts itself upon him for resolution" (82-83).

In the case of Agatha Christie, both the general setting, described by Knight as the "English country house" (2004, 89) and the opening scenes are characterised not only by their private nature, but also by their domesticity. Christie's opening scenes are often set in the dining room, more specifically around the table during a meal (e.g. *Mrs McGinty's Dead* 7). Even those introductions set in Hercule Poirot's study depict the detective as engaging in his day-to-day domestic rituals, frequently involving the preparation of food or drinks (e.g. *Dumb Witness*). The meal and the dining-table rituals serve as symbolic representations of peace and order. Elinor Ochs et al. (1989) observe that formal centralised dinners, i.e. those where diners are seated around a table and participate in the same activity while eating are themselves highly ritualised affairs

> entailing conformity to numerous eating conventions. Many dinners involve opening and closing rituals, such as saying grace and asking permission to be excused. Further conventions include where to sit, which utensils to use, how close the serving dish should be from the plate, how much food one should serve oneself, how to request food, how to respond to offers of food, when to speak vis-a-vis eating, the order of eating different foods, which foods must be eaten, quantity of food which must be eaten off plate and so on. (240)

In other words, the meal is a ritual of order. Everything has its place and everyone involved has their own assigned role. In this sense the dining room at mealtime, as used by Christie, is the ideal setting for the opening scene of a crime story. Furthermore, the domestic setting is yet another aspect which feminises Christie's detectives. Christie's crimes are generally committed between family members or among a close circle of related persons; the criminals primarily threaten the personal safety of individuals within the home rather than menacing the wider public or even the entire society. In other words, the crimes are restricted to the domain generally understood as the feminine sphere (Knight 2004, 92).

1.3.2. Time or No Time?

Detective fiction is a genre which is characterised by the distortion of time (Hanson 2004, 9). Firstly, it is possible to observe a "dual movement" of time: the investigation moves simultaneously "backward to causes or origins" and "forward to effects or conclusions" (Hodgson 1992, 320). Secondly, the story is conditioned by a temporal inversion; the murder itself, chronologically the first event to occur, is the last. Thus each detective story can be divided into two temporal series: "the days of the investigation which begin with the crime, and the days of the drama which lead up to it" (George Burton quoted in Todorov [1966] 2008, 227). According to Todorov these aspects mirror the two elements of each narrative, the first of which is the sujet/plot, unlimited by constraints of physical time, which is represented here by the process of investigation in which the detective collects bits and pieces of the real events randomly, and not in the order in which they actually happened. The second element is the fabula/story, the actual story of the crime, which took place before the beginning of the narrative. The detective novel forms two separate time sequences from material which in other narratives would frame as just two aspects of one single chain of events (Todorov [1966] 2008, 227). However, one of the time sequences—the story of the crime—must always be absent from the actual narrative, otherwise the story of the investigation would lose its purpose.

Thus readers of detective stories follow the detective's movement forward in time towards the retrospective reconstruction of the events of the crime. This breaking of the boundaries between present, past, and future means that the detective story is not in fact set in any of these timeframes. The narrative becomes a timeless ritualistic tale. Nonetheless, authors who wish to maintain a sense of verisimilitude try to anchor the story to a specific time setting through the use of allusions to real-life events and persons. LeRoy Lad Panek (1987) observes that

> Golden Age writers usually make a point of dropping the name of at least one historical criminal during the course of their novels: one cannot read many novels of the era without encountering Crippen, Palmer, Joseph Smith, Burke and Hare, and other notorious real criminals. Bringing in

> historical criminals established the bona fides of the writers (and readers) as criminologists (123-24)

However, as was suggested in section 1.1.1, authors mix these references to historical characters and events with references to fictional detectives and criminals and their feats, and use these to perform the same function of lending credibility to the text. Thus they "with one hand give hard facts about criminology and with the other hand establish a playful sense of unreality" (124) further complicating the sense of time in the stories, whether fictional or real.

It can be seen from the above discussion that the detective story is set neither in the present, nor in the past, nor in the future. Nor is it set in a real time, or in fictional time. Dick Allen and David Chacko state that the world of a detective story is fixed not in a real past, but rather in a conserved image of a time. This time is not fluid, but this does not seem to matter; it serves to render the story timeless, independent of time (1974, 348). McCaw elaborates this view of a "conserved image of time," claiming that the time of the detective novel is a nostalgic time—a longing recollection of a past that never truly was (2010, 50).

"Many twentieth-century writers of classical detective stories reflect the nineteenth-century novel in their treatment of society in the form of nostalgic fantasies of a more peaceful and harmonious social order associated with the traditional rural society of England" (Cawelti 1976, 98). This is certainly true in the case in the Sherlock Holmes stories, which represent "a lovingly detailed picture of late Victorian England" (Grella 1970, 35), and it is also apparent in the unchanging quasi-Victorian provincial towns or manor house of Agatha Christie's mysteries. If Christie ever mentions contemporaneous events or their consequences, such as Poirot's flight from Belgium in the First World War or Hastings' past as an army officer wounded in the same war, these are only details which have "nothing directly to do with the plot" (Knight 2004, 90). The almost universal presence of the nostalgic time in Golden Age detective novels reflects the feeling prevalent in the turbulent period of the early 1900s, when people facing rapid social and ideological change experienced a growing nostalgia for an imaginary better past inhabited by a more content population (Grella 1970, 47-8).

1.3.3. Detective Story as Set in a Nation

While the importance of time and place in classical detective novels is clear, it can also be argued that the concept of the nation is an equally important element of the setting. Ochs et al. assert that all narratives are central to the creation of group feeling, manifested through "a general sense of co-membership" (1989, 253). In a crime narrative, the group which is emphasised the most is the nation. Erdmann claims that the contemporary crime novel has become a kind of *heimatroman* or "homeland novel;" in this context, the term homeland standing for "everything that the home locality involves—such as types of buildings, traditional costumes, customs and values, local dialects—with an emphasis on rural rather than urban life. It can also be understood [...] as the primordial tie to an ethnic group" (2009, 16). To a certain extent, this is also true of the classical detective story.

As early as the beginning of the twentieth century, French and English crime literature "was expected to exhibit a certain national flair" (14). Crime authors relied heavily on national stereotypes in terms of both characterisation and in the creation of setting (22). These stereotypes can be understood as forming an integral part of the crime formula: the standard and stereotypical depictions of the Englishman, the Frenchman and the Arab represent a rule of characterisation, and the typical English country manor house became the customary setting of the Golden Age crime novel (see 1.3.1). Thus "[w]hile literary theory and cultural criticism in the late twentieth century questioned the basic features of identity, that is, gender and nationality, as historical constructs, crime fiction sought to affirm a sense of national and gender identity all the more intensively" (Erdmann 2009, 20).

As a rule, classical British crime stories are set exclusively in England, most frequently in its southern part known as the Home Counties. Scotland, Wales or Ireland do not usually enter the picture. Thus the Golden Age novel is concerned with the confirmation "of a dominant form of Englishness" (Rowland 2001, 62). McCaw agrees, claiming that "[f]or many readers and viewers it is Christie's quintessential Englishness that is central to her appeal: 'Christie offers us a world of perfect order [and] we have a desire to believe the world is an English village" (2010, 41). In other words, Golden Age crime authors present a simplified, stylised depiction of Britishness, or more accurately Englishness, limited to a definite set of images. According to Susan Rowland (2001), Christie's Miss Marple is depicted as "a collection of stereotypical Englishness" and Hastings is endowed with so many clichéd traits of an English gentleman that he becomes a parody rather than a depiction (63). As will be shown later, these stereotypical depictions are not always used to uphold, but are also often used to undermine the general preconceptions about nation and the sense of a nation's unity.

However, in order to be able to create a unified and symbolic image of Englishness, authors needed to establish a clear-cut divide between what was English, and therefore local and familiar, and what was different and, by extension, foreign. The method employed to differentiate between the two was the technique which Edward Said labelled "orientalism," i.e. the construction of Western identity by "projection onto a homogenised Eastern "other" of precisely what the occidental is supposed *not* to be: irrational, savage and dark" (Rowland 2001, 62, original emphasis). Thus the English character is defined by means of a set of negative oppositions, underlining its difference from the other (67).

In earlier works of crime fiction, these oppositions were employed to highlight the nature of the other as a menace to the integrity of the English nation. For example in A. Conan Doyle's stories, the other was often associated with crime and guilt, while conforming to English values was connected to ideals of morality and innocence. The shifty foreigner was very frequently also the thief or the murderer. This practice, which was employed well into the twentieth century, not only reflected England's "need for a European scapegoat" to achieve "a symbolic displacement of post-Second World War anxiety" (McCaw 2010, 43), but was also evidence of a more general "anxiety over colonial relations of all kinds," so often personified by Christie's groups of English tourists in the former colonies of the British Empire who are shown as being very aware of "their own otherness in foreign lands" (Rowland 2001, 71). The ever-present racism and nationalism and the post-colonial awareness of difference permeate the Golden Age crime novel. Even if these attitudes are not represented directly in the behavior of characters or by ascribing the guilt to the foreigner, they are at least visible in "rhetorical modes of presentation" (65). For example in P. D. James's novels, characters appear to be politically correct and racist attitudes are condemned, however the stories still reveal a strong distaste for multiculturalism and argue against the integration of other cultures into British society (Rowland 2001, 67).

Authors have repeatedly used the implication of racism or have pandered to the assumed racism of their readers in order to add complexity to their plots. In Ngaio Marsh's novels, suspects often include a number of foreigners who "attract suspicion, so advertising English racism, but are very rarely guilty" (Rowland 2001, 65). This technique was also frequently employed by Sayers and Christie. Their detectives are never overtly racist, however the other characters (and, by implication, also the readers) often are, and as such are distracted from the correct solution by their instinctive distrust of "a suspicious Arab" or a furtive Greek husband (Rowland 2001, 66). The criminals themselves make use of this racist undercurrent and mask themselves as foreigners or instead cast aspersions of guilt at a foreigner in order to draw suspicion away from their own culpability. Thus they "project their criminality as 'other' or foreign to their own psychic construction of Englishness" which is equated with morality and innocence (69).

However, although racism and nationalism permeate the Golden Age crime story, these concepts and feelings are not always wholeheartedly embraced. The New Zealand born Ngaio Marsh identified her detective as English, but at the same time used otherness to criticise and dissect the conceit of Englishness. In her stories the culture of the Maori is depicted as possessing such integrity that it becomes immune to crime, and is contrasted favourably with English culture, in which an inherent corruption leads inevitably to crime (Rowland 2001, 66). Christie, too, mocked the self-conscious awareness of the English and their need to conform to an idealised national identity. This is especially visible in the interplay between her two characters, detective Hercule Poirot, whose "neatness, fussiness, [and] demands for fine food and central heating" (Rowland 2001, 63) are in complete opposition to the perfected masculinity of the stiffly gentlemanly and stereotypically English Captain Hastings. In the interactions between the pair, it is always Poirot who has the upper hand and who is demonstrably less naïve and more insightful. This ironic treatment of stereotypical Englishness is accentuated by Hasting's name, which alludes to the famous battle in which the English were conquered by the perennial other in the English psyche, continental Europeans (63).

The mockery of Englishness seen in crime fiction can be considered as a reflexion of the growing sense of instability within the nation itself. Authors who were faced with social and cultural changes presented by modern life began to lose faith in the belief that the nation was a coherent unity characterised by common traits. It gradually became apparent that the supposedly unified nation was in fact deeply divided. Firstly, Dorothy L. Sayers and other female authors of the Golden Age realised that women were treated as "a colonised other within English society" (Rowland 2001, 72); the underlying assumption within English society was that a woman could never be as truly English as a man, a conceit which suggests that the seemingly coherent community is in fact split in two. Furthermore, even the quintessentially English manor house or country estate began to be perceived as nothing more than a nostalgic reminder of the nation's past and forgotten glory, and that this nostalgia was at root "psychically as well as criminally sick" (72). The murdered corpses which littered the English country homes and vicarages of Golden Age detective novels indicate that crime permeates the environment.

Paradoxically, it is precisely through crime that authors tried to reunite this internally divided nation. In her novels, Agatha Christie presented the English village as an "idealized world," "a world that is unified and operating according to age-old principles." However, the actual characteristics which made this fictional world English, the "bonds of solidarity and fellow feeling," were not named or were very slight and "this is where the representation of crime becomes so crucial. For it is the communal response to crime that reveals the underlying collective identity;" without it "there is no clear social adhesive, little to define what Englishness really is" (McCaw 2010, 44). Traditional crime authors made use of this interconnection between crime and social coherence, and many novels of the time support Émile Durkheim's assertion that crime is a necessary element in society because it helps society to recognise its common values and unifies its members against a common enemy, the disruptor of the established order (McCaw 2010, 45).

However, gradually even this "likemindedness" in response to crime (47) began to dissolve. The social and ideological changes which took place following the Second World War were so profound that the image of a nation as a defined and static entity no longer applied and the national landscape of the detective novel was uncovered as a myth, a "fantasy derived from nostalgia," "a fly-in-amber land, in which were perpetuated the ways and the values of a society that had begun to fade away" (47). In their later novels, detective fiction authors unmasked the true nature of Englishness as a collection of empty signifiers devoid of any real content. National identity has become a model of the real "without origin or reality: a hyperreal." Consequently, crime, rather than fostering a sense of national identity, had begun to use the concept for its own purposes, such as in Agatha Christie's *Nemesis* where the patriotic Houses and Gardens of England tour serves as a backdrop to a scene of crime and suspicion among its participants (McCaw 2010, 52). All feelings of community within the nation were lost and Englishness became a "theatrical notion." National identity was revealed as something which is neither natural nor true, but is instead "made up" and lacking in substance (Rowland 2001, 63). Alison Light (1991) claims that the masquerade or the "fake" is indeed the driving force of Christie's stories. Her world is a world of farce where "[v]olubility stresses the ephemeral as though meaningfulness itself had been thrown into the melting-pot" (68).

This awareness of the emptiness of the notion of English national identity led to a questioning of the past, the time which helped to nourish this notion. As was demonstrated above, the writing of classical crime authors "seems fixed in a mythic time, 'a golden age' apparently outside history" (Light 1991, 63). Crime authors and even the characters themselves are aware of the fictionality of such a mythical time. P. D. James's detectives Adam Dalgliesh and Cordelia Gray, for example, "sense that the desire for a sacred past Englishness is a fantasy not borne out by history. These detectives know that England never was the ideologically whole, undivided nation they long for" (Rowland 2001, 70). The lovingly remembered time when the English nation constituted a united community with shared values, was acknowledged by many Golden Age authors to be largely imaginary. And this "manufactured past" (McCaw 2010, 51), unreal yet nonetheless enchanting, serves as a parallel to the equally enchanting distinct and unified nation that never was.

Notes

[1] Agatha Christie's comments are part of an original recording transcripted by Selina Mills and Rosie Waites at BBC. See partial transcript at <http://news.bbc.co.uk/today/hi/today/newsid_7612000/7612534.stm>

CHAPTER TWO

THE FOOD FORMULA

The last two decades have seen the birth and rapid rise to prominence of a new field of study in the humanities—food studies. The theoretical study of food had been marginalised and neglected for so long by academia that even in 2008, when Warren Belasco published his book defining key concepts in the field, he admitted that often when he told his colleagues or friends about his area of specialization, he was faced with their unbelieving stares or even deprecation (2008, 2). Belasco therefore asked himself why it is that the consumption of food, one of the few inevitable elements of life, which is shared by all individuals and societies, is so invisible to researchers and scientists.

The reasons, he argues, spring from the deep-seated patriarchy, which have for long pervaded education and research in the West. Traditionally, food is the domain of women; it belongs to the insignificant private domestic sphere and it concerns the profane body and its desires, which, according to classical Western philosophy, need to be repressed. On the contrary, research is the pursuit of the pure masculine mind, rational and liberated from the restricting limits of the body. Thus in the patriarchal world order, the two fields of research and food are not compatible (Belasco 2008, 2-3). Another obstacle which slowed the development of the study of food is that it requires a holistic, general approach. Food is a subject pertaining to a number of disciplines, including (but not limited to) biology, sociology, anthropology, and economics. In order to be able to study food, the researcher cannot specialise. They must become, as Belasco put it, a generalist, someone who has access to information from many areas and who can thus provide an overview and put the individual data into a broader perspective, a feat which is often impossible to specialists (7).

However, in reality the union between food and research is not only possible, but has proven to be a fruitful one. As Carole M. Counihan and Penny van Esterik (2008) observe, interest in food studies has expanded dramatically, especially over the last ten years. Not only does the discipline of food studies continue to grow in itself, but it also penetrates other fields such as psychology or geography, where it is used as a method of revitalising research and providing a different perspective (1). Paradoxically, the reason for the rapid growth of the field lies in the reasons behind its former stagnation: the growing prominence of women's studies has resulted in the acknowledgement of the importance of the hitherto neglected "female" spheres of interest. The private and domestic domains have been legitimised as subjects of scientific interest (1).

Another strong force which has contributed to the growing interest in food studies is the increasing insecurity and fear connected with food. Consumers in the West are slowly beginning to realise that food production has lost its local character and that it has become a global pursuit in which agricultural and food producing companies are important players in politics and in the economy. This new awareness gave rise to the aforementioned fears and consequently to various movements campaigning for a more ethical, healthier, and more environmentally conscious style of eating (Counihan and Esterik 2008, 2). Finally, Belasco adds one more reason for the rise of food studies, namely that this subject reflects the new interests in “matters of taste, craft, authenticity, status and health” shared by educated Western middle classes, whose members form the greatest part of academia (2008, 6).

As mentioned above, food studies is a holistic and interdisciplinary field. Despite this fact, it is possible to distinguish three distinct general research approaches, which are taken by the majority of food scholars. The first of these is the anthropological/sociological approach, utilised by a number of contemporary scholars, such as Carole Counihan, Warren Belasco, or Jack Goody. In addition, interest in food can also be detected in the works of classic anthropologists such as Claude Lévi-Strauss or Margaret Mead. Other authors and scholars, such as Sidney Mintz or Wolfgang Schivelbusch, opt for a historical approach to food. In addition, food has recently been discovered as a topic by philosophers, which in turn gave rise to the third approach to food studies, namely the philosophical approach. Food philosophers such as Lisa Maree Heldke, Dave Monroe, and David M. Kaplan ponder a wide range of food related questions.

The academic study of food has been supplemented by an ever-growing number of food professionals, chefs, cookbook authors, and nutritionists writing about food. As Fabio Parasecoli (2008) puts it “food is pervasive” (2) and this is reflected by the close attention that the media and the public at large now pay to prominent celebrity chefs or nutrition specialists whose self-appointed role is to tell the public what is, in Marvin Harris’s words, “good to eat” ([1985] 1998). However, the vast amount of often conflicting information about food now available has left the public more unsure and confused than ever before. Signe Rousseau (2012) observes that the hero-worship of TV chefs is just one of a number of symptoms which suggest that people feel they need help and advice in determining what they should eat (xxii-xxiii). This atmosphere of food fear and confusion has given rise to a growing number of food activists and movements, such as Carlo Petrini's Slow Food campaign or the Local movement championed by Gary Paul Nabhan.

As the issues associated with food continue to form a pervasive force in contemporary discourse, interest in food has spread from the domain of food studies and the food industry to other fields. Scholars researching art, gender studies, architecture, mass media, and literature now adopt food as a method for use in their work (Counihan and van Esterik 2008, 1). This chapter briefly examines the multitude of approaches to the study of food undertaken by anthropologists and sociologists (2.1), historians (2.2), philosophers (2.3), and literary theoreticians and critics (2.4). Moreover, it explores how food can be useful in the study of formulaic forms of writing, in particular the genre of detective fiction (2.4.1). The last section attempts to show that the formula of the classical detective story, as understood by structuralists such as Cawelti, is indeed not so different from the standard formula of food preparation: the recipe.

2.1. Anthropology and Sociology of Food

Food is an indispensable element in the lives of people in all cultures and societies and as such it has been of interest to classic anthropologists ever since the discipline first emerged. One of the first scholars to conceive of food as a subject for research was Margaret Mead (Counihan and van Esterik 2008, 3) in her pioneering work on the eating habits of post-war USA. Mead defined the food habits of a community as a "standardized set of behaviors in regard to food manifested by individuals" and saw them "as systematically interrelated with other standardized behaviors in the same culture" ([1943] 2008, 18). In other words, food is understood as being closely linked to all other phenomena in a culture and it is not possible to decipher changes in and implications of eating habits without taking into consideration a wide spectrum of other cultural structures. Mead maintained that in all cuisines a number of "available foods are arranged" into patterns, i.e. into dishes and meals (21). These patterns are formed and influenced by a whole spectrum of geographical, economic, and cultural factors such as income, availability of crops, religious taboos, etc. (22).

Mead's work demonstrates that food is by no means an isolated phenomenon and that it therefore cannot be successfully studied in such a manner. In her essay "The Problem of Changing Food Habits" ([1943] 2008) Mead highlighted the necessity of a holistic and generalist approach to the study of food and stressed the importance of integrating knowledge from various specialised disciplines into one framework (17). She argued that measures devised by mid-twentieth century nutritional specialists in order to feed post-Second World War Europe and introduce a healthier diet into affluent America often failed because these specialists did not take into consideration the far-reaching consequences of food, eating, and changes in foodways. "Only by putting each recommended innovation and the methods suggested for bringing it about against the total cultural picture, is it possible to guard against initiating changes which, while nutritionally desirable in the narrow sense, may be socially undesirable in a wider sense" (18).

Two decades later Claude Lévi-Strauss published "The Culinary Triangle" ([1966] 2008), an essay in which he summarised his structuralist approach to food (Ashley et al. 2004, 30). Lévi-Strauss presented a classification of food based on a system of binary oppositions (raw and cooked) modelled according to theories of structuralist phonctics formulated by Roman Jakobson (Ashley et al. 2004, 30). Mirroring the phonetic "vowel triangle" and "consonant triangle," Lévi-Strauss set to construct a "culinary triangle," the minimal system of types of foods and methods of food preparation ([1966] 2008 36-37). In his triangular system, the abstract categories of raw, cooked, and rotted correspond to methods of food preparation, i.e. roasting, boiling, and smoking (37). These categories enter into relationships of opposition; for instance, the relationship between boiled and roasted reflects the opposition between culture and nature. Moreover, it is possible to include various other elements in this framework, and thus arrive at the realization of an "unconscious language" by which a society expresses the patterns of its organisation (43). In Western societies boiling is associated with water, the private sphere (preparation of food at home), the family, the indoors and femininity; roasting, in contrast, connotes fire, the public sphere (prepared during celebrations for large groups), community/society, the outdoors and masculinity (38). Thus food is turned into a language-like structure, which can communicate a wide range of cultural meanings.

Lévi-Strauss's work led to further studies by structural anthropologists into the concept of food as a sign-system. In her publication *Purity and*

Danger: An Analysis of Concepts of Pollution and Taboo ([1966] 2002), Mary Douglas attempted a structuralist analysis of religious and ritual taboos including the Kosher laws of the Jewish faith. A semiotic approach to food inspired by structuralist linguistics was also advocated by Roland Barthes. In his essay "Towards a Psychosociology of Contemporary Food Consumption" (1961), he claimed that the foodways of a nation have a much deeper meaning than that acknowledged by political scientists or economists. He maintained that different types of food are not only substances but also "institutions" which "necessarily imply a set of images, dreams, tastes, choices, and values." In other words, food is not just a physical fact or a product, but it is also "a system of communication, a body of images, a protocol of usages, situations, and behavior" ([1961] 2008, 28). Barthes believed that "as soon as the basic needs [for nutrition] are satisfied [...] *food has a constant tendency to transform itself into situation*" (34, original emphasis).

While structuralists such as Lévi-Strauss, Douglas or Barthes studied food as a social phenomenon with a wide array of symbolic meanings, theorists who favoured a materialist approach adopted the opposite point of view. Marvin Harris viewed foodways of cultures not as bearing meaning, but instead as being guided solely by the laws of convenience, economy, and nutritional value. In his book *Good to Eat* ([1985] 1998), he examined and analysed various food taboos (especially those connected with meat) in cultures across the world on the basis of these laws. The fourth chapter entitled "The Abominable Pig" (67-87) is a direct response to the structuralist reading of Jewish food taboos conducted by Mary Douglas. Harris instead proposed a materialist explanation and showed how the taxonomy of forbidden animals was justified by the climatic and geographical conditions in the regions in which Jews originally lived.

However, in spite of their different approaches to food and sometimes even opposing points of view, all of the authors mentioned above agree on the need to study food as a phenomenon per se; they agree that it would be too simplistic to examine food solely through the lens of nutrition sciences or economy, thereby reducing it to a substance composed of various chemical elements necessary for the human body, or even to consider it as nothing more than a profit-bearing commodity. This need is also acknowledged by a number of contemporary food anthropologists and sociologists. Today, that which Mead, Strauss, or Barthes considered a necessary step to take to understand food has become reality and the field is far too broad to be summarised within the scope of a single chapter. Bearing this in mind, the following paragraphs attempt to trace only the main concerns currently dominating the extensive amount of research in the field of food anthropology.

Although contemporary food anthropologists and sociologists deal with a wide array of topics, three main domains of interest can be distinguished, namely "food insecurity, eating and ritual and eating and identities" (Mintz and Du Bois 2002, 99). The issues of food security and doubts about the possibility of providing sustenance for the world's rapidly growing population have become the main focus of attention for contemporary food experts. The problem of the availability of food is intertwined with concerns over the unequal distribution of food—the richest individuals in the world consume twenty-five times more than the poorest (Belasco 2008, 107).

Furthermore, consumption levels among the increasingly affluent populations of developing countries such as China continue to rise which in turn creates a need for intensive agriculture and animal husbandry, both of which cause serious damage to the environment and lead to the overexploitation of the world's reserves of drinking water (108-110). Food anthropologists attempt to trace the evolution of these problems, map their political, economic and environmental implications, and attempt to estimate how the issue of food security might develop in the future. They observe numerous aspects influencing global food supply in their analyses, including "changes in intergroup relations within socictics; mass production of foods; biotechnology; movements of peoples; increasing globalization of foods themselves; and war" (Mintz and Du Bois 2002, 104). In addition, they examine the complex power structures arising from the system of food production, distribution, and consumption in capitalist societies (Counihan and van Esterik 2008, 9).

While researchers dealing with issues of food security and insecurity address contemporary socio-economic problems, others continue the work of their structuralist predecessors and concentrate on the symbolic nature of food and its expression in food rituals. Kima Cargill (2007) observes that cultural and religious rituals almost always involve food or the process of eating (327). A close connection exists between food and the symbolism and belief systems of a culture; in fact, a culture's foodways represent a symbolic system in their own right. As a symbolic system, food can be used as a means of communication, both in a religious sense and in day-to-day encounters with other members of a community. As Mintz and Du Bois put it, "[n]ot only do ritual meals connect participants to invisible beings, but they also perform critical social functions. Eating in ritual contexts can reaffirm or transform relationships with visible others" (2002, 107). However, in order to form a symbolic system from food, it is necessary that it be consumed "in ritual contexts," i.e. "the symbolic meaning depends not simply on what is served but on how food is actually used not only in the rituals, but the routines and conventions of daily eating" (Marshall 2005, 70). The process of eating in each community is guided by spoken and/or unspoken rules and meals are prepared and consumed in a series of standardised operations. These repeated actions transform the process of eating into a ritualised act (69-70).

The ways in which food is interconnected with religion, ethnicity, and other markers of identity is another crucial issue studied by food anthropologists. In fact, food itself is one of the most important markers of identity. "[F]ood serves both to solidify group membership and to set groups apart" and it "functions in social allocation, in terms of ethnicity, race, nationality, class, and (less precisely) individuality and gender" (Mintz and Du Bois 2002, 109). The first of the important elements of identity shaped through food is ethnicity or nationality. As with all other aspects of identity, a sense of an individual's or group's own ethnicity is born from difference. "Hence an ethnic cuisine is associated with a geographically and/or historically defined eating community" (109). However, this sense of ethnicity, as Sidney Mintz and Christine M. Du Bois observe, is not something predefined and unchangeable, but is instead a constructed notion; it remains something which is largely imagined in much the same way as respective cuisines can only be imagined (see 3.3). Nevertheless, once these ethnic/national cuisines come to existence—even if only in a nation's imagination—they are able to influence and reinforce the sense of identity (Mintz and Du Bois 2002, 109).

Class is another aspect of identity which is closely connected with the food which one eats. Wynne Wright and Elizabeth Ransom (2005) observe that "over the past two decades food has increasingly become a signifier of social class and cultural capital" (310). An individual's status in society can now be either reaffirmed or undermined according to their diet and eating correctly has become an important signifier in upward social mobility (310). A number of authors, for instance Jack Goody (*Cooking, Cuisine and Class: A Study in Comparative Sociology*, 1982) or Harvey A. Levenstein (*Paradox of Plenty: A Social History of Eating in Modern America*, 1993) take class difference as the starting point of their studies of food.

However, of all the identity markers connected with food and eating, none has recently received so much attention as the interconnection of food and gender (Mintz and Du Bois 2002, 109). The interest in the study of food from a gender perspective, and especially the interest in the relationship of women to food, should not strike one as surprising, as it was indeed the discipline of women's studies which paved the way for the acceptance of food studies as a respected academic field (see above). Nevertheless, although food has historically been strongly associated with women, recent researchers such as Fabio Parasecoli also pay attention to the relationship of men to eating and to how food shapes masculinity in its various forms.

A number of authors, both classic (Claude Lévi-Strauss, Mary Douglas) and contemporary (Belasco, Counihan, Deborah Lupton, etc.), have observed that food is loaded with a wide range of gender associations in all cultures. Food and reproduction are the two activities that bring the sexes together: men and women need to engage in a collective effort in order to secure sustenance and procreation (Belasco 2008, 36). Moreover, the activities of eating and sexual intercourse exhibit a number of similarities: both involve crossing individual body boundaries, are inevitable to sustain life (Counihan 1999, 63), both engage the senses, are enacted in strongly intimate settings, and involve use of the mouth (Belasco 2008, 35-36). Counihan describes food and sex as "metaphorically overlapping," adding that "gifts of food may represent offers of sex, and sex may be described through food images" (Counihan 1999, 63). Consequently, both activities are governed by sets of rules and taboos determining the settings in which, and the persons with whom, they can be performed.

This interconnection of food and gender is not only general and symbolic, but is manifested in the concrete everyday eating habits of women and men. In all cultures, maleness and femaleness are defined through the consumption of specific foods (Counihan 1999, 63); more specifically, gender identities are defined by what one is and is not supposed to eat (3). It has been shown that people in Western societies have deep-seated beliefs about which foods are feminine and which are masculine, and which foods are appropriate or inappropriate for members of each sex to consume (Lupton 1996, 104).

In summary, over the last two decades a huge amount of research has been conducted in the fields of food anthropology and food sociology. Authors have observed the role of food in almost all aspects of the lives of individuals and societies and have also examined many of the most pressing issues of contemporary civilisation, such as food insecurity, world hunger, food safety, and the influence of food consumption and production on the world economy and global politics. Others have continued the work of classic anthropologists and discussed food as a system of symbols and a means of cultural communication, especially as manifested in the ritual forms of eating. Finally, a large group of scholars have dealt with the ways in which food and identity are intertwined and studied how food helps shape and undermine an individual's or a community's sense of ethnicity, class, and gender. The following section offers an overview of the historical approach to food; it also traces the developments of some of the phenomena studied by food anthropologists and discusses the ways in which foodways change over time.

2.2. History of Food

In his ground-breaking book *Histoire de l'alimentation* published in 1894, Louis Bourdeau was one of the first scholars to call for a more serious approach to the subject of food history, arguing that food is the single element which has influenced all people at all times and in all societies economically, socially, and philosophically ([1894] 2005, 4-5). He went on to criticise the fascination of the scholars of his era with the "*monde idéal*," which he considered as being far removed from the needs and demands of "*la prosaïque réalité*" (5). In his book Bourdeau intended to trace the development of the nature and production of foodstuffs; typical methods of conservation, preparation of various meals or food products (drinks, bread, etc.); and the manner of serving them ([1894] 2005, 6) to fill a gap that he believed existed in the study of history.

As Michele Field (2007) observes, Bourdeau's call for the recognition of food history went largely unheeded; even a century after the publication of his landmark study, "there was such a vacuum in reliable food scholarship" that any historian writing on food was faced with the prospect of a circular research which constantly returned to the same publications, most notably to one of the few comprehensive reference books on food to date, Alan Davidson's *Oxford Companion to Food* (Field 2007, 20). Over the last few decades this situation has gradually changed. In 1981 Alan Davidson co-organised the first Oxford Symposium on Food and Cookery (Field 2007, 20) and 1989 saw the establishment of the International Commission for Research into European Food History, an organisation which would later sponsor European research in the field (Atkins, Lummel and Oddy 2008, xv). Consequently, in 2002 John C. Super went as far as to claim that "[t]he transformation of food from a marginal subject of interest to a few agricultural historians to one recognized for its potential for exploring new dimensions of the past is now almost complete" (165).

As more and more historians choose food as the subject of their research and as the published work on the subject continues to grow, it is now possible to overview some of the general approaches undertaken and the topics which are most frequently studied. The three most dominant approaches to writing food history are as follows: 1) the comprehensive approach, 2) the specialised approach, and 3) the popularising approach. The comprehensive approach aims to cover as broad a scope as possible, and authors opting for this approach therefore usually cooperate in teams on reference books or encyclopaedias, or publish collections of papers. According to Super, some of the most important reference works defining the field of food history include Jean Louis Flandrin and Massimo Montanari's *Food: A Culinary History from Antiquity to the Present* (1999), which presents a general overview of the development of food and eating in Europe, together with Alan Davidson's *Oxford Companion to Food* (2006), Kenneth F. Kiple and Kriemhild Coneè Ornelas's *Cambridge World History of Food* (2000) or Raymond Grew's *Food in Global History* (1999). All of these authors attempt to place food into broader contexts of culture, society, politics, economy, and health, taking into consideration as many factors and sides of the issue as possible.

In contrast, other authors choose to specialise and concentrate on a single period, nation, food item or method of preparation (Super 2002, 168). Numerous histories with a single crop, dish, or food group as their focus have been published to date, including Wolfgang Schivelbusch's *Tastes of Paradise: A Social History of Spices, Stimulants, and Intoxicants* (1993); Mintz's *Sweetness and Power: The Place of Sugar in Modern History* (1986); and Du Bois, Chee-Beng Tan and Mintz's *The World of Soy* (2008). Some examples of histories focusing not on a crop but covering a geographically, culturally, or temporally limited area are Andrew Coe's *Chop Suey: A Cultural History of Chinese Food in the United States* (2009) or *Culture of the Fork: A Brief History of Everyday Food in Europe* (2001) by Giovanni Rebora. Finally a number of authors, including some of those mentioned above, have attempted to popularise food history and food writing by tailoring their work for a more general audience (Super 2002, 168). These include Andrew Dalby (*Dangerous Tastes: The Story of Spices*, 2000) or Diane M. Spivey (*The Peppers, Cracklings and Knots of Wool Cookbook*, 1999).

In addition to the different approaches adopted, food historians also differ in the topics chosen for their research. These vary greatly and cover all periods of history, from the Palaeolithic to the twentieth century and deal with cuisines of all continents. Despite this diversity, Super maintains that it is possible to trace four main themes dominating the field of food history. These are “diffusion, ‘other,’ cuisine, and nutrition” (2002, 169). Diffusion traces the discovery of individual foodstuffs, the development of eating habits and their changes over time. Historians interested in this aspect of food ponder issues such as “the transition from hunting and gathering to agriculture, the rise of grain-based diets, the emergence of cooking, and the complex social relationships associated with food” (Super 2002, 169). Currently, the main focus of this field of research is Europe and the Americas, although some studies have also been carried out on the ways in which “spices and aromatics [...] link Europe, the Middle East, and Asia” (170).

On the contrary, researchers discussing the "other" deal with eating and cooking in various cultures across the world. These authors understand food “as a physical property and a social symbol” which “separate[s] groups, distinguishes them from others in their own society, and from those beyond.” These concurrent functions of dividing and unifying are highlighted in the case of food taboos, whether cultural or religious, which represent “an extreme method of separation” (171). When cuisine is at the centre of attention, historians understand food as “one part of a historical matrix that shifts and changes through time” (171) and study it as an element of social structure. They concentrate on analysing eating habits, rituals of preparation and consumption of meals and the distinct relationships created through these processes in different societies. In other words, they view food as “grounded in the economic and political realities of the time” and of the culture in which it is eaten (172). Finally, authors frequently choose nutrition as the starting point for their research. Nutrition historians ask “basic questions about food availability” in various communities at different points of time. They discuss topics as food availability and scarcity, food inequality, luxury foods, malnutrition and famine (172). They investigate “changes in patterns of eating, the general levels of nutrition and the consequences for health and life expectancy” (Woolgar et al. 2006, 1).

This overview demonstrates that although food history has expanded greatly over the past two decades as more and more scholars turn their attention to it, the field is far from unified. The interests, methods, and approaches are highly diverse and are often not limited to the realm of history alone. As in food anthropology, the current trend in food history is to abandon a purely historical approach in favour of an all-encompassing interdisciplinary one. Bentley notices this trend, claiming that there is a “growing academic interest in the cultural study of food” and scholars such as Mintz, Levenstein, and Belasco focus on “cultural and social histories of food” (Bentley 1994, 523). Not only do they document history, but they also use "food as a vehicle for examining larger cultural, political, and social changes" (524). Authors observe the influence of historical events (such as the World Wars, the Great Depression, or the Industrial Revolution) on foodways; they also describe a nation/community's "food consumption and habits" and their change in time, take note of "corporatism and materialism" (524), "increasing mechanization of food production," "proliferation of corporate food products," "standardization of tastes and diet," etc. To sum up, a growing number of scholars work on the borderline between history and sociology, examining the "relationship between food and other indexes of social change" (526).

C. M. Woolgar et al. (2006) also observe this trend, noting that

> [i]n the past twenty years [the study of food] has changed a great deal and a multi-disciplinary approach has become essential to encompass the historical, archeological, and scientific record. During this time, historians have opened up sources in new ways; zooarchaeologists and archaeobotanists have processed and assimilated archaeological material from a wide range of sites; and scientific techniques [...] have begun to allow an assessment of the cumulative impact of diet on the human skeleton. Nonetheless, the wide variety of information about diet and nutrition has rarely been drawn together. (1)

They go on to argue that historians and scholars working in other fields need to start cooperating, because a topic as all-encompassing as food cannot be understood when approached from only one perspective; in order to achieve "a holistic view of the subject," plurality of approaches is necessary (2) (see similar argument by Belasco in 2.1).

As can be seen from the summary above, this shift of perspective has already begun. Moreover, historians of food do not venture only into the fields of sociology and archaeology; in his *Paradox of Plenty: A Social History of Eating in Modern America* (1993), Levenstein combines history and sociology with economics in his discussion of the effects of abundance in contemporary USA (Bentley 1994, 525). In *Meals to Come* (2006) Belasco moves into the field of "history of the future" and offers a vision of the future of food through the lens of an eclectic mix of economics, social and cultural studies, mass media studies and political science. In *Building a Housewife's Paradise: Gender, Politics, and American Grocery Stores in the Twentieth Century* (2010), Tracey Deutsch takes a post-modernist stance towards food, analysing the "broad significance of exchange and consumption to power relations in modern life" from the point of view of political science and gender studies. She concentrates on the demographics of the US population, on patterns of consumption, and on how they "undergirded U.S. politics for much of the twentieth century" (9). Joan Fitzpatrick's *Renaissance Food from Rabelais to Shakespeare* (2010) presents an examination of various texts discussing food—historical documents, cookbooks, literary works—combining history with literary criticism, while Massimo Montanari intertwines history with language in his study of proverbs about food titled *Cheese, Pears, and History in a Proverb* (2010).

In summary, contemporary food historians do not restrict themselves to a purely historical approach to their subject. Instead, as Montanari put it, scholars attempt to observe food "under a *macroscope*" (2006, vii, original emphasis). They believe that to understand the complex relationships created by food consumption and production, and the various influences which they have had on other historical events, it is necessary to find a way to integrate knowledge from diverse fields, including but not limited to "nutrition, literature, linguistics, myth, folklore, history, and medicine" in order to achieve "the broadest perspective possible" (Montanari 2006, vii).

2.3. Philosophy of Food

The idea of food as a philosophical topic was long neglected by thinkers in the West. In traditional Western philosophy, food was regarded as an issue which pertained to the inferior world of the body and the physical rather than the superior world of the mind and the ideal, and was therefore considered unworthy of serious attention. This approach was advocated by philosophers in the idealist tradition in particular. Plato neglected the body and the physical on the grounds of his assumption that the material world was merely a reflection of the perfect or ideal world. This perfect world could only be imagined or described by human representation, but could never be realised. Thus in Plato's "hierarchical model of the world [...] ideas were supreme," whilst the "world of the senses, bodily pleasures, and humdrum" was marked as inferior and not deserving of serious attention (Symons 2007, 24).

Plato not only thought of food and bodily pleasures as unimportant, he also considered them dangerous. Jessica Moss (2006) writes: "Plato is suspicious of pleasure. He devotes the whole of the Philebus and a significant portion of the Gorgias to attacks on hedonism. He declares that 'the soul of a true philosopher...keeps away from pleasures and appetites and pains and fears as much as it can' and denounces pleasure as 'evil's greatest lure" (503). According to Michael Symons, Plato believed that "[f]eeding reduced people to the level of animals, and [that] the appetites needed strict controlling." His class system corresponded to this view: the upper classes were to be composed of monarchs and thinkers, while food production should be confined to the lower classes (Symons 2007, 24). Moss explains that Plato believed pleasure to be dangerous because "it is a *deceiver*" (2006, 504, original emphasis). In his view, the pleasures of the body can and often do conflict with the rational principles of morality and goodness and should therefore be controlled. In other words, the mind always desires to do good but the body does not, and thus the body should be subordinated to the rule of the mind.

The desire for food and the pleasure of eating fall under the category of unreliable bodily pleasures. P. K. Skiadas and J. G. Lascaratos (2001) observe that while Plato acknowledged the necessity of humans to eat, he allowed for it only as "the provision of food for existence and life" (533). He believed that "variety of nourishment results in corruption and illness" and advocated self-restraint. He maintained that "dietary restrictions" ensured a healthy and moral life (535). Plato was also suspicious of cookery (*opsopoietiki*), which he did not consider an art, but merely a "habitude" (536).

The Platonic dichotomy of mind and body, in which the mind is the superior, more valuable element, and his consequent dislike of pleasure were adopted by his followers in ancient Greece, and later by medieval philosophers in the Christian tradition. In the third book of his *Nicomachean Ethics*, Aristotle made a clear distinction between pleasures of the body "and those of the soul, such as love of honour and love of learning" ([350 BC] 2009, 10). He went even further in his division of pleasures by claiming that pleasures derived from the senses of sight, hearing, and smell were different from those derived from taste and touch. The latter two were the basest and most bodily of all senses, shared by humans and animals alike, and as such were considered "slavish and brutish" (10).

The pleasures arising from them, namely the enjoyment of food, drink, and sexual intercourse, should be subjected to temperance and restrictions, as "self-indulgence would seem to be justly a matter of reproach, because it attaches to us not as men but as animals. To delight in such things, then, and to love them above all others, is brutish" (10). According to Aristotle, these brutish delights tend to "go wrong," meaning that people tend to overindulge in them thereby leading to immoral and irrational behaviour. Therefore the pleasures of taste and touch which one experiences "should be moderate and few, and should in no way oppose the rational principle." In summary then, Aristotle's definition of a moral person is one whose body is controlled by her/his reason: "The temperate man craves for the things he ought, as he ought, and when he ought; and this is what rational principle directs" (12).

The work of Thomas Aquinas is in many ways a continuation of the Platonic and Aristotelian philosophical tradition. In Questions 141, 148, and 147 of *Summa Theologica* ([1265-74] 2000) he discussed the issues of temperance, gluttony, and fasting, respectively. Aquinas, like Plato and Aristotle before him, was a proponent of temperance, i.e. moderation and self-control. He also understood temperance as pertaining to the bodily pleasures of taste and touch, those, which he, as with Plato and Aristotle, labelled animal-like, and requiring the restraint of reason (2000, 3211-12). In addition, Aquinas developed the opposing concepts of gluttony and fasting. Gluttony is any excess pertaining to the consumption of food, i.e. a conscious exceeding of "the measure in eating, from a desire for the pleasures of the palate" (3258) and is considered a sin (3261). Aquinas also considered a developed taste and a delicate palate as gluttonous and criticized people who require "dishes that are expensive; [...] dishes too elaborately prepared, that is, daintily; [...] inordinateness [...] in the taking of the food, either by anticipating the due time of eating, which is too soon; or by not observing due mode and manner in eating, which is too eagerly" (3261).

In contrast, fasting is described as a legitimate religious practice to be undertaken in order to meet certain ends: "First, to repress the concupiscences of the flesh; [...] because by fastings chastity is preserved. Secondly, it is taken up that the mind may be more freely raised to the contemplation of high things; [...] Thirdly, to satisfy for sin" (3245). Thus in Aquinas's, Plato's, and Aristotle's philosophies alike, the body and its pleasures were considered dangerous and harmful as they could stand in the way of moral and reasoned behaviour, and therefore it was advised that these corporeal impulses be avoided or repressed by the mind.

However, the philosophical rejection of the body typical for authors in the idealist tradition was not universally shared. Certain philosophers chose the opposite approach and placed food at the centre of their theories. One of the most notable examples can be found in the work of Epicurus, who directly challenged Plato's rejection of the body and its drives; his philosophy instead placed the body before the mind as its necessary condition and he consequently viewed eating as the basis for all thinking. According to Symons (2007), some of the central elements in Epicurus's teaching placing him in the tradition of body philosophy were his esteem for the material world and the senses, his advocacy of pleasure (albeit with limits) and his acknowledgment of the importance of friendship, community, and conviviality (14).

Epicurus's lifestyle and philosophy strongly resemble those advocated by contemporary food movements. He and his disciples resided in a school called the Garden, which was located outside the city of Athens where the community were able to produce their own food. The community was characterised by its egalitarian spirit—men, women, and slaves all received equal treatment. Epicurus's moral system was constructed through empirical observation; right and wrong stemmed from the practical results or the "contentment" achieved through the actions which people performed in everyday life (Symons 2007, 15). Epicurus was a philosopher of the private and of the individual, as opposed to Plato, who dealt with the public. He saw the quest for wealth and power as ultimately fruitless and preferred the "security of living unknown," in friendship and conviviality, and a society that was a network of intimate relationships rather than a corporate structure of power and control (Symons 2007, 27).

"Epicurus was viewed in ancient times as a gardener, cook, and cookery writer" (Symons 2007, 18) and as such he "based his philosophy on meals" (17). Like Plato or Aristotle, he "recommended a simple life" of moderation, but at the same time he acknowledged that there were limits to everything, even to frugality, temperance, and reason (Symons 2007, 19). Symons observes that Epicurus's teaching could easily become a basis for contemporary foodies' philosophy in that it advocated empirical observations, the enjoyment of the pleasures of food in good company, and the bodily experience of eating as a basis for a feeling of unity with the cosmos. Moreover, he maintained that sharing food helps to teach generosity, etiquette, and the value of companionship; and that close connection with the production and preparation of food can instruct one about natural cycles, ecological systems, and even the working of elementary particles (21). Food enables "learning through observation, satisfaction, and conversation rather than through ideologies and dogmas," which helps to protect the Epicurean thinker from becoming "overawed by political and religious authority, preferring reclusive reassurance." Finally, a food philosophy can become a universal philosophy because its appeal is universal—ultimately, all people eat (22).

However, as Symons notes, despite the efforts of individual philosophers to force a re-evaluation of the West's relationship with food and the body, there long had been a "deep-seated antagonism within high Western culture" (23) towards all things physical, especially towards pleasure or enjoyment (see above). This slowly begun to change in the nineteenth century, the era of gastronomy and the gourmet. Stephan

Rössner (2007) claims that gastronomy was born of the French Revolution. Professional chefs, formerly employed exclusively by aristocratic households, were suddenly forced to abandon their positions and seek employment elsewhere. Thus the modern restaurant was born, an institution which catered to the needs of a growing class of affluent commoners (531). These new consumers shared a desire for the pleasures of "elaborately prepared fine food" which had hitherto been reserved solely for aristocratic society (Parkhurst Ferguson 1998, 602). Nevertheless, the doctrine of the Catholic church preaching against pleasure and indulgence, and the advocation of sobriety and self-control by traditional secular philosophers meant that hedonism and gastronomy continued to be labelled as either sinful or as forms of "social vice" (607-8). These attitudes were slow to change, but eventually they did. Gastronomy became understood as both "a science and an art" and the gastronome was now

> considered something of a philosopher-diner, the antithesis, in any case, of the unreflective eater whose lack of self-control led to the gluttony reproved by the Church. [...] This modern construction of culinary fervor sloughed off negative connotations onto the gourmand, the glutton (*glouton* or *goinfre*), or the *gastrolâtre* (someone who "makes a god of his stomach"), thereby securing for the gastronome the lofty position of high priest for this new cult. (609)

The establishment of gastronomy as a legitimate pursuit was accompanied by a rapid "[r]ise of culinary discourse" (611). As more and more texts on food and eating were published, there was a gradual change in the perception of gastronomy; from an extravagance of a few enthusiasts it turned into a proper scientific field. The most prominent food professionals or gastronomes writing at the beginning of the nineteenth century were the gastronomic journalist Alexandre Balthazar Laurent Grimod de la Reynière, writer of "culinary treatises" Antonin Carême, and Jean Anthelme Brillat-Savarin, whose work can be seen as a precursor to what is known today as the sociology and philosophy of food. "These three authors were witnesses to, even as they were agents of, the modernizing gastronomic society. Each aimed to systematize culinary knowledge; each contributed to the formalization and, hence, the very definition of modern French cuisine" (Parkhurst Ferguson 1998, 611). Brillat-Savarin went one step further and aimed at popularising gastronomy, turning it into a "topic of general discussion and analysis beyond those directly concerned with material production and consumption" (Parkhurst Ferguson 1998, 616). Thus, in nineteenth century

France a new philosophy, the philosophy of food, was born, and "[n]ever again could food be confused with either a sin or a mere bodily function" (617).

Nevertheless, it took more than a hundred years before gastronomy became a fully accepted part of philosophical discourse. Thanks to the rise of the alternative philosophies of feminism, post-colonialism, and multiculturalism in the 1980s, the tenets of traditional Western thinking were questioned and eventually overthrown; as a result, the discussion of issues which had long been neglected, such as those of women, bodies, and food, became possible (Symons 2007, 27). Although the discussion of food is relatively rare even in contemporary philosophy, interest in the subject is ever growing as can be seen in the emergence of volumes such as Deane W. Curtin and Lisa Heldke's *Cooking, Eating, Thinking: Transformative Philosophies of Food* (1992); Fritz Allhoff and Dave Monroe's *Food and Philosophy: Eat, Think and Be Merry* (2007); or Kaplan's *The Philosophy of Food* (2012).

Contemporary philosophical discussion of food covers a broad range of subjects. Some authors, such as Symons (see above), analyse Epicureanism as a philosophical approach and consider the benefits which can be gained from thinking critically about food. Others investigate issues of taste, focusing on taste in food rather than in art or aesthetics. For these authors "personal taste or choice emerge as critical issues" and they question how subjective these issues really are, and also "to what extent [they] are free or controlled" (Wrye 2007, 46). The authors try to establish whether tastes in food can be learnt and cultivated, or whether they are, as Pierre Bourdieu maintains, socially constructed and influenced by an individual's community ties and class affiliation ([1979] 1984, see also Wrye 2007, 46-47, Iggers 2007, 94). Other scholars, for instance Carolyn Korsmeyer (2007), focus on the opposition between "delicious" and "disgusting" and observe how individual foods fall into or cross the boundaries between these categories, and how even the disgusting can become a source of delight and pleasure (145).

Another group of thinkers deal with the aesthetics of food and ask whether it is possible for cooking to be considered a form of art, and also whether food itself can be an object of beauty and art. They note that while food, paradoxically, does not fall under any traditional art category, it is still common practice to speak of it as art. Monroe ponders the question of whether the utilitarian and perishable nature of food impedes its becoming a true art object (2007, 133-44), while Kevin W. Sweeney (2007) wonders if food can be objectively and reflectively appreciated (117-32). Sheila Lintott (2007) opts for an even more unconventional approach, attempting to determine "the role of aesthetics in eating disorders" and whether it is possible to define these disorders as a quest for the sublime (68).

The philosophical subject which has probably been most extensively studied in relation to food is the ethics of eating. Approaches to food ethics vary greatly, from discussion of medical ethics, ecology, and health in publications such as Gregory E. Pence's *The Ethics of Food: A Reader for the 21st Century* (2002) to studies of post-colonial and social ethics represented by *Exotic Appetites: Ruminations of a Food Adventurer* (2003) by Lisa Maree Heldke. Moral philosophers of food attempt to ascertain whether eating is an ethical act and, if so, how people should eat.

The concept of ethical eating is closely connected with fears about food availability, the future of agriculture, and food safety (Belasco 2006, vii-viii). "For many years, agronomists, politicians, economists, philosophers, and poets have been arguing over whether Progress—defined as more convenience and more meat for more people—is sustainable." This debate has reached new intensity in the twenty-first century as fear of climate change and destruction of the environment continues to spread among the general consciousness (Belasco 2008, 105). Belasco and others now wonder what can be done to ensure health and nutrition for the growing world population without destroying the planet and, in addition, how this can be done ethically.

In response to these concerns, food activists have proposed a variety of alternative ethics of food, including vegetarianism, punk cuisine or organic farming (Counihan and van Esterik 2008, 6). These new food movements characterise themselves as responding to contemporary food insecurity, as well as to the paradox that although food has slowly moved to the centre of attention and more and more information on eating is available, "[m]ore people than ever before in history have absolutely no involvement in producing the foods that sustain them" (Nabhan 2002, 26). According to Gary Paul Nabhan (2002), a member of the Local food movement, contemporary consumers have become

> food worriers [who] fatalistically concede that we hardly know anything about who grew our food and how, but we are fixated on whether today's fare is more nutritious or less so, more tasty or more toxic, higher in fiber, folic acid, fat, and antioxidants or less so. As conscientious consumers we are told that we should be preoccupied with issues regarding the chemical composition, the days since initial packaging, and the densities of insect parts and fecal coliform found in the grains ground down to make our daily bread. Nonetheless we don't much fathom from whom or from whence they came. (27)

Nabhan proposes what Belasco has labelled an "anthropological fix" to this paradoxical relationship of consumers to food and to food scares. He advises consumers to eat locally and to produce as much self-grown food as possible in order to escape the negative influence of media, corporations, and institutions on their personal well-being (Belasco 2008, 122)—a focus on individuality and self-reliance which is reminiscent of the teachings of Epicurus.

Carlo Petrini, the founder of Slow, similarly responds to food fears and insecurities by proposing that consumers should reject imported or industrially produced food in favour of organically grown, locally sourced products (Schneider 2008, 384). Petrini goes even further, linking the decrease in local food production to the dissolution of community and family ties, and claiming that anxiety about food reflects more abstract anxieties about national/local identity, tradition, and heritage (A. Leitch 2008, 384). However, Petrini differs from other moralists of food in that he introduces the aspect of pleasure into the discussion. Slow Foodists propose a different solution to the problem of food insecurity than that envisioned by Belasco's anthropological fix. Instead of calling for a lowering of expectations and asking that consumers try to be satisfied with less than they currently enjoy, they stress that the pleasure which can be gained from life and consumption should still remain a priority (A. Leitch 2008, 394).

Slow Foodists place the pleasure of eating and faithfulness to tradition in food-making procedures before any other value, even that of food safety. Their emphasis on the centrality of pleasure in food ethics is such that they are often faced with accusations of being "a bunch of good-timers interested only in stuffing [themselves]" (Petrini 2001, 10). However, it is disingenuous to suggest that 'stuffing oneself' is the aim of Slow Food. Their objective is to create a new gastronomy, one that not only ensures that the nutritional needs of the world's population be met, but which also has broader economic and cultural dimensions. The purpose of Slow Food is to place food and pleasure of eating at the centre of society. This implies an abandonment of traditional morality defined by reason, asceticism, and resistance to desires, and instead teaches us to embrace pleasure as a means of reconnecting with our past, securing for ourselves a sustainable future, and establishing meaningful relationships with ourselves, others, and our environment. Slow Food rejects the traditional Western refusal to acknowledge the body, as well as the materialist belief that what is good to eat is dictated only by the laws of economy and necessity. Instead, we are asked to spend more time, money, and energy to eat less, but with more pleasure.

Such a hedonistic approach to food ethics is rare among contemporary thinkers. Indeed, pleasure seems to be a repressed topic for moral philosophers even in the twentieth and twenty-first century, when papers on hedonism tend to be structured as defences, rather than as descriptions or explanations (John Wild: "The Resurrection of Hedonism" [1927], Laurence J. Lafleur: "In Defense of Ethical Hedonism" [1956], Fred Feldman: "The Good Life: A Defense of Attitudinal Hedonism" [2002], or Roger Crisp: "Hedonism Reconsidered" [2006]). Both Feldman and Crisp devote a substantial part of their papers to responding to objections to hedonism. Crisp notes that one of these objections stems from the Aristotelian rejection of bodily pleasures as unclean, immoral, and pertaining to animals, and for this reason Crisp labels it the "philosophy of swine rejection" (2006, 622). Although Crisp's paper is in favour of hedonism, he still refuses to accept these "unclean" bodily pleasures and instead opts for the term enjoyment. Similarly, Feldman believes that "pleasure' properly applies to feelings of various sorts. All that is required is that the one who experiences the feeling enjoys it" (2002, 605). He goes on to differentiate between sensory or bodily pleasure and a sense of enjoyment, and for him it is exactly this kind of enjoyment "that makes life better." He calls it "attitudinal pleasure"—"a way of being aware of a state of affairs" (607). He admits that "[s]ome people are convinced that there is a deep conceptual link between the attitude of enjoyment and the feeling of sensory pleasure" (609), but he hesitates to accept this view.

One of the examples of a moral philosopher who awards sensual pleasure a place in their ethical system is Michel Onfray. In Onfray's popular philosophy, hedonism goes hand in hand with atheism and both allow him to oppose the traditionally prescribed repression of the body. As outlined in *La puissance d'exister* (2006), his ethical theory shows a clear break from traditional Western idealism. Instead, he argues for a morality founded on "an introspective attitude to life based on taking pleasure yourself and pleasuring others, without harming yourself or anyone else" (Melville 2007, 27). In summary, even the defences of hedonism as a moral philosophy carry the heritage of a long tradition of the subordination of bodily experiences to mental ones. Those who acknowledge and accept the importance of the body and of sensual pleasures, such as Onfray or Petrini, still represent a minority.

It is notable that the advocates of the philosophy of pleasure are more often found among the ranks of popular writers and philosophers than of academics. If scholars are still fighting against the continuing influence of the idealist tradition, perhaps the task of formulating a new philosophy of pleasure and the body must fall to someone else. Fritz Allhoff and Dave

Monroe believe that this new type of philosophy of food has become the domain of the chef her/himself, and they devote a whole section of their publication *Food Philosophy: Eat, Think and Be Merry* to contributions from food professionals (2007, 8-9). Jennifer Iannolo (2012) agrees with this view in an interview with chef Thomas Keller: "I've been talking to different chefs about food philosophy because to me, [they] are more food philosophers than anything." Iannolo holds the belief that the various approaches to cooking of different chefs result from their reflections on food and eating and from their personal philosophies of food.

Indeed, chefs such as Keller or Mark Tafoya publish cookbooks which offer not only recipes, but also insights into and reflections on food. They also contribute to periodicals and essay collections or, in Tafoya's case, edit food magazines (i.e. *The Gilded Fork*). The philosophy of the chef-philosopher is clearly a hedonist one, but it is also sensualist, paying attention to the body and celebrating bodily pleasures. *The Gilded Fork's* philosophical manifesto states:

> For us, the sensual experience is an ethereal one, where food is an intimate subject we approach with utmost sincerity; but the sensuality is equally an intellectual pursuit—the why behind the rapture. And lest we ever take ourselves too seriously, we always like to have fun with it. Fun and lots of sass where applicable.
>
> Rather than spotlight the trendy, we are focusing on the roots of cuisine itself, and celebrating the art of experiencing food, wine and culture via the senses in cooking, in tasting—and in understanding.
> (Iannolo and Tafoya 2012)

As Matt DeLucia (2006) argues, "[t]he modern chef is no longer focused or committed to one restaurant, or to one menu, or to one kitchen. They have become restaurant designers, cookbook writers, and business plan experts. They have had to become media experts, do interviews, and demonstrate their abilities on television." It can be seen from the above that they have also become philosophers advocating a new form of hedonism.

2.4. Food and Literature

As the previous three sections demonstrate, the study of food has now become an accepted and important part of contemporary scholarship. David Bevan observes that "[a]fter *homo sapiens*, *homo ludens*, *homo necans et al*," the contemporary age can be characterised by "the pervasiveness and the significance [...] of *homo edens*" (1988, 3). Furthermore, this pervasiveness has led to the birth of a new discourse of food and "what Brillat-Savarin projected over one hundred and fifty years ago has acquired a resonance and a centrality today that is admirably and exhaustively inscribed in text" (Bevan 1988, 3). However, the discussion of food is by no means limited to scholarly texts of philosophy, anthropology, and semiotics. Kerri Majors (2012) claims that "food is an essential ingredient in fiction" (68) not just in contemporary Western literature, but also in literary works "from practically any period or cultural tradition" (Keeling and Pollard 2009, 4). Yet despite its omnipresence, food has frequently been neglected by literary theorists and critics (6).

The reason for this paradox, Majors believes, lies in the negative connotations ascribed to fiction featuring food. "Food in fiction equals beach reading, as in 'not serious'—certainly not literary, and maybe even pornographic"[1] (2012, 79). This dismissal of food as not serious enough stems from traditional Western philosophy, as described in section 2.3, in which food was considered to be too trivial to be of interest to highbrow critics and theoreticians (Keeling and Pollard 2009, 6). Majors wonders whether "this uncertainty about food in literature might be related to its ephemeral nature. You make it, you eat it, and it's gone" (2012, 79).

However, even if food in the real world is short-lived and perishable, food in literature is permanent; moreover, it is fictional and replicable, and, as James Brown (1984) points out, "[f]ictional meals are above all literary signs: consequently they are subject to the same kinds of analysis as any other literary phenomenon" (quoted in Keeling and Pollard 2009, 6). Indeed, the study of food as a literary sign can provide significant insights when analysing a literary text. Food is the basic element around which human relationships, communities, societies, and even whole cultures are built, and as such it "is also fundamental to the imagination and the imaginary arts" (5). Food is an inseparable part of cultural rituals and therefore it is not only a reflection of culture, but also plays an active part in constructing it. Thus food ceases to be merely a practical matter of nourishment and becomes instead a matter of imagination, and consequently of art and literature (6).

A number of influential scholars have acknowledged the centrality of food to society and to literature. Mikhail Bakhtin addressed the issue of food as cultural sign in *Rabelais and His World* (1965); Roland Barthes did so in *Mythologies* (1957), a semiotic analysis of food further elaborated on in his "Toward a Psychosociology of Contemporary Food

Consumption" (1961, see 2.1). The topic was also addressed by Louis Marin in *Food for Thought* (1989) and by Julia Kristeva in *Powers of Horror: An Essay on Abjection* (1982) a work which discusses "food loathing as a means of deconstructing cultural signifying regimes" (Keeling and Pollard 2009, 8). Analyses of food in literature also appear in interdisciplinary texts, such as in Carolyn Korsmeyer's *Making Sense of Taste: Food and Philosophy* (2002), Michael Symons's *A History of Cooks and Cooking* (2004), and in Joan Fitzpatrick's *Renaissance Food from Rabelais to Shakespeare: Culinary Readings and Culinary Histories* (2010).

While the above-mentioned authors discuss food only in connection with other issues which are more central to their work, some scholars choose food as their primary concern. Among the first to do so was Norman Kiell, whose *Food and Drink in Literature: A Selectively Annotated Bibliography* published in 1995 remains the only "book-length bibliography of food in literature" to date (Keeling and Pollard 2009, 9). This volume is a reference book containing two alphabetically listed bibliographies, one dedicated to food in literary texts and the other to drinks, covering authors from Horace to Joseph Conrad. David Bevan's *Literary Gastronomy* (1988) is a critical analysis of food in twentieth century literature, which also addresses culinary texts. Similar publications include Barbara Scrafford's *Literary Feasts: Recipes from the Classics of Literature* (2004), Anna Shapiro's *A Feast of Words: For Lovers of Food Fiction* (1996), a food-based reading of twenty-five classic novels and stories supplemented by a selection of the author's own recipes, or John Wilkins's *Food in European Literature* (1996), a discussion of food symbolism in various literary texts from Portugal, Italy, France, England, and Ancient Greece and Rome. Mary Anne Schofield adopts a more interdisciplinary approach in her *Cooking by the Book: Food in Literature and Culture* (1989), which studies food as a rhetorical device in literary texts, mass media, advertising, and philosophy.

In addition to collective volumes such as those listed above, a number of monographic studies by single authors have also been published in the field over the last two decades. In *Eating Identities: Reading Food in Asian American Literature* (2008) Wenying Xu examines food symbolism in the writing of Chinese-American authors in an effort to study the problems of culture, politics, and identity. In *Culinary Fictions: Food in South Asian Diasporic Culture* (2010) Anita Mannur also takes the relationship between Asian-Americans and food as her starting point. She observes the link between food and ethnic identity, and also between food and gender in the work of Asian-American writers. Sarah Sceats focuses on the question of gender and her *Food, Consumption and the Body in Contemporary Women's Fiction* (2004) analyses the role of food in creating femininity in various forms. Andrea Adolph chooses a similar approach for her *Food and Femininity in Twentieth-Century British Women's Fiction* (2009), in which she discusses the manifold implications of female characters' relationships to food. And while all of the authors mentioned so far are mainly interested in how food shapes and reflects identity, Susanne Skubal addresses a different issue in her *Word of Mouth: Food and Fiction after Freud* (2002). This publication examines food from the psychoanalytic point of view, focusing on the role of oral experience and its various representations.

As culinary literary criticism is a relatively new field, most of the work is still published in the form of articles. Kara K. Keeling and Scott T. Pollard (2009) observe that the "key moment in the development of food studies in the humanities was the founding of *Gastronomica: The Journal of Food and Culture*, which began publishing in 2001" (7). *Gastronomica* focuses on food studies as "an existing field on its own, deserving its own journal, in which they feature a wide variety of interdisciplinary scholarly and general audience articles" (Keeling and Pollard 2009, 7). Thus the journal also provides a forum for culinary literary critics and theoreticians, which, according to Keeling and Pollard, "is much needed, given that although many analyses of food in literature are being produced, there is no strong venue devoted to the topic" (8).

In summary, a number of scholars have recently become interested in the field of food literary criticism and there has been a significant rise in the amount of published research. Despite the wide range of approaches adopted by different authors (e.g. Skubal v. Mannur), it is nonetheless possible to trace a number of similarities in the corpus of work. Firstly, a majority of authors deal with the function of food as a symbol or literary device. Food is often "used to create a mood or convey an idea" (Schoenberg and Trudeau 2006). As a powerful symbol of the home, of safety and of satiation, food is frequently adopted as a means of underlining the contrast between states of harmony and disharmony. Dining rituals help authors to depict the opposition between an apparent superficial order and the deep-seated conflicts hidden within a group, community or society. The organisation of meals and ritualised activities connected with eating reflect "social order and civilization" and are "representative of the limitations" it imposes on various groups. Secondly, food is often "used to increase the realism in [...] writing" (Schoenberg and Trudeau 2006). In her 2011 interview for NPR, contemporary crime author Donna Leon observed that her detective is "an Italian, so it would be extraordinary if he did not eat well at least once a day. I follow him through his normal life; he talks to his kids, he talks to his wife, he goes about being a detective. But he also has to eat." In reality people need to eat and they do so frequently; therefore if the characters eat as well, it makes them seem more real.

In addition to lending reality to their characters through food, authors also use food to characterise them and indicate "their status in society." Majors points out that meals are often "a natural extension of [the] character and the setting of the novels" (2012, 67). She claims that food is "critical to understanding" a character (68) and that it can indicate relationships between characters, as well as help to create relationships between readers and characters (69). In other words, food can "do the serious literary work of revealing characters without ever drawing attention to" itself (70). Finally, food can also be an important tool for setting the scene and highlighting the style of a piece of writing (73). This is particularly true in contemporary writing, where food consumption and preparation scenes function in much the same way as "landscape descriptions in nineteenth-century novels, as setting and mood, as well as projections of a character's state of mind" (75).

When analysing food as a literary or cultural sign rather than as a device, critics pay particular attention to the ways in which food can reflect, construct or deconstruct identity, and either denote or mask otherness. "Food has been acknowledged as a key indicator of ethnicity" (Schoenberg and Trudeau 2006) and as such is often analysed in the work of ethnic authors (e.g. A. Mannur 2010, Wenying Xu 2008). Sala Levin (2012) notes that food is frequently employed "to highlight otherness" and can function "as a social wedge" separating different communities (72). Authors dealing with immigration, expatriation, and assimilation often use food to mark ethnic/national identities, while equating "assimilation with the adoption of [foreign] foodways." Levin observes that in Jewish literature food is tied to ritual and to the feelings of guilt caused by the abandonment of one's own tradition and heritage (73).

Food is also frequently linked to gender, and especially to the various roles and identities performed by women. Food is a means of discussing femininity and domesticity; it can symbolise oppression, but at the same time it can contribute to the struggle against patriarchy, in which women "are nothing more than bodies, unworthy even of nourishment" (Schoenberg and Trudeau 2006). The portrayal of eating disorders is used "to address issues of gender, language, and sexual politics" and eating rituals serve as "a metaphor for the power struggle inherent to family dynamics" (Schoenberg and Trudeau 2006). Levin adds that depictions of cooking and eating in a family can be used as a forum for the discussion of the "maternal role" of women. Due to its connection with domesticity, the mundane, and the profane, food can become a means of exploring "all the trappings of daily life" (2012, 73). Finally, food is prominent in children's literature or literature about children, as "[f]ood experiences form part of the daily texture of every child's life from birth onwards." When writing about childhood, authors "continually hark back to childhood experiences of food, even when the intended audience is adults rather than children" (Keeling and Pollard 2009, 10).

All of these examples demonstrate that food forms an integral part of many literary texts and is used as a device, a symbol or a theme by fiction authors. However, while some authors use food as a mere addition to their texts, others produce texts devoted solely to food, drink, and eating. This type of text, which is known as culinary writing or food writing, first developed in France in the nineteenth century (see 2.3) and has grown in prominence since then; today, culinary texts are more popular than ever before. Darra Goldstein of *Gastronomica* observes that "[i]t sometimes seems [...] as though everyone is writing about food" (quoted in LeMay, 2011). However, despite the popularity of food writing and the amount of culinary texts in existence, the field has not yet been established as a relevant topic for academic study. In his essay titled "In Defense of Food Writing: A Reader's Manifesto," Eric LeMay (2011) sums up this paradox:

> That food writing needs a defense might strike you as odd. [...] food writing now shows up everywhere, on best-seller lists and Twitter feeds, in academic catalogs, splashy newspaper sections, and photo-drenched magazines. [Food writing] addresses a basic need. We need to eat. [...] Food has an importance that would seem beyond question and instead of defending food writing, we might ask why bookstores aren't organized into four basic sections: Food, Clothing, Shelter, and Other.

Recently, authors have come to question this rejection of food writing as insignificant or inartistic. John T. Edge (2011) believes that the role of food as an inseparable part of every human's life can provide important insights into human nature and help to relate the experiences of people from various social, ethnic, and religious backgrounds. He stresses that it is not only important to study unusual or high-quality food, but also all other types of food, including junk food or spoilt food, because each of these foods represents the people who cooked and ate it. Even more radically, Adam Gopnik (2005) questions the very standards of what can and cannot be considered sophisticated and artful, asking: "Why should the search for caramelized cauliflower be any less significant than Ad Reinhardt's search for the pure-black painting, or John Cage's for pure silence?"

However, to determine whether culinary writing is literature, it is necessary to find out what types of texts constitute the genre. This question is difficult to answer, because the field is extremely varied; the University of Guelph's library, for example, acquires approximately 5000 new culinary books each year, including "books about wine, food traditions, journals and manuscript cookbooks ... correspondences of food writers and copies of their articles" (Konieczna 2005). Moreover, food writing does not always have to be solely about food; it can also take the form of a memoir or memoir-cookbook fusion, such as Laura Elise Taylor's *A Taste for Paprika* (2007), in which "[e]very chapter is based on a grandmother cooking with her granddaughter and telling stories about life" (Konieczna 2005), or even of books for children (Rosenbaum 2009, 297). Furthermore, not only do culinary authors produce different genres, they also employ different methods. In "Dining Out: The Food Critic at Table," Gopnik distinguishes two basic approaches to food writing:

> the mock epic and the mystical microcosmic. The mock epic (A. J. Liebling, Calvin Trillin, the French writer Robert Courtine, and any good restaurant critic) is essentially comic and treats the small ambitions of the greedy eater as though they were big and noble, spoofing the idea of the heroic while raising the minor subject to at least temporary greatness. The mystical microcosmic, of which Elizabeth David and M. F. K. Fisher are the masters, is essentially poetic, and turns every remembered recipe into a meditation on hunger and the transience of its fulfillment. (2005)

But despite this remarkable variety, all food writing has something in common—choosing eating as the main topic for their books and articles demonstrates the intention of culinary authors to focus "on the ordinary," on the everyday and trivial (Edge 2011). Food writers try to prove that there is a deeper cultural and social significance to food than is acknowledged by contemporary society, which frequently reduces food to a mass of vitamins, calories, fibre, and fat the sole function of which is to provide only what is necessary for the continuation of the life of the physical body (LeMay 2011). LeMay attacks this viewpoint, which he calls "nutritionism," as he believes it "strips our food of its connection to culture." He believes that the purpose of food writing is to remind us "that food is 'really' about culture [...] Food writing defends readers against nutritionism's reductive bio-vision of food [...] It restores to food everything else, everything more, that food is about, which is just about everything."

2.4.1. Food and Crime Fiction

Now that the omnipresence and all-encompassing nature of food, and consequently of food writing, has been recognised, food permeates more spheres of life and more literary genres than ever before. At the same time, more crime mysteries are being published today than even during the Golden Age of detective fiction (Carvajal 1997). So it is not surprising that the last couple of years have seen the birth of what is known as the culinary mystery. In this sub-genre, the main plot is supplemented by "actual recipes" and "gumshoes not only track killers and determine motive but also grill sherry-flavored tuna or bake batches of chewy 'chocolate comfort cookies" (Carvajal 1997).

Culinary novels of various genres first emerged in the 1980s and 1990s and this style of writing has continued to grow in popularity ever since. One of the first examples of such a novel is Nora Ephron's *Heartburn* (1983), which combines "instructions for comfort food with a story of a pregnant cookbook writer who discovers that her husband is having an affair" (Carvajal 1997). Some contemporary culinary mystery authors include Diane Mott Davidson (*The Grilling Season*, 1998) or Joanne Fluke (*Peach Cobbler Murder* 2005). However, it is Virginia Rich, former food editor at *Sunset Magazine*, who "is often cited as the creator of the modern 'culinary mystery' subgenre, writing three culinary mysteries in the '80s featuring amateur sleuth/cooking school teacher Eugenia Potter" (Burton Smith 2010).

In the hybrid genre of culinary mystery, food descriptions or recipes are just as prominent as or even more so than the mystery itself. Majors points out that popular mysteries with chef/sleuth protagonists often feature instances of food porn:

> "Food porn" once meant visual or verbal representations of food as erotic, even as a substitute for sex; however, it's come to apply to any visual or written representation of food that glorifies ingredients and flavors. [...] In fiction, then, "food porn" might be applied to any "long, loving descriptions" of food that have a verbal glossiness to them, the kind of sheen associated with pornographic magazines. (2012, 77)

However, although both the culinary mystery and food porn are relatively recent phenomena, food has been a part of crime stories ever since the birth of the genre. In his article "Murder on the Menu" (2010) Kevin Burton Smith observes that "right from the start there's been a curious link between food (and drink) and crime fiction." Food played an important role in some of the earliest classical mystery stories, for example in the early Sherlock Holmes mysteries or in the short stories of Edgar Allan Poe. In "The Casque of Amontillado" (1846), "the narrator/murderer uses a cask of a rare and valuable sherry to lure his former friend to a secluded wine cellar—and his doom" (Burton Smith 2010). Burton Smith labels Rex Stout's detective Nero Wolfe "the world's premiere foodie detective" and points out that the Nero Wolfe books—exactly like contemporary culinary mysteries—included full-length recipes. But as Burton Smith concludes, "the ultimate confirmation of the food-crime analogy is the mystery-themed cookbook." *The Nero Wolfe Cookbook* was published by Rex Stout himself in 1973, and other similar books followed, including *The Lord Peter Wimsey Cookbook* by Elizabeth Bond Ryan & William J. Eakins in 1981 or *The Sherlock Holmes Victorian Cookbook: Favourite Recipes of The Great Detective & Dr. Watson* by William Bonnell in 1997.

Over the last couple of years, a number of literary theoreticians and critics have noticed the interconnections between food and crime fiction and there now exists a number of articles and book-length studies dedicated to the topic. In her *A Critical Study of Female Culinary Detective Stories: Murder by Cookbook* (2009), Nieves Pascual Soler analyses how cooking and eating are connected to the process of detection and how they help shape the identity of the detective-cook in contemporary culinary mysteries. Rita Elizabeth Rippetoe examines dietary habits in hard-boiled detective novels; her *Booze and the Private Eye: Alcohol in the Hard-Boiled Novel* (2004) analyses how alcoholic beverages function "as contributions to the theme of the man with a code" prevalent in this genre (3). She also pays attention to the roles which drinking plays in characterisation, plotting, and relationship creation (5). V. Louise Saylor's article "The Private Eye and His Victuals" (1984) also concentrates on the hard-boiled novel. It looks at how food aids character development in stories by the contemporary authors Richard Hoyt, Michael Z. Lewin, Lawrence Block, and Robert B. Parker. In "Food and Crime" (2010), Angelica Michelis attempts to discover how food and eating are related to crime and criminal investigation in contemporary crime novels, while Rebecca L. Epstein ("Crime and Nourishment: The Food and Foodways of Hollywood Gangster Films," 2005) and Christopher E. Forth ("Nobody Loves a Fat Man: Masculinity and Food in Film Noir," 2008) concentrate on the role of food in crime films.

The above-mentioned authors observe that food and drink perform a number of crucial functions in crime stories. Most frequently, food is used as a symbol of security and order and is juxtaposed with the violent and dangerous world of the detective story. Burton Smith claims that it is "no surprise detectives care about their food. In a world where evil is alive and well, and what passes for justice is too often random, food may be the one tiny piece of our helter-skelter world we can put right; a place where we can be kind to others. And ourselves" (2010). Popular culinary mystery writer Diane Mott Davidson confirms this view, stating that readers of crime novels "want to believe that justice will prevail, but they also know some dark things will happen." Food can than function as "a life-affirming counter to the darkness" assuring the anxious reader that all will turn out well in the end (interview by Carvajal 1997).

Another important role of food in detective stories is to create verisimilitude. In real life people eat, so if the characters in a crime novel eat as well they begin to seem less imaginary, more physical and consequently more real. Rippetoe claims that mimetic fiction, including crime fiction, "attempts to display the world as we know it, a world in which details matter" and thus contains elaborate descriptions not only of important events or landmarks, but also of the ordinary, of everyday life, including food and drink (2004, 23-24). Thirdly, as in other literary genres, food and drink can be used in a crime story as tools for constructing the narrative. Food can become a vehicle for the plot; it can serve as a clue, a murder weapon or even as a technique in the investigation. Moreover, authors frequently employ food to characterise both protagonists and minor characters (Rippetoe 2004, 7). Finally, many authors of culinary novels exploit the connection of food with sensualism and pleasure. The culinary romance novelist Jacqueline Deval claims that "food mixes well with writing because many readers are 'sensualists' who yearn to enter another world. 'Experiencing what the character is thinking and feeling and sensing is akin to having a good meal" (interview by Carvajal 1997). Kerri Majors observes that this is also true of writing featuring instances of food porn: the detailed descriptions of the food and the preparation process serve to "arouse our appetites" (2012, 78).

In summary, food and crime fiction appear to be closely interconnected. As was shown above, food has a prominent place in both classical and contemporary mystery stories. Jackson even claims that although the backgrounds of detectives featured in contemporary crime fiction are extremely varied, "[c]haracters working with food or in other domestic spheres constitute one disproportionately large group" (2002,

11). It is assumed that this link between cooking and mystery solving follows from the fact that both a recipe and a mystery are types of formula.

In his publication *Adventure, Mystery, and Romance: Formula Stories as Art and Popular Culture* (1976) Cawelti explores the concept of formula and how it applies to various works of popular literature. He defines formula as "a structure of narrative or dramatic conventions employed in great number of literary works" (5). Moreover, he distinguishes between two specific uses of the term formula: it can refer either to the plot type or to the manner in which individual parts of the story are treated (e.g. the stereotypical depiction of characters). Cawelti then proceeds to identify individual formulas, classifying mystery and its subcategory, the classical detective story, as one of the five main types (42). It follows from the definition of formula that it should be predictable, unoriginal, prearranged, and generally valid. However, Cawelti claims that in order to become really successful, the formulaic story has to alter the expected pattern in one way or another. The story has to be universal, but at the same time special; unoriginal, but at the same time new and unique (12).

In other words, a detective formula is a recipe for writing a mystery or a crime story. If an author wishes to create such a story, she/he needs to follow a set of rules in a certain order and use specific ingredients otherwise the desired result is not achieved. The list of ingredients includes characters (the detective, suspects, the victim, the criminal), the crime and its investigation, and setting. But at the same time a truly brilliant author—exactly like a brilliant chef—must sometimes break the rules in an unexpected way and treat her/his readers to a hitherto unknown flavour. Panek observes that the most successful writers of the Golden Age "flouted the rules with abandon" and, on the contrary, those who adhered to the rules too rigidly, ended up creating "rotten fiction" (1987, 123). Another parallel between a mystery and a recipe is that in a detective story, murder is not understood as sinful, immoral, violent, and horrible, but is instead, like a tasty dish, seen as a way to pleasure. And like food, a mystery brings its readers not only pleasure, but also suspense as they wait for the solution to be prepared and revealed, feeling first the anticipation and then the gratification when the finished product is presented and their curiosity sated (Cawelti 1976, 55).

However, if we think of a mystery as a recipe, we may also wish to ask exactly who the chef is. Cawelti likens detectives to psychoanalysts because they too are specialists in uncovering what is hidden inside the mind, reading clues correctly, and noticing small, seemingly meaningless incidents (93-95). However contemporary culinary mystery authors come up with a different analogy. In their stories the detective is turned into a chef. The producers of "Food Detectives," a TV show running on the *Food Network*, suggest the same analogy and the main star of the programme, "Ted Allen and his band of culinary sleuths conduct experiments to find the truth behind all of your burning food conundrums."[2] And indeed, in both classical and contemporary mystery novels it is the detective who gathers all the ingredients: the murder, the suspects, and the witnesses, the place and time, and then investigates and evaluates them, adds everything which is necessary and throws away all that is excessive in order to produce the main dish: the brilliant solution.

Notes

[1] see 2.4.1 for a definition of food porn
[2] <http://www.foodnetwork.com/food-detectives/index.html>

CHAPTER THREE

FOOD AND IDENTITY

Identity is a recurrent notion in contemporary humanities. Over the past century it has come to be considered "a powerful organizing presence in social life" and one of "the most compelling of contemporary concerns" (Leve 2011, 513). The prominence of discourses on identity can largely be accounted for by the emphasis placed by democratic capitalist societies on individuality, but also by post-modern relativism which has resulted in the dismantling of borders between the subjective (i.e. identity) and the objective (i.e. culture). As Lauren Leve (2011) states, identity has become a "metaculture: culture [...] not just in itself but for itself" (514). The understanding of identity as "culture" can be justified by the fact that identity, in contrast to personality, is not only determined by the traits of individuals, but also by thc structure of the society in which they live (Woodward 2004, 6). In other words, "identity is a person's knowledge that he or she belongs to a social category or group" (Stets and Burke 2000, 225). This would suggest that identity is to a large extent dependent on the opposition between sameness or similarity and difference. A person identifies with others who are like them; they choose to belong to the same category or group, while they differentiate themselves from those who are not (Woodward 2004, 6).

However, identity is not a one-way process. On the contrary, it is composed of two complementary elements: firstly of how individuals see themselves and secondly of how they are seen by others, and these two views of an individual are by no means always the same. The sense of a person's identity is further complicated by the possibility of possessing "multiple identities" which can appear in different situations or periods in an individual's life (7). Another factor worth considering is the tension between one's chosen or desired identity and their actual identity, which can be conditioned by external factors or even by one's own body, its needs, age, or shape (8).

The question of identity and the tensions between various identities—real, imaginary, true, fake, multiple, desired—form one of the most prominent themes in crime fiction. The focal point of the detective story's plot—the investigation—is in fact a process of uncovering and delimiting the identities of individual characters. Furthermore, as crime fiction is a genre preoccupied with the question of social order (see 1.1), the "quest to discover the identity of the person responsible for a particular crime has come, in many cases, to serve as a pretext for, or to provide a framework for a wider interrogation of society or of what constitutes criminality" (Krajenbrink and Quinn 2009, 1). It is assumed that Agatha Christie used her characters' identities exactly for this end: to explore the Britain of her times and to investigate and question the key elements of British identity, namely class, gender, and nation.

Erving Goffman (1956) observed that all identities are in fact performances, which are staged, consciously or unconsciously, for the benefit of an audience. It follows that in order for the audience to decipher one's identity, it is necessary for it to be encoded into a specific symbolic system. However, this symbolic representation does not have to be something explicit, such as a national flag or a rosary; in fact, identity is manifest in everything, even in the most commonplace elements of daily life. Judith Williamson, for instances, notices the symbolic function of fashion choice:

> When I rummage through my wardrobe in the morning I am not merely faced with the choice of what to wear. I am faced with the choice of images: the difference between a smart suit and a pair of overalls, a leather skirt and a cotton skirt, is not one of fabric and style, but one of identity. You know perfectly well that you will be seen differently for the whole day, depending on what you put on; you will appear as a particular kind of woman with one particular identity which excludes others. (quoted in Woodward 2004, 13)

As with fashion, food can also function as a symbol of identity, as was discussed in section 2.1. It is the aim of this chapter to explore this symbolic function of food in Christie's novels, the various functions it serves in depicting the characters' identities, and the ways in which Christie used it to poke fun at stereotypes or even to express social commentary.

3.1. Food, Class, and Christie's Characters

Throughout the twentieth century, sociologists and economists alike acknowledged the power of social class in shaping relationships within a society. William K. Gabrenya Jr. (2003) observes that class continues to play a crucial role even in present-day Western capitalist societies (1). The results of research conducted by Mark Tomlinson and Alan Warde (1993) over the period of over twenty years suggest that twentieth century Britain was (and contemporary Britain still is) a classed society. Tomlinson and Warde (1993) argue that "[c]lass is a more persistent form of social differentiation than many contemporary marketing and cultural studies accounts might suggest" and as such remains, despite claims to the contrary, an important aspect of an individual's identity.

An individual's membership of a certain social class is influenced by their possession of "objective resources" (Kraus, Piff and Keltner 2011, 3), or what Pierre Bourdieu labelled cultural and economic capital. The possession of such capital "is signaled via symbols of wealth, preferences, and social behaviors (e.g. manners, language use)" (Kraus, Piff and Keltner 2011, 3). It follows that a person's daily rituals and consumption habits are among the most useful class markers or, as Michael W. Kraus et al. (2011) put it:

> From the macro to the minute, social class is a deep and pervasive social environment, differentiating people in the most rudimentary elements of their lives, including their neighborhoods, schools, diets, preferred forms of recreation, and places of worship [...]. Daily life is suffused with social class. (246)

Class is both an economic and cultural phenomenon. Although differences in the disposable incomes of working class, middle class, or upper class households can to a great extent account for the differences in the tastes, consumption patterns, and beliefs of these groups, this is not the only factor. Bourdieu observes that members of different classes possessing more or less equal financial means (e.g. a well-paid manual worker and a poorly-paid teacher) still differ considerably in what they choose to spend their money on ([1979] 1984, 177). This "unified lifestyle" within a class, i.e. class culture, is crucial to "the processes of social integration and belonging" (Tomlinson and Warde 1993). Class culture is "not learned by experience, but rather [...] passed down over generations within families and communities through socialization and enculturation practices" (Gabrenya 2003, 6). According to Bourdieu belonging to a class culture by choice, as opposed to belonging to a socioeconomic class out of necessity, is most manifest in the food choices which individuals or groups make and in the food rituals they choose to observe:

> The art of eating and drinking remains one of the few areas in which the working classes explicitly challenge the legitimate art of living. In the face

> of the new ethic of sobriety for the sake of slimness, which is most recognized at the highest levels of the social hierarchy, peasants and especially industrial workers maintain an ethic of convivial indulgence. ([1979] 1984, 179)

Thus when a family spends money on "heavy, fatty, fattening foods" or, on the contrary, regularly dines on lighter meat and fresh vegetables and fruit, this does not only reflect the income of that family, but also the ideology of the class to which the respective family believes they belong (177).

The objective resources available to an individual or group, i.e. a group's actual socioeconomic class, and their subjective evaluation of their own class are not always consistent (Kraus, Piff and Keltner 2011, 6-7); consequently it is possible for an individual or group to adopt a culture of a class to which they do not belong. While this can in some cases be attributed to misjudgement, in others it serves as a method of improving one's status, and yet in others it represents a manifestation of the freedom of the upper class who are not ruled by the laws of necessity, and who can freely choose to either indulge or be ascetic (Bourdieu, [1979] 1984, 177-8, 199). Thus class identities are constructed through the interplay of various economic and cultural factors and individuals' voluntary choices either to adhere to or to shun a certain class culture.

3.2. The Class of Producers and the Class of Consumers

In chapter one it was shown that the genre of the classical detective novel is a highly classed one. Firstly, crime novels address audiences of a specific class, in particular the educated middle or upper-middle class, as opposed to other popular genres such as the horror or the adventure novel. Secondly, class plays an important role within the stories themselves as the crime story as a rule takes place in a strictly delimited setting, more specifically an upper or upper-middle-class one (see 1.3.1). Both, the detective and the minor characters are almost exclusively members of the upper or upper-middle professional classes. Working class characters are scarcely present and if they do appear, they are not central to the plot.

Class is indeed a constant presence in the novels of Agatha Christie. In line with the classical crime story tradition, she mostly chooses her characters from the upper classes of society. Some of her recurring stock types include an impoverished upper class spinster or governess, a young or middle-aged gold-digger, a rich old widow, unemployed aristocratic youth, an heir/heiress, and a businessman-cum-profiteer. The setting is also generally upper class; the stories are often set in a mansion of an old (and often impoverished) aristocratic family (*Towards Zero*, *The Mysterious Affair at Styles*) or in households of the *nouveau riche* (*Crooked House*, *Hercule Poirot's Christmas*). What is characteristic of Christie's portrayal of characters is the satirical tone she often employs. Each character exhibits some exaggerated traits of which they are unaware; each of them has their petty problems and secrets, which they consider of great importance. Thus while Christie accepts bourgeois society and its sensibility as the standard, she simultaneously mocks it and reveals its weaknesses (as in the case of the *nouveau riche* immigrant family in *A Pocket Full of Rye* who change their name to blend in with the aristocracy, but who can never change their habits and questionable morality).

In accordance with the conjectures of Bourdieu or Tomlinson and Warde concerning the connection between class culture and food, Christie frequently makes use of food habits and rituals to display or highlight the social class of her characters. In fact, Christie's characters as a rule fall into two distinct classes which are defined on the basis of food; food producers (those who prepare food for others, i.e. the working class) and food consumers (those who consume food prepared by others, i.e. the middle and upper class). In other words, the class of each of Christie's characters can be determined by whether or not they cook.

The division into food producing and food consuming classes is a theme which is acknowledged by various authors. Lydia Zepeda (2007) observes that shifting the burden of foodwork is one of the main goals of the higher levels of any society. Food production jobs are "generally low paying, high stress, often physically demanding, and have rapid turnover" (40). Furthermore, they require little training and as such are typically considered as occupations which are more suitable for the lower classes of society, providing little cultural and economic capital. The low wages earned in the food production industry reflect the low value that society places "on those who are preparing and serving us food" (40). Belasco agrees, claiming that "[w]hether female or male, foodwork is strenuous, hot, tedious, repetitive, and often unappreciated" (2008, 45). When the mother of Lynn Marchmont, the protagonist of *Taken at the Flood*, is forced to take up a job in the kitchen (37) this symbolises not only the physical decline of her ageing body, but also the family's loss of status, which is finally confirmed at the end of the book when Lynn marries farmer Rowley instead of the wealthy heir David Hunter.

Christie's division of characters into consumers and producers (or servants) reflects Bourdieu's division into the tastes of luxury, by which he meant the tastes of those who have the means to choose what they eat, and the tastes of necessity, representing the tastes dictated by nutrition and economy ([1979] 1984, 176). Consumer classes wish to distance themselves as much as possible from the material and bodily aspects of nutrition or, as Priscilla Parkhurst Ferguson (2004) puts it, they wish to set up the "fundamental opposition between cooking (or cookery), with its German roots, and cuisine, with it French flair" (20, original emphasis). In cookery food features as a "material product that engages the senses and appeases appetites," while in cuisine it becomes "a symbolic creation tied to the intellect and the spirit" (16). This "denial of function" (Bourdieu, [1979] 1984, 176) is achieved through the aestheticisation and ritualisation of the process of eating and also by distancing oneself from the processes connected with food production and preparation:

> the bourgeoisie is concerned to eat with all due form. Form is first of all a matter of rhythm, which implies expectations, pauses, restraints; waiting until the last person served has started to eat, taking modest helpings, not appearing over-eager. A strict sequence is observed and all coexistence of dishes which the sequence separates, fish and meat, cheese and dessert, is excluded: for example, before the dessert is served, everything left on the table, even the salt-cellar, is remover, and the crumbs are swept up. (196)

The ritualisation of meals in consumer class households is a recurrent motif in Christie's stories. The daily food ritual is described repeatedly and in detail. According to the novels, a typical upper-class day starts with early morning tea, served generally in bed at a fixed time, most frequently around 8 o'clock (*A Pocket Full of Rye* 27, *Nemesis* 109), followed by breakfast served from 9 to 11 a.m., either in a breakfast room (*The Seven Dials Mystery* 15-16) or in the bedroom (*Evil Under the Sun* 77). Rules abound at lunchtime too; it is forbidden to rise from the table before the meal has been finished, and while seated one must converse with the diner at their side (*Elephants Can Remember* 14-15). After lunch, guests are allowed to leave the table and coffee drinking and polite conversation ensue (16-20). Dinner is the most ritualised and formal of all meals; the number, gender, and status of guests at a formal dinner is strictly prescribed and even a change of clothes is required (*The Secret Adversary* 142; *Passenger to Frankfurt* 163). The men-women ratio needs to be balanced and the party is generally composed of "diplomats, ministers, industrialists and socialites" intermingled with a number of "smoothovers," educated professionals whose role is to facilitate and brighten the conversation. Even the process of leaving the dinner table is standardised; women rise and leave the room first and men can only follow a couple of minutes later (*Passenger to Frankfurt* 118). The importance of eating meals at specific times during the day is highlighted by the practice of sounding the gong to signal that a meal is ready and that the group should move to the dining room (e.g. *Sleeping Murder*, *And Then There Were None*, *Dead Man's Folly*).

Drinks are also subject to norms, and the exact time of the day dictates which drinks can be served. Refreshments (i.e. alcoholic beverages) are served before lunch, at about twelve thirty (*Nemesis* 176) and before dinner (218) and the tea ritual takes place twice a day, in the morning (*A Pocket Full of Rye* 5-7) and in the afternoon (*Why Didn't They Ask Evans?*, *Murder Is Easy*). When Mrs Burton-Cox visits detective author Mrs Oliver late in the evening, Mrs Oliver observes: "Now what will you have? A glass of sherry? It's too late for tea, of course. Or would you prefer a cocktail of some kind?" (*Elephants Can Remember* 209). In other words, not only is there a specifically designed time to consume a drink or foodstuff, but the respective drink or foodstuff is forbidden outside its ritualised time slot. The presentation of food and drink is of high importance, as well, as it contributes considerably to the aestheticisation of the eating experience. Chinese porcelain is mentioned repeatedly in the novels (e.g. *Murder Is Easy* 285) and it is of such value to the characters that issues over the inheritance of a Spode porcelain dinner dessert service causes an enraged argument among family members (*After the Funeral* 282).

According to Bourdieu, the extensive stylisation of eating is a means of negotiating the eaters' "relationship to animal nature, to primary needs and the populace who indulge them without restraint," or rather the eater's superiority to such a populace. In other words, "it is a way of denying the meaning and primary function of consumption" ([1979] 1984, 196). Only extreme circumstances force Christie's upper class characters to eat their meals outside standard rituals of formal dining, such as in *And Then There Were None* where the death of both servants and the fear of a serial murderer on the loose forces the characters to prepare and eat their meals together, standing at the kitchen table (227).

However, the adherence to upper class rituals and the choice of foodstuffs to be eaten can also serve another purpose, as proof and validation of an individual's social status. Those who possess a great deal of economic capital but lack cultural capital try to acquire or imitate the tastes of those possessing the latter quality (Bourdieu [1979] 1984, 185). On a number of occasions Christie's characters utilise food in order to prove their class membership. Christie used this practice as a hint indicating that the character is a fraud, either a *nouveau riche* lacking in cultural capital or an impostor or trickster. The industrialist Lord Whitfield surrounds himself with exotic objects from the colonies, because, as Christie ironically notes, pineapples spell "distinction and good taste" to him (*Murder is Easy* 216). Nonetheless, this solitary attempt at refinement cannot hide his working class origins which are definitively proved by his breakfasting heartily on kidneys (49). Mike, the working class protagonist of *Endless Night*, marries a rich heiress, but is unable to adapt to his new social surroundings. He struggles to memorise what drink goes with what food, what foods to order, how to enter a restaurant, or how to tip; problems which his new wife Ellie, a woman born into money, does not have to bother with (132). Similarly, the identity thief Comte de la Roche who features in *The Mystery of the Blue Train*, exaggerates his (fake) aristocratic status in order to deflect suspicion by his food choice of "omelette fines herbes," "entrecôte Béarnaise," "savarin au rhum," and "a very fine old brandy" (199-200).

On the contrary, members of the food producing classes, more specifically the various servants such as cooks, waiters, parlour-maids or butlers, do not have the freedom to choose their food neither on the basis of the taste of luxury, nor in order to impress or trick others. Their food choices are limited to the cheapest, most filling, and most agreeable of the available alternatives (Bourdieu, [1979] 1984, 177). Thus when they are presented with an opportunity to indulge they do so eagerly with a sense of "readiness to take advantage of the good times" (183). This is also the case with the servants in Christie's stories. When Frances Cloade, an aristocrat, insists on drinking plain black coffee without sugar her maid finds it strange, as she would undoubtedly take coffee with lots of milk and sugar in it if she had the means (*Taken at the Flood* 42). Similarly, when Jane the hairdresser receives a pay rise, she immediately decides to be extravagant and goes for a lunch to an expensive restaurant with live music (*Death in the Clouds* 181). The same pattern of action is followed by Tuppence, one of Christie's few non-upper-class protagonists. After a short spell of unemployment, Tuppence suddenly comes into money. As soon as she is promised the cheque she begins contemplating a lunch at an expensive restaurant, dreaming of unlimited *hors d'oeuvre*, *lobster á l'Américaine*, chicken Newburg, and *pêche Melba*—"an extremely unwholesome menu" (*The Secret Adversary* 42-43).

The need to cater to the "vulgar" demands of the body (Bourdieu [1979] 1984, 177) connects the lower class characters in Christie's novels with nature and also with animals and their constant need to secure sustenance. Indeed, animal-like characteristics are consistently ascribed to servants by upper class characters in most of Christie's novels. In *And*

Then There Were None, one of the characters observes the composure of the butler Rogers in the face of the death of his wife. When Rogers does not mourn but instead continues to carry out his food preparation duties, the other remarks: "Wonderful animal, the good servant. Carries on with an impassive countenance" (147). In *The Mysterious Affair at Styles* the housemaid Dorcas is described as "the very model and picture of a good old-fashioned servant" (29). After interviewing her, Captain Hastings remarks: "As she stood there, with her honest face upturned to mine, I thought what a fine specimen she was of the old-fashioned servant that is so fast dying out" (73). Dorcas is depicted here not as an adult human being, but rather as a child ("honest face"), and her subordinate position is emphasised by the position of her body—she has to turn up her face to look at Hastings, her superior. In the second part of the remark she is degraded to the status of an animal when she is described as an endangered species. The supposed animal nature of the servants is connected with their perceived innocence and inferior intellectual capacities. Poirot, for example, observes that servants are unlikely to commit murder (*Dumb Witness* 163); he later suggests that the mentality of servants is not adapted to sophisticated crime (397).

Therefore, firstly due to the wish of the upper classes to remove themselves as far as possible from the strenuous and bodily aspects of eating, perceived here as the preparation of food and from the necessity of eating, and secondly due to the supposed intellectual inferiority of the food producing classes caused by their materialistic relationship to food, the servants are rendered invisible in the upper-class households of Christie's stories. The cook never leaves the kitchen; she does not know her employers personally, and they do not know her. Thus the waiting staff, the butler and the parlour maid represent the only link between cooking and eating, between the producer and the consumer. In *Why Didn't They Ask Evans?* the two protagonists, Frances and Bobby, observe that "one never tips a cook. One never sees her, for one thing.' 'No, and she never sees you..." (334). When Mr Enthwistle remarks that "Georges [Poirot's butler] materialised with some *pâté de foie gras* and hot toast in a napkin" his word choice ("materialise") indicates that for the people being served, the serving staff is not only invisible but even non-existent except for the moment when they are catering to their needs; once this duty is performed, they de-materialise again (*After the Funeral* 107).

However, despite the servants' perceived invisibility, they are a vital element in the life of the consumer classes. Not only at home, but also during their travels (*Murder on the Orient Express*, *Destination Unknown*) and even when held captive (*And Then There Were None*), the upper class rely on others to prepare their food. When Anne and Harry, two of the characters in *The Man in the Brown Suit*, escape to a deserted island to hide, they still hire a native woman to serve and prepare their food (265), and when Anne proposes that she will cook for Harry so that they could stay alone, he replies: "I don't suppose you know anything about cooking" (271). Thus, the relationship between the two classes is characterised by mutual interdependence, where food producers depend on the consumers for employment, but consumers rely on the servants to provide nourishment, safety, and health.

As a result of this symbiotic relationship, the potential carelessness or even malice of the staff could endanger the employers. Sir Eustace's constant complaints about servants highlight the fact that his mood and well-being are largely dependent on the behaviour of his subordinates (*The Man in the Brown Suit* 174). Any possible malice on the part of the serving staff could even have lethal consequences. The upper classes are conscious of this fact and frequently accept the presented meals with distrust, a result of the persistent fear of being poisoned by the serving/cooking staff. In *By the Pricking of My Thumbs*, the inhabitant of a luxurious nursing home believes she is being slowly poisoned and that her organs will then be offered for sale (35), and an aristocratic doctor circulates the story of a serial murderess who had found work as a family cook and who then began adding poison to the family's food (211).

Despite this mutual interdependence, the servants in the novels remain in a subordinate position in the end and never exploit the power which they hold over those whom they serve, a fact which represents yet another proof of their supposed animal-like innocence. Moreover, the ultimate freedom, the possibility to cross class boundaries, is reserved solely for the upper classes. Members of old aristocratic families and millionaires can freely choose to engage in working class pursuits. Such is the case of the heiresses Ellie, who first enjoys an expensive dinner at a restaurant and next eats cheap workers' food in the streets of Paris (*Endless Night* 131), or Frances, who can party with the golden youth at the most expensive London venues (*Why Didn't They Ask Evans?* 21), and also go for a picnic of beer and sandwiches with her working class acquaintance (59). On the contrary, Mike, Ellie's husband who has married her for money, must observe all of the upper class conventions and rituals if he wants to be accepted (see above), and Frances's working-class friend Bobby refuses to accompany her to one of her London parties on the grounds that he would not blend in with her stylish friends (*Why Didn't They Ask Evans?* 59).

It follows that Poirot's class membership gives him an enormous advantage in his investigations: as an upper class detective he can move seamlessly from a chat with middle class Superintendent Spence over a glass of shandy (*Hallowe'en Party* 49) to a discussion of a murder over a cup of afternoon tea with aristocrat Sir John Cavendish (*The Mysterious Affair at Styles* 43) or even to sharing food preparation techniques and trying to guess the identities of possible murderers with Marjorie the cook in her kitchen (*After the Funeral* 221).

3.3. Food, Gender, and Christie's Characters[1]

Like class, gender is one of the crucial elements of an individual's identity. It is an institution that is "embedded in all the social processes of everyday life and social organizations" (Risman 2004, 430). The category of gender is not predefined as a given, but is instead, in Judith Butler's words, "performed;" various gender identities "are continuously (re)created" and (re)negotiated through one's actions in a given social setting (Lyons and Willott 2008, 694). But in spite of the constructed nature of gender identities, gender difference is "universally used to justify stratification" (Risman 2004, 430). Thus, the construction of gender is a two way process in which individuals engage in acting out or producing their gender identities which, in turn, shape the individuals themselves (432). Gender thus becomes "embedded not only in individuals but throughout social life" (431).

Food and food choice play an important part in constructing, altering or disrupting gender identities. Food is an extremely gendered phenomenon connected with the body, with sex, power, patriarchy, and oppression of women (see 2.1 and 2.4) and the "idea that men and women have differing perspectives and priorities in relation to such issues as diet and health, and even the ethical dimensions of food choice, seems an eminently plausible one, requiring little more than an appeal to "common sense" to confirm it" (Beardsworth et al. 2002, 470). As early as in the 1960s, Lévi-Strauss made note of the associations between food and gender (see 2.1). Contemporary scholars have also dealt with more specific influences of gender on food choice and eating styles. In a study conducted by Deborah Lupton (1996), respondents were asked to decide whether different foods were appropriate for different genders, and if so, to explain their choices using specific examples. The interviewees, almost unanimously, responded positively to the question. Moreover, there was considerable agreement on the particular foods which pertain to individual genders. Feminine foods were characterised as "light, sweet, milky, soft-textured, refined and delicate" (Lupton 1996, 106), whilst masculine foods were "[h]eavy' foods [...] those that are hard to digest, weight on your stomach, are chewy, rich or filling, or are 'unhealthy" (107). The two types of foods that were considered quintessentially feminine and masculine were sweets or candy and red meat, respectively (104). According to Eric B. Ross (1987), the evolution of this phenomenon can be traced throughout history. Prehistoric hunters, unwilling to give up their nourishing meat, kept the killed prey to themselves, forcing women to look for vegetarian alternatives (18). This situation did not change even in the modern period. In the nineteenth century English workmen consumed the bulk of the households' stock of meat, while women had to rely on carbohydrate-rich foodstuffs such as bread and jam (30).

Moreover, sweetness is traditionally connected with innocence and love, while meat has closer connotations with sex (37); and although sexuality is acceptable, even required, from men, it is regarded with suspicion in women, and many Western societies considered women eating meat as excessively sexual and immoral. In order to avoid the impact of meat they were advised to eat vegetables or sweets, or at least to disguise the taste of meat with (preferably white) sauces (50). Even in many modern cultures, the high-calorie, high-protein meat is often considered the only "real" food and meatless dishes are despised. At the same time, men are seen as best suited to eat meat (50); women, children, the elderly, or sick are all marked as inferior on account of their inability to digest it.

The relationship between meat and sugar in the domain of food is reflected by that of alcohol and abstinence in the realm of drink. Non-alcoholic drinks, light drinks, and coffee are associated with women (Lupton 1996, 106), while strong drinks and spirits are seen as predominantly masculine. However, the association of women with coffee is a relatively new phenomenon. When coffee first gained prominence in England, it was considered a masculine drink, because of its drying character and its stimulating effects on the brain. The feminine drink of the time was beer, connoting moisture and affecting the body. Women were banned from coffeehouses, which were dedicated to talks of business and finance (Schivelbusch 1993, 37). Only gradually did women penetrate the coffeehouse, and this development took place as men began to reject the coffeehouse in favour of the private club, an establishment which was still exclusively masculine. By the middle of the nineteenth century, the coffeehouse had become a feminine place; drinking coffee completely lost its association with business and instead became inextricably connected with female gossip (69). Coffee and tea drinking rituals evolved into ornamental affairs supplemented with props (china, silverware) which were used in order to achieve an aesthetic effect (177), a further reflection of the view that a woman is a decorative, purposeless creature.

In a study similar to Lupton's, Antonia C. Lyons and Sara A. Willott (2008) analysed how gender influences the drinking habits and views on alcohol of a group of young adults. They note that "alcohol consumption has been linked to the construction of traditional masculine identities" and that "gender stereotypes link drinking to manliness" (695). They go on to investigate the drinking patterns of women and ask why there has been an increase in the amount of alcohol consumed by women over the last couple of decades. The findings of their research suggest that even in the twenty-first century, "male drinking practices" persist as a form of ascertaining one's masculinity, and they report that the pub remains "a site of male power and legitimacy" (695). Moreover, they observe that masculine identities are always defined in opposition to femaleness and men engage in "a desperate struggle to avoid and negate any accusation or appearance of femininity" (695). When it comes to the drinking habits of women, the authors note that "drinking alcohol may also be seen as a way of 'doing gender' and accomplishing both traditional and non-traditional gender identities" (696). Young women engage in public drinking and traditionally masculine forms of alcohol consumption (binge drinking, displays of public drunkenness, drinking contests) in order to gain the power and superior social position otherwise reserved for men (700).

However, despite recent changes in drinking habits of women, "the hierarchical structuring of gender remains, with behaviours aligned to hegemonic masculinity being valued." Women are forced to attempt to become more masculine in order to improve their position in society. Moreover, not all women are given the possibility to do so by appropriating male drinking habits. Married women, mothers, or older women "are condemned for their drinking" by both men and other women (704) and even young and independent women are expected to exercise more "self-policing and self-restraint" than men (706). Finally, the type of alcoholic beverages preferred by women differs from that consumed by men. While drinking beer remains a strictly masculine activity, and is especially associated with "hard masculinity," women are expected to consume "cocktails, spirits, wine and champagne," or drinks "described as glamorous and sparkling." A woman drinking beer is often perceived as unfeminine or even disgusting, and her choice of beverage can suggest that she is not "well brought up" (701).

While Lupton or Lyons and Willott observe how specific food items or drinks are gendered, Alan Beardsworth et al. concentrate on how gender roles affect food work and determine who has the responsibility to make decisions about food. The findings demonstrate that in contemporary Britain "a married woman's obligation to produce elaborately prepared traditional meals for her husband provides an expression of her domesticity and subordination" (2002, 473). The "tasks of preparing food still firmly belong to women" and men only rarely engage in foodwork, and if they do so, it is generally only to "help." In spite of this, women "do not enjoy the power which would allow them meaningfully to control their own and their families' food intake" (Dixey 1996). In other words, the "choice of meals is determined by husbands' preferences" or by "the man's work pattern," and the male of the house must be provided with square meals even if the family suffers from a constrained budget (Dixey 1996). However, in a parallel to the work of Belasco (2008, 41-43), Rachael Dixey observes that a woman's role as the main food producer can not only be a means of oppression and restriction, but also of power. Some women deliberately choose to dissuade men from cooking. Their kitchens become a space where they can exercise their own power and "responsibility for this vital area of life can give [them] some control over the household and a sense of self-worth" (Dixey 1996).

3.4. Constructing and Destructing Gender Stereotypes

In her treatment of food, Christie acknowledged the omnipresence of gender-based food stereotypes and employed them when characterising her minor characters, who often fit into traditional gender roles. Christie especially exploited the contrast between the vigorous man with a hearty appetite and the fragile lady or young girl who eats little and lightly. On numerous occasions her male characters can be observed enjoying breakfasts of coffee or tea, toast and marmalade, scrambled eggs, bacon, cold ham, cereal (*A Pocket Full of Rye* 27), kidneys on plentifully heaped plates (*Murder Is Easy* 49), or cold ham and haddock (*Why Didn't They Ask Evans* 319). In contrast, their female counterparts seem to be content with only one piece of toast, coffee, and orange juice (*A Pocket Full of Rye* 27), toast and weak tea (*Why Didn't They Ask Evans* 319), or they even skip food entirely, drinking just a cup of coffee and a glass of juice (*Endless Night* 210).

Christie also made use of the traditional view of men as meat-eaters and women as sugar-eaters. While the staple of a true gentleman's diet is a Porterhouse steak (*The Mystery of the Blue Train* 339), women seem to share the opinion of Ariadne Oliver, that "[s]weet things [...] really give you a lot of vitality" (*Elephants Can Remember* 147). In *The Man in the*

Brown Suit, the protagonist Anne explains her choice of comfort food after being held captive for a couple of hours as follows: "A man, I suppose, would have had a stiff peg; but girls derive a lot of comfort from ice-cream sodas. I applied myself to the end of the straw with gusto. The cool liquid went trickling down my throat" (223). Similarly, afternoon tea served in a man's household is accompanied by cooked sausages (*Hallowe'en Party* 66), but when it is served by a woman, it consists of scones with homemade strawberry jam or little drop cakes (*After the Funeral* 156). Moreover, not only do women prefer sweet food and men meat, but each sex seems to despise the food of the other. In *Elephants Can Remember* Ariadne Oliver is disgusted by her companion during coffee because she eats in a "carnivorous way" (21). On the other hand, male characters in the novels display horror at the prospect of being offered meatless dishes. Poirot and Captain Hastings, in *Dumb Witness*, quickly excuse themselves when they are invited to dinner by two vegetarian spiritualists, after which Hastings remarks: "Thank goodness, Poirot, [...] you got us out of those raw carrots! What awful women!" (159).

Sweetness is associated with women not only in terms of their choice of food, but also in their character. Women, especially young women and girls, are referred to as sweet-tempered, having a sweet voice, or even playing sweet music throughout most of the analysed novels (*The ABC Murders* 104; *Nemesis* 159; *Endless Night* 171; etc.); on the other hand, older unmarried or unattractive women, who are considered to have lost their perceived femininity, are described as being sour-faced hags (*Five Little Pigs* 208), speaking in acid voices (*Endless Night* 196) and having vinegary faces (*Nemesis* 167).

This preference for sweets over meat and the general tendency to follow a lighter diet renders the female characters powerless. Indeed, there are striking parallels between the food eaten by sick characters and that of women, both in terms of the food itself and the way in which it is consumed. Delicate ladies usually eat in bed (*Evil Under the Sun* 191), however, when male characters do this, it indicates sickness (*After the Funeral* 41). Moreover, the craving for sweets ascribed to women parallels that of very young children, who are often appeased by or find comfort in candy (*After the Funeral* 11, *The Murder at the Vicarage* 51). Thus, by their assigned foodways women are rendered vulnerable and incapable of taking care of themselves; they become people who need to be managed by others, more specifically, by men.

Alcohol is also considered to be an inappropriate drink for proper women, children, and the sick. When women entertain each other they serve tea, coffee, cake, and sweets (*Passenger to Frankfurt* 252) and they are generally only seen drinking under extreme circumstances, such as in the case of Mrs Hubbard, who is offered a glass of cognac as a remedy after fainting (*Murder on the Orient Express* 223). However, "refreshments," i.e. alcoholic drinks, represent an inevitable element in meetings between men. Alcohol drinking rituals serve as a testing ground for traditionally masculine virtues: competitiveness and aggression. In a working-class pub, the drinker who is the last standing after a drinking bout is the winner. The failure to take part in a round of drinks or the inability to "hold one's liquor" leads to loss of rank and subsequently to subordination (Schivelbusch 1993, 171-173). Here again the idea that a woman, a person not fit to drink alcohol, is equivalent to a weak man is perpetuated. Even alcoholism, unpardonable for women, is tolerated in men. In *Murder on the Orient Express* the drinking habit of the detective Mr Hardman is treated with acceptance, and viewed as rather natural in a man (234).

On the contrary, if a man does not drink, he is often looked down upon by the other characters or is perceived as having a weak personality (*Three Act Tragedy* 108, 112). In *Dumb Witness* the protagonist admires her alcoholic father and looks down on the abstaining doctor, claiming that real men can take alcohol and only weaklings drink water (41). Elsewhere the ways in which two brothers drink their wine reveal the difference between their characters; the meek and calm Yahmose slowly sips from his glass, while the wild and strong Sobek "tosses it off" and "smacks his lips" afterwards (*Death Comes as the End* 186). In addition, male characters often speak about non-alcoholic drinks in derogatory terms in order, to highlight their "hard man" status and to differentiate themselves further from femininity. Thus tea is referred to as "cat lap" (*Taken at the Flood* 254), and when Mr Symmington's companion Elsie offers him a nice hot cup of tea after he has discovered that his wife is dead in *The Moving Finger*, Jerry, the protagonist disparages her choice of beverage: "Personally I should have given the poor devil a stiff whiskey and soda. He looked as though he needed it" (94).

Another significant phenomenon observed by researchers and reflected in Christie's novels is that in a vast majority of cases, food production work is carried out by women. All of the middle or upper class households depicted in the novels, with three notable exceptions (see below), employ a female cook (*The Clocks*, *Passenger to Frankfurt*, *Murder on the Orient Express*, *Nemesis*, etc.). The kitchen is understood as a women's place, where the female pursuits of cooking and chatting are carried out (*Death Comes as the End* 23). This custom is broken only in extreme circumstances; one example of this is in *And Then There Were None*, when the death of Mrs Rogers the cook leaves her husband (the butler) as the only servant on the whole island, and he is therefore forced to prepare lunch. However, Mr Rogers is anxious about his cooking skills, and unlike his wife he only serves a cold meal of tinned ham and tongue (156). Later, after the butler also dies, the remaining women take up kitchen duties (200), and only after Miss Brent is taken sick and there is just a single woman left on the whole island does a man finally start helping in the kitchen (210).

However, although Christie frequently made use of stereotypes of masculinity and femininity in characterisation, she equally frequently employed food to subvert the traditional notions of what a man or a woman should be like. Reversals of gender roles appear throughout the analysed novels. The young adventuress is one of Christie's typical stereotype-subverting characters. Lynn, the former army nurse and protagonist of *Taken at the Flood*, dreams of an adventure-filled life and is reluctant to settle down and become a country housewife. She rebels against being placed in a position of weakness by emphatically refusing to take her meals in bed like a lady (27). Similarly, the teenager Linda rebels against the patriarchal society as represented by her extremely feminine stepmother who is obsessed with men and staying slim. Linda, on the contrary, scorns traditional femininity and to show this, she refuses to breakfast in her room: "Oh, I get up. Breakfast in bed's so *stuffy*." (*Evil Under the Sun* 132, original emphasis). Joanna, the young and modern protagonist of *The Moving Finger* is described as drinking alcohol: "She is very pretty and very gay, and she likes dancing and cocktails and love affairs and rushing about in high-powered cars" (13), and the young adventuress Tuppence equals her male partner Tommy in intellect as well as in appetite (*The Secret Adversary* e.g. 42, 73). Similarly, the young New Woman Bridget underlines her independence, courage, and intellectual capability by drinking alcohol and is annoyed when she is served traditionally effeminate tea in a "dainty" china set (*Murder is Easy* 285).

Women who overeat are also seen as a challenge to dominant ideas concerning correct food habits. According to Lupton's research the general opinion is that a man needs to eat large amounts of food, even to take two helpings per meal. Furthermore, Lupton claims that a man is expected to eat greedily, in large gulps (1996, 104-106). Women, on the other hand, are believed to need less food, or at least lighter and less nourishing food, and to eat these reduced portions slowly and with care. This stereotype influences the feeding of children too; in many households, boys are generally given larger and more nourishing helpings of food than girls, as it is believed that they should become bigger, stronger, and more active (105). Girls in the Western world are taught that they need to become small thin women. According to Counihan, the cult of thinness is derived from the mind/body dichotomy so important in Western culture, in which the dominant males are associated with the powerful mind, and the subordinate females with the insignificant body (1999, 77). Thus the thinness and weakness of the female body caused by under-nourishment serves as a symbolic representation of its cultural subordination (62).

However, despite the fact that women in Western society "are trained to be nonaggressive, pacifying, and self-sacrificing" and not express their emotions (84), they still find ways to rebel against the status quo and these acts of dissent often involve food. Sometimes the rebellion assumes the extreme form of eating disorders, when women turn their aggression against their own bodies and either starve or fatten themselves in order to escape their condition of female sexuality (84-91). Such behaviour can be observed in a number of Christie's characters. In *Passenger to Frankfurt* an old matron fattens herself into immobility while hosting opulent feasts as a means of asserting her power. The sheer bulk of her body simultaneously desexualises her and renders her dominant and powerful (181-184). The mother of an Egyptian royal family, Esa, insists on being constantly provided with fruit from a plater by her side (*Death Comes as the End* 110-115) and demonstrates her elevated status by distancing herself from the mundane troubles of life; she instead spends all of her time enjoying "well-cooked" "fat meats," vegetables, honey, and wine (177, 209, 216). Similarly, although to a lesser degree, Miss Marple's asceticism and indifferent attitude towards eating rid her of both a curved figure indicating femininity and the craving for sweet foods typical of other female characters in the novels.

Instances of men robbed of their power through food also appear in the novels. In *Murder Is Easy* Mr Horton is a henpecked husband, controlled by his wife and forced to do all of the housework, including cooking (149). For decades, women were confined to the domestic spheres of life and their public voices were silenced by burdening them with the demands of the household and food preparation (Belasco 2008, 44). Moreover, even the achievements of women in the domestic sphere were attributed to men; although women did all the shopping, cooking, serving, and cleaning, it was always the man of the house who was considered the "breadwinner." In professional kitchens the head chef is invariably a man, while women are delegated to the role of helpers (47). In Mr Horton's case these roles are reversed and his invalid wife takes over the power in their relationship and delegates him to the feminine role of household help and cook. In order to reassert his masculinity, Mr Horton indulges in drink (*Murder is Easy* 113-16).

Food as a means of gender role reversal serves as a useful tool in characterisation. However, Christie uses the same method in order to feminise the genre of crime fiction as such. At the beginning of the twentieth century, traditional detective stories required a male protagonist. However, as we have seen, the newly emerging classical crime novel attracted a growing number of female readers, and many of the authors were female as well. These authors began attempting to feminise various aspects of their novels. Nevertheless, the introduction of an actual female detective was problematic. The traditional detective was placed firmly in the realm of the mind, the rational, and the masculine. As it follows from the nature of the formula that it "can be bent [...] but not fundamentally altered" (Pascual Soler 2009, 10), the new feminised detective also had to be modelled according to the masculinist assumptions inherent in the genre. Although Christie decided to use a woman as her sleuth in the case of Miss Marple, she still felt the need to conform to the demands of the male-dominated genre (Knight 2004, 162).

It is possible to suggest that Christie tried to negate the masculinity inherent in the figure of the detective not through the creation of a completely female protagonist, but instead by strongly desexualising her detectives. In order to do so, she exploited what Counihan labels the "possibility of destruction of gender identity" (1999, 66): she attributed stereotypically female traits to her male detective and vice versa. First she invented Hercule Poirot, a male character who defies many of the preconceived ideas about masculinity. When she later created an actual female detective in the form of Miss Marple, she again relied on the technique of desexualisation in order to prevent her character from clashing with the established formula.

Firstly, Christie made use of the dictum of traditional Western society, which tells women that their identities consist solely of their bodies and appearance (Counihan 1999, 89). Christie's female detective Miss Marple is depicted as rather untidy; she is by no means elegant, and she does not show any real concern for her appearance. Poirot, on the other hand, pays extreme attention to his attire; he even sacrifices comfort for elegance (e.g. in *The Mysterious Affair at Styles*, *Hallowe'en Party*), his staple moustache is always impeccably groomed, and his surroundings are tidy and neat. Moreover, he is depicted as being delicate and of fragile health, for instance when he overdresses for a short summer drive in an open car in *Dumb Witness* (62) or when he suffers from motion sickness in *Death in the Clouds* (23). Secondly, Christie also relied on depictions of their foodways in order to reverse the protagonists' gender identities, and she did so with even greater frequency than is the case with their appearance.

In his approach to food, Poirot is distinctly feminine. He inclines to all of the aspects of a woman's diet listed above: he takes delight in delicate and ornamental food and he consumes a large amount of sweets. He even engages in the preparation of food. In *The Mystery of the Blue Train* Poirot serves food to his counterpart, an English gentleman (339), and in *Dumb Witness* he attempts to share some of his culinary techniques with his partner, Captain Hastings, an effort which is inevitably met with disapproval (290-291): Hastings considers cooking an activity unfit for real men and therefore not a suitable topic of conversation. Similarly, sweets are generally regarded as feminine and inappropriate for men; however when Poirot entertains he offers his guests coffee and little pastries (*Elephants Can Remember* 145) and his habit of drinking chocolate is a recurrent motif in the novels (*Elephants Can Remember* 163; *Dumb Witness* 53; *One, Two, Buckle My Shoe* 118, 121; etc.).

Chocolate has a special status among sweets, as it is not only a food, but also a drink, and therefore is identified in opposition to other drinks. After its introduction in Europe, drinking chocolate was considered the opposite of drinking coffee, which was at that time thought of as a masculine drink. While coffee was associated with the mind, intellect, self-control, and masculinity; chocolate represented indulgence, body, pleasure, and femininity (Schivelbusch 1993, 87). Unlike with coffee, the associations of chocolate have remained more or less unchanged until the present day. Cocoa is today a drink of women and children and is seen, especially in the Puritan Anglo-Saxon world, as unfit for men (93). It is no wonder then that Poirot's habit of drinking chocolate for breakfast is considered revolting by Hastings, a stereotypical Englishman (*Dumb Witness* 53).

Poirot's other drinking habits are equally unconventional and unmasculine. Poirot avoids strong alcohol, the staple drink of the contemporary Western man (see above); instead, he opts for non-alcoholic or light alcoholic alternatives or an occasional cocktail (*Three Act Tragedy* 44). In *Elephants Can Remember*, Superintendent Garroway is very amused at seeing Poirot drink *sirop* of blackcurrant instead of the customary whiskey and soda, and when he is later told that Poirot drinks *tisane* ("herbal tea"), he remarks: “Ah. Invalid dope of some kind” (181). In *Three Act Tragedy* Poirot again asks his host, Sir Charles, for his staple “glass of *sirop*”, however, his request is met with incomprehension and he discovers that "*sirop* [is] not included in Sir Charles's conception of drinkable fluids" (42).

The position of Miss Marple is more complicated than that of Poirot; as a woman, she cannot be depicted as completely feminine and still fit into the detective formula. In her case, food and eating habits are used to allow her to conform to the masculinist requirements of a classical detective story. Miss Marple and Hercule Poirot represent opposite poles in terms of their approach to food: while Poirot tends to over-indulge in food and is famous for having a sweet tooth, Miss Marple believes in controlling one's bodily desires and is generally indifferent to food, an attitude which is visible in her approach to her garden; she likes taking care of her flowers, but finds growing vegetables "dull" (*Nemesis* 17). While the characterisation of Poirot challenges Western culture's perception that body and its passions and pleasures are set apart from mind and reason (Counihan 1999, 82) by merging a plump body and love of pleasure with exceptional intellectual capacities, Miss Marple combines stereotypically feminine methods of detection, for example chatter and gossip, intrigues and tricks, intuition and reminiscences, with a masculinised approach to food.

In order to reinforce her desexualised image, Christie also renders Miss Marple's drinking habits masculine. While proper women are supposed to indulge only in non-alcoholic beverages, as is shown when Miss Marple is offered fresh lime juice while the rest of the party enjoy a glass of Planter's Punch in *A Caribbean Mystery* (21), Marple is by no means opposed to drinking alcohol. When entertaining a police inspector, she does not offer him tea or coffee, but instead a glass of cherry brandy which she claims to have distilled herself according to her grandmother's recipe. However, the inspector declines, stating that he does not drink before lunchtime, and this role reversal further emphasises the unconventional nature of Miss Marple's drinking habits (*The Murder at the Vicarage* 54).

3.5. Nation, Nationality, and Christie's Fiction

Since their birth in the nineteenth century, the concepts of the nation and national identity have been powerful forces in the shaping of societies all over the world. Benedict Anderson observes that at the end of the twentieth century, unlike only one hundred and fifty years before, the nation state was the norm. Today, the existence of nations and consequently, of differences between them, is often taken for granted.[2] However, what constitutes a nation is by no means a straightforward question. Shared language, which in the nineteenth century was understood as the single most important marker of nationality, is no longer a valid one, with nations like the Swiss or the Belgians being composed of speakers of multiple languages (2006, 135). Recent scientific discoveries illustrate that even race, which was once believed to be a fact determined by genetics, is in fact culturally constructed, as the genetic differences between individual races are negligible (White 2004, 23). Today scholars have come to believe that "it is nearly impossible to define ethnic groups and nations by objective criteria. Defining criteria exist but lie almost exclusively in the subjective realm as ethnic groups and nations (and also tribes and races) are largely self-perceived" (26).

As early as in 1983 Anderson advocated the view that a nation is an idea rather than a fact. He understood it as being subjective, changeable, and constructed; as opposed to objective, fixed, and predetermined. He defined nation as "an imagined political community—and imagined as both inherently limited and sovereign" (2006, 6). Anderson argued that each group larger than a couple of individuals who are able to maintain regular personal contact is by necessity nothing more than an imagined community—we feel an affinity, or what he called "communion" with others whom we do not know and whom, in actual fact, we cannot be sure exist. However, he stressed that such communities "are to be distinguished, not by their falsity/genuineness, but by the style in which they are imagined" (6). Because, as Anne Murcott (1996) puts it, once these communities are believed to be real by their members, they become real in their consequences (29). Moreover, Murcott adds that

> [o]nce a model of nation was imagined, and the means of transporting it far and wide became more and more securely established, it had become available for what Anderson shrewdly calls piracy. By the second decade of the nineteenth century if not before, the idea could readily and widely be borrowed, reinterpreted, or appropriated for new purposes. And in the process newly imagined histories of states, newly formed and re-formed in the name of nation, could be created to become fixed as museum displays. (28)

This malleability of the concept of nation is often exploited by governments engaging in "systematic, even Machiavellian, instilling of nationalist ideology through the mass media, the educational system, administrative regulations, and so forth" (Anderson 2006, 114). It follows that there cannot be one single form of nationalism and a single national identity, but rather "a thousand inchoate dreams" which in "varying combinations" employ the patterns created by previous nationalisms (140).

In order for nationalism or national identity to be born and to continue to exist, it first needs to be created (or imagined) and then dispersed among a population by means of social institutions and through the experiences and activities shared by members of a community. Eating is one of the most important of these activities. Murcott believes that food can be understood as "a medium of communication." Like the mass media, food is "inserted into the interstices of daily life of all of us—almost whether we like it or not" and as such "it can perhaps take its place, along with print capitalism as a [sic] another fluid means of transporting the modular idea of nation" (1996, 30).

Moreover, food is the perfect means for establishing and observing difference, which is crucial for the creation of national identity. Anderson observes that unlike religions, which allow for conversion and as such are inclusive, nations are "imagined as *limited*, because even the largest of them [...] has finite, if elastic, boundaries, beyond which lie other nations" (2006, 7, original emphasis). In other words, members of a nation always differentiate between what is "us" and what is "them" and competitively proclaim that what is "ours" is also, naturally, "the best" (17). Food can serve as the battleground where such competitiveness is engaged, because although eating is a universal activity common to the whole of humankind, the specific foodstuffs that various groups eat vary greatly (Murcott 1996, 23). Parkhurst Ferguson shares this view, claiming that by "what recipes exclude as well as include, in what they assume as much as what they specify, cookbooks define what is appropriate and what is not. They tell us what is French or Italian or Provençal or Tuscan, and what is not" (2010 102). In addition, the timeless quality of national dishes and their perceived antiquity can establish a nation as a community which has always existed and always will. Food can serve as "the expression and affirmation of a national identity that somehow exists outside of history [...] a nation without history, without politics, a nation rooted in terroir and tradition" (105).

The nation and nationality play a crucial role in detective fiction, as was discussed in detail in section 1.3.3. According to McCaw, "traditional detective fiction illustrates an implied (sometimes explicit) connection between crime and national identity" (2010, 41) In early works of British detective fiction this connection was embodied in the opposition of British versus the foreign and the implied parallel opposition of moral versus criminal, respectively. The foreign element, whether represented by a German spy, an American fanatic or an immoral person "polluted" by their experiences abroad, represented the types of forces that disrupted the healthy English core (41). However, this simplified approach was abandoned in the works of later crime authors, including Agatha Christie. While Christie's stories "utilize stereotypes in their articulation of a vision of rural England," with the "archetypal English village" at the centre, and evoke a "shared culture," or even, in the words of Ferdinand Tönnies ([1957] 2004), a "perfect unity of human wills as an original or natural condition which is preserved in spite of actual separation" (37), the same stories are also used by the author as a means of poking fun at the stereotyped idealised Englishness and uncovering it as theatrical, unreal or even decayed.

Christie often relied on food in her construction of national stereotypes, both of the English and other nationalities. Englishness is associated with a wide variety of meals and foodstuffs, including the English breakfast, afternoon tea, steaks, apples, or tarts with cream. In *Nemesis* Christie enumerated the contents of a conventional dinner in a conventional English household: "a small joint of mutton" accompanied by a dish of "roast potatoes" is followed by a "plum tart with a small jug of cream" and pieces of "rather indifferent pastry" (88). When Poirot plans to entertain a respectable English lady, he commissions his butler George to "provide a meal of square crumpets richly buttered, symmetrical sandwiches, and other suitable components of a lavish English afternoon tea" (*Hickory Dickory Dock* 14). Lord Horbury, the quintessential English gentleman, is described as enjoying a breakfast of kidneys while reading the morning newspaper (*Death in the Clouds* 163); he is seen to care only about "horses and hunting and shooting and crops and tiresome old farmers" (165), and defines a marvellous life as one composed of "hunting and tea and muffins and children" (173). Similarly, in *Murder Is Easy*, "plum pudding on Christmas day," "village cricket," English old ladies and open fireplaces are all associated with cosiness and Englishness (8).

However, national identity cannot exist in isolation. In order to define a nation it is necessary to place it in contrast to some other nation. As Anderson put it, the rhetoric of nationalism always contains the element of competition against a clearly defined other (2006, 17). In addition to identifying certain foods as English, Christie also frequently placed the normal, proper, healthy, and tasty English foods in opposition to the foreign, which are described as abnormal, disgusting or at the very least inferior to the English in quality or taste. In other words, English cuisine is the norm and if the cuisines of other nations differ, they are described as deviating from this norm. In this manner Mr Aarons presents his vision of a proper meal as consisting of "a good Porterhouse steak and a tankard of something worth drinking" or alternatively a steak and kidney pudding, followed by an apple tart with a jug of cream, a sharp contrast to the unsatisfactory French "fallals and whatnots," "ordoovres," "omelettes," and "little bits of quail"; all inferior foods unworthy of a proper gentleman (*The Mystery of the Blue Train* 339). In much the same way, in *Taken at the Flood* an elderly visitor at a village pub disapproves of the international dishes on offer, stating: "And every year things get worse and worse. No service! Food uneatable! Vienna steaks indeed! A steak's either rump or fillet steak—not chopped-up horse!" (261). Even Miss Marple reveals her preference for traditional English food on her vacation in the Caribbean, when after being presented with a breakfast of paw-paws she cannot help wishing that "she could have a nice apple" instead (*A Caribbean Mystery* 37).

Not only foreigners' food, but also their eating habits and table manners are looked down upon as bizarre at best or even uncultured. English travellers in Africa are forced to stop for refreshments "in a primitive structure by the road," where they suffer an interminable wait for "stale cake and lukewarm tea" (*The Man in the Brown Suit* 252). In *Destination Unknown*, the characters are reduced to feeding themselves on a dish of semolina and meat stew set on the floor in a Berber house (138). In *By the Pricking of my Thumbs* Tommy and Tuppence note uncomprehendingly that some nations, like the Irish, enjoy funerals—especially the eating and drinking that comes after them (45). Later their butler Albert is scandalised by the times at which people in the south of Europe eat their meals: "Of course some people do eat dinner late, [...] I went to Spain once and believe me, you couldn't get a meal before 10 o'clock. Ten p.m. I ask you! Heathens!" (189). In *The Murder at the Vicarage* the Japanese are described as consumers of "half-cooked rice" (12), while in *Destination Unknown* Miss Hetherington disapproves of her French co-diners who let their children "sit up far too late. Ten o'clock sometimes before they go to bed, and they go through every course on the menu instead of just having milk and biscuits as children should." What is more, their "parents even let them drink *wine*" (103, original emphasis). As the narrator sarcastically remarks, "[h]orror could go no further" (103).

The superiority of the English over other nations is also highlighted by the fact that English characters are frequently those belonging to the class of food consumers, while it is foreigners who serve as food producers. When natives of various former colonies are depicted in the novels, they are predominantly employed as servants or waiters (*The Man in the Brown Suit* 265, *Destination Unknown* 285, etc.). Immigrants from continental Europe also frequently perform food production tasks—Mitzi, the servant girl in *A Murder Is Announced*, is a Central European war refugee, as is the maid Olga in *Elephants Can Remember*, and Italian or French cooks and waiters appear in a number of novels (*Hickory Dickory Dock*, *A Caribbean Mystery*, *Sparkling Cyanide*, etc.).

These characters are typically depicted as being inferior to the English, or as child-like and naïve; for example "Geronimo, the Italian manservant" is described as "making emphatic gestures with his hands" or having "his wizened monkey-like face screwed up in a comical grimace" (*Hickory Dickory Dock* 86). Moreover, even if some members of the serving staff are English, there is a strict hierarchy determining that the English always hold a higher rank than the foreigners. In *Sparkling Cyanide* an English head waiter, the reliable Charles, is assisted by Italian helpers who, although they are described as "delightful" and "cheery," are also depicted as clumsy and silly (e.g. 145). In *A Caribbean Mystery* the ranking of various members of the hotel staff clearly demonstrates the low esteem with which the respective nations are regarded by the English guests: the service itself is done by "proud" black women, and an Italian head waiter and a "French wine waiter" are "in charge" of the dining room, but everything is supervised by the Englishman Kendall (24). Interestingly, Kendall is "seconded" in this position by his wife (24), indicating that even the most English of women remain inferior to the true English*man*.

The foodways of foreign nations, whether European, American, Arab or African all receive the same treatment as the foreigners themselves. The French represent the only notable exception to this rule. French cuisine, although disapproved of or disparaged by some characters (such as in the case of Mr Aarons), is frequently associated with the aristocracy, with stylishness, and with expensive taste. In *Taken at the Flood*, the impoverished aristocrat Frances Cloade reminisces that in the times when her family were "in funds," they used to hire a French chef (as opposed to a plain English cook), who would prepare elaborate six-course dinners (51).

Pierre Verdaguer (2005) observes that this is not unique to Christie's writing. On the contrary, "Frenchness—and even excessive Frenchness—is associated in Anglo-American crime fiction with upper-class elegance and poise" in a great number of cases (151). French eating habits and other French customs are not necessarily described realistically, as "what matters is less their cultural accurateness then the illusion of cultural otherness they create" (153). Christie often used French in preference to English terms for meals, such as in *The Secret Adversary* (*lobster à l'américaine* or *pêche Melba*, 42; *sole à la Jeannette*, 257) and as Verdaguer observes, such use of French vocabulary is, like the French food the characters consume, "in most cases [...] essentially decorative" (2005, 154).

Nevertheless, even if the exceptional case of the French cuisine is taken into consideration, the previous paragraphs demonstrate that in an overwhelming majority of instances, the English characters in Christie's novels regard foreign cuisines and eating habits with suspicion, if not with disgust. However, disregard of the others' food is by no means limited to the English. Christie's foreign characters frequently approach English food in the same way as the English approach theirs: with mockery, disdain, or even superiority. In *Hickory Dickory Dock*, the African student Mr Akibombo complains that the English diet gives him "disquieting sensations in his stomach" (267). In the same novel Italian cook Maria claims that she cannot prepare the promised risotto because the suppliers brought her "the wrong rice" and suggests making spaghetti instead, leading to the following argument with her supervisor:

> "We had spaghetti last night."
> "It does not matter. In my country we eat the spaghetti every day—every single day. The pasta, it is good all the time."
> "Yes, but you're in England now."
> "Very well then, I make the stew. The English stew. You will not like it but I make it—pale—pale with the onions boiled in much water instead of cooked in the oil—and pale meat on cracked bones." (88)

Similarly, the Central European housemaid Mitzi claims that "English cooking tastes like water" (*A Murder Is Announced* 136) and dismisses English cakes as tasting of sand (211). Disregard for English cuisine and drinks, is sometimes expressed even by Poirot. When a police inspector comes to see him, Poirot's butler George suggests they offer him beer instead of Poirot's signature *sirop de cassis*, to which Poirot replies: "How horrible! But how British!" (*After the Funeral* 207) and in *Murder on the Orient Express* the American traveller Mrs Hubbard declines the offer of a cup of tea with biscuits, as she finds it too English to her taste (232).

These outsider perspectives on Englishness serve as a tool which enables Christie to poke fun at the stuffy stereotypes of the nation. Indeed, David Malcolm and Cheryl Alexander Malcolm (2008) observe that

> Christie's stories do not promote a nostalgic vision of pre-war England as a site of harmony and an acceptance of its social order—such an understanding of Christie may have been promoted by late-twentieth-century television adaptations of her work. Rather, the Poirot stories set amongst the upper classes show that the traditional pillars of society are not morally intact and many of them cannot be trusted. (73)

Similarly, McCaw notices that Christie was able to tap into the growing belief which took hold in the twentieth century (especially after the Second World War) that Englishness had become “fraught with tension” and “hard to sustain in any meaningful sense” (2010, 46).

The belief that true national identity had been lost in the past became the first response to the breakdown of what was believed to be traditional Englishness (McCaw 2010, 46). Food which is labelled as being typically English is often described by the characters as something they used to eat as children, in those "better times." In *Evil Under the Sun* Miss Darnley describes her childhood as “very English,” consisting of “[t]he country—a big shabby house—horses, dogs—walks in the rain—wood fires—apples in the orchard—lack of money—old tweeds—evening dresses that went on from year to year [...]” (30). Similarly, in the pseudo-Victorian Bertram's Hotel, which still offers full English breakfasts and five o’clock teas, the characters feel as if they were “stepping back a hundred years” and could enjoy “the old English dishes":

> there's a marvellous old-fashioned beef-steak pudding! You've never tasted anything like it; and great sirloins of beef and saddles of mutton, and an old-fashioned English tea and a wonderful English breakfast. And of course all the usual things as well. And it's wonderfully comfortable. And warm. Great log fires. (*At Bertram’s Hotel* 17)

This evocative description prompts another visitor to reminisce about an idyllic past; "Yes, yes... I remember when I was a child... Sideboards groaning with hot dishes. Yes, it was a luxurious way of life." (19)

However, Christie was not satisfied with the simplistic claim that true Englishness had been destroyed by the modern way of life. Instead, she problematised English nationalism as such by making the concepts of English superiority and exceptionalism seem self-centred or even absurd. In *Sparkling Cyanide*, for example, Anthony, a secret agent of Spanish origin, sits in a café with his English colleagues, drinking what he derisively labels “an English café's idea of a nice cup of coffee” and admits to being forced to take the drink “for the sake of being admitted on equal terms to the other two men's conference” (305). In *A Murder Is Announced* even the English characters themselves recognise the absurdity of adhering to the national cuisine as a patriotic exercise, when one of the characters, Miss Hinch, after having eaten a rich chocolate-butter cake prepared by the foreign cook complains that although “foreigners certainly understand confectionery [...] What they can’t make is a plain boiled pudding.” After this remark “[e]verybody was respectfully silent, though it seemed to be hovering on Patrick's lips to ask if anyone really wanted a plain boiled pudding" (215).

In fact, Christie utilised her most frequently recurring character, Hercule Poirot, in order to hold a mirror up to the English characters. The Belgian Poirot is purposely designed to be as un-English as possible; "Unlike the tall Englishman Holmes, Poirot is a small and fussy foreigner, 'a funny little man with [an] egg-shaped head and the enormous moustaches' and almost effeminate in his behavior" (Malcolm and Malcolm 2008, 72). And it is partially his separate nationality, which allows him to solve the mysteries, as his judgement is not clouded by the prejudices of his English companions (72). Poirot is a Belgian, a fact which he often has to stress to others (*Hickory Dickory Dock* 51, *The Big Four* 194) and as such he is unclassifiable as the Belgian nation is devoid of any stereotypical qualities in the eyes of the other characters. Thus, in Verdaguer's words, his foreignness becomes "a cultural testing ground" (2005, 156) where the English norms are contrasted with those of another and evaluated. Poirot's foreignness functions as a space in which the author can explore the English "preoccupations with their own national issues or their longing for a better world. [...] a setting in which [...] encounters with the cultural Other can be fictionalised" (159).

Finally, in a number of novels Englishness is represented as neither a dream of the past, nor as an illusion upheld with comical stubbornness, but rather as a carnivalesque sinister performance which masks an inherent decadence and immorality. In these novels Christie turned Englishness into a "theatrical notion" and presents "the sense of national identity as 'made up" (Rowland 2001, 63). She depicts "a society of strangers whose social exchanges have become theatrical and dissevered from a sense of place" (Light 1991, 62). Thus when in the *Hallowe'en Party* a child is drowned in a bucket of apples intended for a game of bobbing, Ariadne Oliver observes that "[n]othing could be more agreeable than a juicy English apple. And yet here were apples mixed up with broomsticks, and witches, and old-fashioned folklore, and a murdered child" (63). In *Endless Night* the protagonist Michael, a healthy and vigorous young Englishman with the tastes "of a Victorian squire," which are frequently contrasted with the meagre appetite of his American wife (210), turns out to be a psychopathic murderer.

The process of conversion from the nostalgic memory of 'good old England' to the uncovering of the theatricality and unreality of any such notion is visible especially in *At Bertram's Hotel*. While at the beginning of the novel the hotel's restaurant is depicted as an old-fashioned place serving meals as they used to be served (see above), as the story proceeds the characters acknowledge that "le Five-o'-clock is as dead as the dodo!" (178). The ideal Englishness, so much admired at first, begins to seem suspicious even as the characters wonder if there could "really be anything seriously wrong with a place that served old-fashioned afternoon teas?" (178). By the end of the novel, this Englishness is revealed to be a fabrication, a performance for the sake of foreign tourists, when the manager's assistant informs the reader that the "same people come back year after year. We have a lot of Americans. People from Boston, and Washington. Very quiet, nice people. [...] They like our English atmosphere" (160). This fabricated Englishness gains an even more sinister dimension when it is revealed that the hotel is in fact only operated as a cover-up for the activities of a crime syndicate. Christie's deconstruction of the concept of English national identity is completed by the closing remark of Miss Marple. When asked whether the revelation of the true nature of Bertram's hotel surprised her, she replies: "Not really. There were so many curious things that didn't seem quite to fit in. It was all too good to be true—if you know what I mean. What they call in theatrical circles, a beautiful performance. But it was a performance—not real" (305).

The preceding paragraphs demonstrate the extent to which Christie's depictions of foreigners rely on stereotypes. However, she employed these stereotypes not only in order to sketch compressed and easily recognisable character types, but also to explore the nature of nationality, especially of Britishness or Englishness, and to question its validity. Furthermore, the subversion of preconceived notions about Englishness also served to make her stories more suspenseful. Readers of her novels are first led to believe that the honest, upstanding tea-drinking Englishmen and Englishwomen are extremely unlikely to commit crimes, a belief which is suddenly proven wrong. Thus Christie was able to achieve two things at once: to create the perfect "least likely person" criminals and to poke fun at what she depicted as stale nationalistic nostalgia.

Notes

[1] An earlier version of sections 3.3 and 3.4 was accepted for publication in *Ostrava Journal of English Philology* 1 (2015).

[2] While even today nationalism is a widely discussed and influential phenomenon, a number of contemporary scholars have questioned its validity. Monica Heller, Charles V. Carnegie, or John Carlos Rowe claim that in the contemporary globalised world the nation-state is no longer an institution capable of dealing with increasingly transnational economic, political, and environmental problems. As

Carnegie (2002) observes, "the principle of nation-state autonomy is logically incompatible with global interdependence" (5). The post-modern understanding of identity as a constructed and fluid phenomenon further challenges the idea of nation as a unified community. We have come to believe that "pure identities" do not exist (10) and therefore it is impossible to mark clear boundaries between different groups. In response to these issues the above authors introduce the term "post-nationalism" in order to describe a globalised reality in which national borders are no longer significant.

Despite these recent developments in social sciences, the concepts of nation and nationality are considered relevant for the purpose of the present analysis. In the first half of the twentieth century, when Christie wrote most of her novels, the political and economic landscape was much less globalised than it is today, and the idea of the nation-state as the "validator of social identity" (Carnegie 2002, 1) was still mostly uncontested.

CHAPTER FOUR

FOOD AND INVESTIGATION

While the focus in the previous chapter was concentrated on characters and their identities, this chapter will deal with another of the basic elements of the detective formula, the plot. In a crime story the plot for the most part consists of the investigation of the crime, a task which is done by means of collecting various material clues, as well as interrogating a sequence of witness. However, while in early crime fiction the detective's technique was based on logic, science, and deduction, new investigation methods were introduced in the Golden Age (see section 1.2). The feminised detective opted for unconventional, feminised techniques, employing domestic knowledge and abductive reasoning.

Domesticity lies at the centre of many of Agatha Christie's novels. As the home is a traditionally feminine domain, setting the stories in the home and using family conflicts to construct plots is a useful tool in feminising the genre. However, as we saw in section 3.5, Christie was also interested in the examination of British nationalism, and the symbolic connection between the nation and the home helped her to explore this issue further. As Anne McClintock (1993) notes, "[n]ations are frequently figured through the iconography of familial and domestic space. [...] We talk of the Family of Nations, of 'homelands' and 'native' lands. In Britain, immigration matters are dealt with at the Home Office; in the United States, the President and his wife are called the First Family" (63). This parallel is based on the concept that both nation and family are understood as realms where one can feel separated from, and also safe from the outside world. The family or the nation represents "us," while the rest of the world represents the "other," which could potentially be dangerous for us.

The understanding of family and home as a basic unit or a miniature version of society and nation has a long history. Wendy Wall (2002) observes that as early as in modern England the home served to provide "the training ground for political order" (1) and the role of the family was to teach individuals the norms of patriarchal world-order (2). In the seventeenth century the "belief that English citizens are bound by the seemingly primal sense of the home" was widespread (10). It is also important to note that it was the woman, or the housewife, who occupied the central position in maintaining the home, and, by extension, in maintaining the state and the nation. The role of the woman of the house was to provide the "self-sufficiency, moral fiber, and industry necessary for England's identification as a nation" (10).

The interconnection between women, domesticity, and nation grew even stronger in the Victorian period, when imperialism became the "complementary ideology" to domesticity (Archibald 1998, 10). A woman who stayed at home, but also a woman who emigrated to marry a colonist was assigned the task of "preserv[ing] the sanctity of the middle-class domestic space from the corruption of the outside world" (8). At this point the home was understood as "fundamentally English" whether it existed on English soil or in the distant colonies (9). Thus at the zenith of imperialism, both the home and England began to be understood as "sacred spaces," centres of the world and of civilisation, where one could feel protected from whatever adversities might be lurking outside and abroad.

In Agatha Christie's novels this very idea of the home and the family as safe havens is undermined. Not only does she explore crime, violence, and hatred within the family, but domesticity and food-related practices and knowledge also form a crucial part of Christie's detectives' method of work. In fact, it is exactly these practices that give her sleuths an advantage over official investigators, because they help them to approach the mysteries from a different perspective, notice seemingly insignificant details, insinuate themselves into the local environment, and extract knowledge from insiders. It is in this way that they finally arrive at the correct conclusion. It follows that the home in Christie's novels is by no means a safe place. On the contrary, it is a place of passion, crime, questioning, spying, and surveillance. What is more, even the family is not portrayed as the close-knit community it might seem to be on the surface, but rather as a group of people unable to trust each other, in which everyone struggles to promote their own interests, no matter at whose expense.

4.1. Kitchen Clues: The Domestic Detective

Food is inseparably linked to the home. Home is the place where people are fed as children, where they return to eat as adults, and where they share either everyday or festive meals with family members and close friends, and so, as a consequence, food is also closely connected with domesticity. Katherine Hampsten (n.d.) observes that in the twentieth century, American mass media defined domesticity as a force bringing "happiness and fulfillment" to human beings, and identified it with "an abundance of food and a well-stocked kitchen." Access to good food at home was believed to ensure an individual's "contentment and security." Women were the instrumental force in bringing about this idealised domesticity. In twentieth-century media discourse, women were depicted as cooks or food providers serving meals to others. Even the possibility of marriage was linked to "a well-equipped kitchen" (Hampsten n.d.). In other words, domesticity, food, feeding and women were understood as being closely interconnected. As Anita Mannur (2010) puts it:

> Preserving the domestic familial structure becomes the responsibility of women; but cooking and food preparation must be acknowledged for the central role they play in upholding the dynamics of domestic familiarity. Preserving the sanctity of the domestic home space, creating a space where members of the household feel nurtured and protected, thus become important touchstones of women's labour. (52)

The act of cooking, and domesticity in general, became the domain of women and a field of feminine knowledge. This notion of domesticity as feminine labour and feminine knowledge was especially prominent in middle and upper-middle class settings and it was reflected in the value systems of these classes (Towell 2009, 4). As guardians of the peaceful and nurturing home, women were seen as guardians of middle-class morality. Moreover, metaphorically, they also became guardians of "true" national identity, which is often scripted "through culinary practice within the home" (Mannur 2010, 58). Thus the peaceful, idealised, and enclosed home is identified with an idealised and enclosed Englishness, and both of them are understood as in need of protection from "the foreign and its intrusion" (Towell 2009, 9).

However, a woman's traditional role within the home is not limited to guarding it against harmful exterior influences. In fact, the very coming into existence of the home is dependent on women. The twentieth-century home is "not a given; it requires imagining into being, and its creation is an index, particularly, of the characters of the women who create it" (Humble 2001, 109). Women are in charge of upholding the basic "tenet of domesticity: the separation of the public and private spheres" (Towell 2009, 5) and of providing "the family (and especially the man) with a barrier to the external dangers" (6).

Images of domesticity, traditional femininity, and of the role of women in the creation and maintenance of domesticity become the substance of what Chiara Briganti and Kathy Mezei (2006) label the domestic modernist novel. According to Briganti and Mezei, the "English domestic novel portrays the social relations and daily life of a contained community (house, village, urban parish, suburb)" (17). This type of novel places emphasis on the "values and rituals" connected with modern domesticity: "separation from the workplace, privacy, comfort, focus on the family" (Reed 1996, 7). Lavaughn Towell (2009) acknowledges the centrality of the private/public dichotomy in both Victorian and twentieth-century crime fiction, claiming that the "trope of separation of work and home as well as creation of an interiority that excludes all the 'evil' from invading the home are important." Families featured in such fiction engage in the concurrent processes of creating "the home in physical and mental form" and reinforcing it "by continuing to keep threats [...] out. If threats made their way in, they were either incorporated or annihilated" (7).

As Briganti and Mezei observe, the modern domestic novel was written in various different styles; "social realism (Winifred Holtby, Storm Jameson), self-deprecatory humour and irony (E. M. Delafield, E. H. Young, Jan Struther), the monstrous (Ivy Compton-Burnett) and the rebellious (Elizabeth Bowen, Rosamond Lehmann)." Examples of the domestic novel also cross the boundaries of different genres, including "drawing-room comedy (Dodie Smith, Stella Gibbons), golden age detective novel of manners (Agatha Christie, Ngaio Marsh, Dorothy Sayers), lyrical exposé of life in the bourgeois home (May Sinclair, F. M. Mayor, Enid Bagnold) and popular saga (Angela Thirkell)," but such works can even be found in the genre of "experimental high modernism (Virginia Woolf, Dorothy Richardson, Katherine Mansfield and Stevie Smith)" (Briganti and Mezei 2006, 18).

However, while modern domestic novels relied heavily on the depiction of stereotypical femininity and traditional, idealised domesticity, they were by no means uncritically acceptant of them. On the contrary, a number of authors, including Christie, purposefully employed these stereotypical depictions in order to question and deconstruct the idea of a peaceful and nurturing home. Christie's stories depict the home as appearing "bucolic" only "from outside, from afar, from the city" (Lyotard [1988] 1991, 193). On the inside one can "all too often tumble upon tragedy, violence and the uncanny" (Briganti and Mezei 2006, 35). As Briganti and Mezei conclude:

> Agatha Christie, the doyenne of nostalgic Englishness, like many other golden age detective novelists whose stories are set in country houses or

> picturesque, cosy villages, exposes one dysfunctional family after another [...] Through the choice of unusual focalizers—a spinster, unwed mother, middle-aged wife, child, or servant, that is, a view from the margins—in the interwar domestic novel, the familiar household is perceived aslant and transformed into the unhomely. Rituals punctuating the life of house, village and parish mask secrets and deceptions while facilitating their occurrence [...]. (35)

As the previous paragraphs demonstrate, traditional domesticity; that, which is typically tied to security, nourishment, food, and women, is one of the driving forces behind the crime novels written by Agatha Christie and other twentieth-century British authors. It also serves to confirm Stephen Knight's observation that the investigation method of Christie's Hercule Poirot, "represents a heightened version of female domestic knowledge as a weapon against fictional disorder" (Knight 2004, 91, see also section 1.2.3). In other words, Christie's feminised detectives rely neither on pure logic, as was characteristic of detectives in the tradition of E. A. Poe's Auguste Dupin, nor on scientific knowledge in the manner of Sir Arthur Conan Doyle's Sherlock Holmes, but rather on domestic knowledge, knowledge of food; knowledge which had traditionally been understood as feminine.

Alison Light (1991) observes that Christie deals with "domestic inquisitions." Her detectives attempt to uncover "family secrets," such as "the inheritance drama, mistaken identities, [or] hidden madness" (62). The main method of both of her most famous detectives, the fussy and frenchified Hercule Poirot and the "shy and twittering spinster sleuth" Miss Marple (62), assumes the form of "family talk" (61). Moreover, Light agrees with Briganti and Mezei by claiming that Christie is "an iconoclast whose monitoring of the plots of family life aims to upset the Victorian image of home, sweet home" (1991, 61). Such a focus on the domestic, ordinary, and everyday on the one hand renders the detective less majestic or God-like, sometimes even comical, but on the other hand provides her/him with a perspective and insight different from other investigators, especially the masculine police, and thus serves to her/his advantage. In other words, the use of domestic knowledge leads to the paradoxical situation in which the detectives are considered marginal and insignificant by the other characters, while simultaneously holding an overwhelming advantage and power over them.

Domestic and culinary knowledge is used for multiple ends both by Christie's detectives and also by other characters. Firstly, information connected to food and eating habits often provides alibis (real or false) for the suspects. In *Evil under the Sun*, Poirot goes to great lengths to establish whether the individual characters took their breakfasts in their respective rooms or in the hotel restaurant (108, 132, 190, etc.). The same technique is employed by the investigators in *At Bertram's Hotel*. Upon arriving at the scene of crime, Chief Inspector Davy, alias The Father, begins his investigation by questioning the hotel's chambermaid Rose Sheldon as to the customary time and manner of serving breakfast (175). Criminals are also aware of the value of formal meals in providing useful alibis. For instance, a serial murderer of women adopts the technique of making sure that he is seen by as many waiters as possible when having his afternoon tea in a café at the time of the death of his victims; when the police later question him, uses these waiters as convenient and impartial witnesses (*Evil under the Sun* 269).

Food can also serve as a clue, especially in the many cases of death caused by poisoning which appear in Christie's novels. In *A Pocket Full of Rye*, *Three Act Tragedy*, *The Mysterious Affair at Styles* and many other stories, the detailed examination of silverware and china, the remains of foods and drinks, or interviews with kitchen personnel help Poirot, Marple or other investigators cast light on individual crimes. In *Sparkling Cyanide*, Anthony arrives at the solution of the mystery thanks to a shrewd idea that comes to him while observing a table laid for tea and coffee and the positions which individual eaters occupy around it. He explains:

> A. Kemp's cup has sugared tea in it. B. Kemp's cup has coffee in it. Two conflicting statements that cannot both be true—But they are both true. The misleading term is Kemp's cup. Kemp's cup when he left the table and Kemp's cup when he returned to the table are not the same. (327)

In addition to being a useful means of establishing alibis and functioning as a clue, cooking and serving food can also be employed by the shrewd feminine or domestically knowledgeable detective as a means of putting her/his witnesses at ease, thereby making them more cooperative and willing to speak. On numerous occasions Poirot hosts, or even cooks dinners for investigators (*Death in the Clouds* 84), informants (*The Mystery of the Blue Train* 339) or even for suspects, such as in *Evil under the Sun*, where he invites all of the party to a picnic in order to observe their behaviour discreetly (278). In *Hickory Dickory Dock*, Poirot even admits to changing his food habits in order to gain information from witnesses:

> Though personally deprecating the five o'clock as inhibiting the proper appreciation of the supreme meal of the day, dinner, Poirot was now getting quite accustomed to serving it. The resourceful George had on this

> occasion produced large cups, a pot of really strong Indian tea and, in addition to the hot and buttery square crumpets, bread and jam and a large square of rich plum cake. All this for the delectation of Inspector Sharpe who was leaning back contentedly sipping his third cup of tea. (107)

In *4.50 from Paddington*, Lucy Eyelesbarrow, the young helper of Miss Marple, uses a similar tactic. Miss Marple sets her up as housekeeper in the house of the suspects in order to spy on them and secretly interrogate them (49-52).

Possession of domestic knowledge gives the detective one more great advantage: it facilitates her/his contact with domestic help and servants, another useful source of information in an investigation. Christie's detectives are knowledgeable in the servants' field of expertise and are therefore able to engage in conversations on shared topics; this allows them to win the trust of the servants and to gain easy access to a number of household secrets. Poirot befriends the cook Marjorie after enquiring about recipes and ingredients in *After the Funeral* (221) and in *Hickory Dickory Dock* he soon becomes the Italian waiter Geronimo's confidante and is able to use him as a spy (179).

Finally, a shared meal is often the perfect opportunity to share information and seemingly idle chitchat over tea; thus food can also become the setting for secret meetings (*The Man in the Brown Suit* 173). Investigators often make use of the familiarity of the local pub or inn and are able to extract useful information and get to know local gossip and any number of guilty secrets (*Why Didn't They Ask Evans?* 157) while mingling with the crowd over a "pint of bitter" (*Taken at the Flood* 110).

What is significant is that the type of knowledge needed to take such a course of investigation as discussed above is never possessed by the official investigators, who are predominantly masculine. In *Three Act Tragedy* Mr Satterthwaite is described as being able to understand the criminal case at hand more than others because there is a "womanish strain in his character" and as a result he has "insight into the feminine mind" (27). A woman-like attention paid to the clothing of others helps Poirot solve the case in *One, Two, Buckle My Shoe*; he is able to infer the identity of the murderer after noticing that she wore old shoes one day and new shoes the next (265). In *Death in the Clouds*, Poirot is the only one to whom it occurs to enquire about the system of serving meals and to ask the plane stewards about disarranged plates and the number of forks and spoons on each table (39-40, 225, 230). Similarly, when the murderer is suspected of having used one of the knives stolen from the dining room as a murder weapon, Miss Marple immediately realises that while a cutlery knife is a poor murder instrument, that night they laid steak knives because steak was on the menu, and these knives "are kept sharp," which makes them possibly lethal (*A Caribbean Mystery* 157). The detective's familiarity with eating rituals can also be helpful in establishing the time at which the crime was committed. For example, Poirot observes that one o'clock is the ideal time for murder, as "at half-past one [...] everyone is quite sure to be in the dining room" (*Evil under the Sun* 273).

Food and eating figure in the investigation process so prominently that even the language used to describe it is often food or cookery related. A false clue is typically referred to as a "red herring" (e.g. *The Sittaford Mystery* 149), the suspects are described as "fishy" (*N or M* 19 or 84) or "seedy-looking" (*Death in the Clouds* 44), and the process of the investigation is labelled grilling (*Endless Night* 122).

However, once again Christie did not limit herself to using food merely as a plot device or as a tool for constructing her mysteries and investigation. Instead, through the very use of stereotyped domesticity she took part in the twentieth-century writers' collective attempt to deconstruct such notions of domesticity. As Towell observes, in classical detective fiction the home and the private, domestic, and familiar are systematically transformed into the uncanny. Towell defines the "unhome-like" or the uncanny in Freudian terms, understanding it as

> that aspect which makes something unfamiliar to characters in a narrative as well as readers when everything leading up to that point had appeared familiar. In other words, characters are apt to experience the uncanny when seemingly familiar places and people become "unhome- like"—they no longer appear safe and inviting. However, the uncanny must come from within. It must derive from an outre element that is also familiar to the person experiencing the uncanny feeling. (2009, 1)

It is this conflict between homeliness into which uncanniness intrudes, or even homeliness itself being transformed into uncanniness, which fuels the majority of Christie's detective mysteries. It is what "strips the reader (and, of course, the characters within the narratives) of a sense of safety—a sense of home" (Towell 2009, 1). Thus, in the classical crime story, as in other middlebrow novels of the twentieth century, the home represents a "grammar" in which that which had been familiar, safe, plain, and thus unimportant gains a new, often sinister meaning (Humble 2001, 108). Such novels reflect "the contemporary sense of a domestic sphere in a state of flux. In many novels the home is foregrounded, becoming the central concern, an emblem of difficult and disturbing change" (111). As Mezei argues, in Christie's work "unheimlich secrets" are constantly being uncovered within the previously seemingly homely settings and crime becomes "domesticated" (2007, 105). Order is not only threatened by outside forces (the public, foreign, strange, urban), but there is "the uncannier, more disturbing threat from inside (the home, the village community) that arises from repressed hates, desires, fears" (110). In other words, in Christie's stories "violence was concealed by the mask of the domestic, hidden by the very thing that made it possible" (Wigley 1992, quoted in Mezei 2007, 110).

In deconstructing the traditional notion of the domestic female, Christie paid special attention to the paradoxical situation in which domesticity simultaneously represents both marginality and power. This paradox arises from the fact that women (or, in Poirot's case, domestic men) "are located both at the center and at the periphery of the familial home space" (Mannur 2010, 52). This conflict is visible in the figure of Poirot, who is frequently considered insignificant, overlooked or even ridiculed by other characters for his unconventional investigation methods, yet who always triumphs in the end. However, it is even more prominent in the character of Miss Marple, an elderly spinster cum amateur detective.

Mezei understands the character of the spinster as a "socially marginal" figure who in spite of, or rather thanks to her insignificance and invisibility is able to exercise surveillance over other characters. As a character who has always been pushed to the margins of family life, the spinster is caught up in the "dialectic between seeing and being seen, omniscience and invisibility" and can assert her "powers of shrewd observation and manipulation" (2007, 104). While seemingly subject to the power of the patriarchal family, "spinsters exercise power through their position at the edge, their surveillance, and their rhetorical tactics" (106), using methods that "are indirect, involving the manipulation of language and the cunning redirection of the readers' and the characters' gaze through (mis)focalization, sleight-of-hand, and narrative ambiguity" (107).

In this way the frail, fluffy Miss Marple, often underestimated by other characters or even described as senile, ends up outwitting all of the official investigators, or, as Mezei labels them, the "blustering males" (2007, 109). Marple's "indirect methods" can be observed in all of the stories in which she is featured. In *Nemesis*, for example, she plays on her old age by pretending that she has forgotten what address she has put on a package in order to obtain it from the post office clerk (167); she later feigns giddiness to gain access to a house so that she can interview its inhabitants (181), and extracts information from chambermaids who bring her early morning tea to her bed (95). In other words, she takes full advantage of being "one of those chatty, fluffy old ladies whom other people expect to talk, to ask questions" which appear to be innocent "gossipy questions," questions "about food she had eaten, servants she had had [...]" (*Nemesis* 84). Thanks to this inconspicuous questioning, she is able to gain crucial information which condemns the guilty and clears the innocent.

The contradictory position into which Miss Marple is placed thanks to her domesticity, marginality, and femininity is examined closely in the first chapter of *The Mirror Crack'd from Side to Side*. Here the apparent insignificance of Marple is brought to the fore; she is rendered frail and powerless on account of illness and old age and is harassed by her over-cheerful caretaker, who treats her as a "slightly mentally afflicted child" (18). However, instead of rebelling against this perception, Miss Marple decides to use it to her advantage. She acts completely in accordance with her caretaker's preconceived notions, feigns fatigue, and burdens her with plenty of insignificant errands to run in town, when, in fact, all the frailness and powerlessness is just a ruse which allows Marple to set off on a spying mission without drawing attention to herself. Christie made this clear when she remarked:

> So Miss Knight started off happily, after a last glance at the frail old lady resting so peacefully by the window. After waiting a few minutes in case Miss Knight should return for a shopping bag, or her purse, or a handkerchief [...], Miss Marple rose briskly to her feet, cast aside her knitting and strode purposefully across the room and into the hall. She took down her summer coat from its peg, a stick from the hall stand and exchanged her bedroom slippers for a pair of stout walking shoes. (21, emphasis added)

The juxtaposition of the image of a frail lady seated in the armchair and that of a brisk adventurer wearing a pair of "stout walking shoes" precisely mirrors the contradiction between the marginal and powerless member of the family and the all-seeing spy; the two roles which are embodied within the figure of the spinster. Thus by employing domestic methods of investigation, using food clues, and by depicting marginality as a surveillance technique, Christie was able to accomplish the transformation of domesticity into power, independence, and adventure.

4.2. Food, Body, Intuition: The Abductive Detective

When discussing the genre of classical crime fiction, rationality is a frequently mentioned concept. In chapter one, I defined extreme rationality as one of the special powers of the detective helping her/him to solve crimes; I also saw it as the thing which enables the reader to enjoy the pleasures of playing puzzle games devised by crime authors, or even as the very quality that a detective novel wishes to restore to the seemingly chaotic world, in the realm of imagination, at least. Rationality thus appears to be the "basic tenet of golden age British detective fiction," as classical detective novels are fuelled by the belief that the "human mind—reason—will eventually triumph over the chaotic phenomena of the world. The detective represents this rational power, and solution of the crime depends on this faith" (Wu 2007, 4).

However, in spite of its strong emphasis on rationality, classical detective fiction "abounds with primitive elements such as rituals and sacrifices on the level of story telling and that of story content" (vii) and "irrational elements [...] parallel or underlie the appearance of rationality" (5). In her novels, Christie constantly juxtaposed the rational, logical, and deductive with the irrational and uncanny, and what had at first seemed to be the former is in the end often revealed to be the latter. Chia-ying Wu (2007) believes that this juxtaposition of the rational and irrational is manifest in the investigation methods employed by Christie's detectives, who tend to rely on what is labelled "common sense" much more than on "conventionally-recognized specialized knowledge in solving crimes":

> Talents—such as intuition—that were regarded as feminine and groundless are praised by her detectives as having a solid rational ground. The vehicle of reason, the detective, that used to be male turns out to be female and at a useless age—as materialized in Christie's spinster detective Miss Marple. (Wu 2007, 10)

Joseph Agassi (1982) agrees with this view, claiming that the very quality which makes crime fiction so fascinating is that

> it gives expression to one major emotional conflict we have about reason and its emotional significance. We hold as obvious both the view that reason is mechanical and that reason is mysterious. [...] One way to resolve this ambivalence is to declare the mechanical to be a magic ritual preparatory to the mystic insight (1982, 105)

and in this way bridge "the gap between the realistic and the romantic; between the cold calculating and the warmhearted intuitive" (105).

The detective, a character occupying a position superior to any other in a crime novel, represents the ideal agent for this act of bridging. Another thing which singles out the detective from all of the other characters, besides her/his ability to reconcile the contradictory elements of rational and intuitive, is her/his infallible sense of justice (see section 1.1.3). In a classical crime story, unlike in the real world, the reader can always be sure that the detective will behave morally and will always fight for the right side.

Traditionally, rational morality, or morality in the Kantian sense, is connected with the repression of the body, with the sacrifice of bodily pleasures and needs for the sake of duty, or simply with asceticism (see 1.1.3 or 2.3). William James Hoverd and Chris G. Sibley (2007) observe that the connection of fasting with virtue, and, on the contrary, of eating or overeating with immorality is very strong even in contemporary society. Indeed, obesity, as the tangible proof of a person's unrepressed appetite, is sometimes even labelled sinful in its connections to the biblical vices of gluttony and sloth (391). In contemporary Western societies, "the obese body is implicitly perceived as evidencing a lack of moral personal responsibility" and "an excess of body fat is seen as negative and discriminatory." On the contrary, the ideal body is considered to be a body which has been "subjugated" through the practices of fasting (or dieting) and physical activity aimed at losing body fat. Moreover, not only is a person who indulges in the pleasures of appetite considered immoral or at least flawed, but it is also believed that overeating impedes thinking (see 1.1.3).

A number of Christie's characters, especially those who perform intellectual work or work demanding exceptional skills, act according to the belief that morality equals asceticism. In *The Man in the Brown Suit* the protagonist's intellectual father is contrasted with her simple-minded protectress through their respective attitudes to food. The father, a scientist, only deals with food when he is forced to, he is "concentrated on his profession and detached from necessities of daily life, he [eats] what anyone put before him, and [forgets] to pay for it" (16-17). Moreover, he does not appear to take any pleasure in eating, which is shown in the way he once "almost accidentally put marmalade on his kippers at breakfast" or on a later occasion almost choked on an "immoderate mouthful of kipper bones" (20). Mrs Flemming, the protagonist's protectress, stands in sharp contrast to this approach; she is regularly described as dull, boring or even stupid. The only conversation topics in which she seems to be interested, much to the protagonist's disappointment, are "children, how hard it is to get good milk for them and [...] rows with dairymen"; these are exactly the down-to-earth, food-connected topics which her intellectual father tries to avoid at all cost (33). Similarly, when the secret government agent Stafford Nye sets out on a mission in *Passenger to Frankfurt*, he refuses to devote any time to food or rest before more important matters are dealt with. Instead, he subjugates his body and forces it to remain active with an endless supply of coffee, which he drinks day and night. In the first chapter alone, five instances of his preparation or drinking a cup of coffee are mentioned (37, 77, 80, 87, and 88).

Asceticism and the exercising of conscious control over the body are also characteristic features of Miss Marple. In line with traditional morality, Marple is frugal, modest, and she puts duty before pleasure as a rule. In *Nemesis*, for instance, she is described as having utilitarian habits, such as sitting in a "straight-backed chair" or heating her room with only a "small wood fire" (29). What is more, she is modest even in her desires. When asked what she will do once she receives the large sum of money promised as a reward for her detective work, she replies she will donate to a number of charities and only after that take her own pleasure (26). This pleasure, too, is extremely humble: instead of the luxurious cruise proposed by the solicitor, she wishes to "indulge" "a little more moderately" in a meal of partridge, a box of marrons glacés, and a visit to the opera (27).

Similar incidents are depicted on numerous occasions throughout all of the Miss Marple novels. Marple's asceticism is especially apparent in her attitude to food. In *A Caribbean Mystery* she sets out on a mission to stop a murderer from killing their next victim. On her way, she is first stopped by the hotel manager who offers her a glass of her favourite "fresh lime" (99). However, Marple refuses, as she has important business to attend to first. Similarly, when the manager's wife Molly takes an overdose of sleeping pills, instead of going out dancing and attending dinner with the rest of the hotel guests, Marple offers to sit at the sick woman's bedside in the place of one of Molly's two friends, because: "they were both young women who liked enjoying themselves [while] she herself preferred a light meal early and so that would suit everybody" (60).

Furthermore, Marple's morality is shown not only in her unwillingness to indulge in eating for pleasure, but also in the manner in which she chooses her food. In an essay arguing against picky eating, Matthew Brown (2007) claims that the practice of being picky with one's food follows from the erroneous belief that what we choose to eat or not eat is purely a matter of subjective taste. In a rather Kantian manner Brown condemns this subjectivist approach to food, claiming that what one likes or does not like is not inherent but learnt, and as such can be changed; that indeed one has a duty to change it in order to behave morally (193-194). In his explanation of what it means to be moral, Brown also addresses the issues of duty, both the duties one has towards others and towards oneself. When a person is not willing to try new foods, they not only express their closed-minded attitude towards food, but also towards life in general, a deficiency which limits their possibilities of gaining experience and of self-growth. "It violates the duty you have to develop you [sic] own capacities and excellence" (196). Moreover, picky eating, argues Brown, is not only immoral in relation to oneself, but also "harmful to others and to your relationships with them." By refusing to eat everything, one inconveniences others, either the people who wish to share meals with her/him or those who have prepared the meals for her/him; moreover, it can hurt the feelings of all involved (201). Picky eating violates etiquette, but above all it prevents one from sharing interesting and pleasant experiences with family, friends or members of foreign cultures and as such can be considered as an immoral form of behaviour (202-203).

Miss Marple is definitely not what could be labelled picky in her food choices. On the contrary, she clearly shares Brown's moral attitude towards eating in which any pleasure to be gained from food is sacrificed in the name of one's duty towards oneself and others. In *A Caribbean Mystery* she eats an exotic dessert, a passion fruit sundae despite the fact that she is also offered an English alternative; she does so not only in order not to bother her hosts, but also to expand her own horizons (26), although privately she admits to preferring the more traditional diet (37). Thus Marplc is engaging in what would be understood as moral in Kantian terms, sacrificing pleasure or the very needs of her body in order to perform the duties dictated to her by reason. Similarly, in *A Pocket Full of Rye* Marple returns home late at night after having solved the case only to find that her servant has left her house uncleaned; she also discovers that her domestic help serves only herring for supper. However, Marple does not comment: she is "too kind" to do so (186).

Nevertheless, despite being extremely moral in terms of duty and pleasure, Marple frequently makes exceptions to morality in order to speed up and facilitate her investigation process and on occasion she uses her superior status to manipulate circumstances or other characters for her needs. She can often be seen lying, or at least omitting or withholding crucial information, tricking her opponents, snooping and eavesdropping, and generally engaging in behaviour which she would consider immoral in others (see 1.1.3 for examples), a procedure of which Kant strongly disapproved ([1785] 2008, 26).

In general, although fictional detectives are on the one hand "incorruptible and determined pursuer[s] of justice," on the other hand they frequently behave immorally "in small ways," such as the protagonist of Raymond Chandler's stories, who sees no real problem with "sleeping with his beautiful clients" or "beating a small-time operator in order to receive significant information" (Agassi 1982, 106). Similarly, in his essay on picky eating Brown allows for exceptions to the rule of duty for himself (he claims never to be able to eat faeces), as well as for others, e.g. vegetarians or people with a heightened sensitivity to tastes (2007, 199). He himself admits that his maxim of avoiding pickiness is not a universal one, stating that "[i]t may be that, after approaching some food with an open mind, learning about it, learning about yourself, and trying different ways of enjoying it, you still just do not like it. As we know, not everyone is capable of exactly the same taste experiences, so we should expect some disagreements" (201).

This diversion from Kantian morality is a result of a shift in focus from the mind to the body and its needs. However, when the "body enters the picture" (Pascual Soler 2009, 7), it is necessary to find a morality that does not spring solely from the domination of the mind (i.e. the masculine) over the body (traditionally labelled feminine). Moreover, such morality must not require asceticism, but should instead embrace pleasure (24). It is assumed that moral pleasure can be achieved through eating.

The process of eating has often been considered a simple matter of fulfilling one's bodily needs, and as the body was excluded from the realm of morals, so was food and eating. According to Roger J. H. King (2007) the prevalent opinion is that we eat what we like and what we are used to, "what's cheap or fast or convenient" (178). However, King and others such as Belasco or Petrini, point out that food is a social phenomenon with a profound influence on oneself and others, and as such has an ethical dimension (see 2.3). King claims that "[c]onsumption, whether of food or other commodities, is an activity about which we can, and should, think ethically. There are better and worse ways to consume—ways that are morally defensible and ways that are morally problematic" (2007, 178).

Despite the fact that King's approach to food is concerned with what it means to eat morally, he does not consider how morality is connected with pleasure and the fulfilment of desires. However, these very issues are addressed by members of the Slow Food movement. The Slow Food movement gained notoriety and a strong public voice after its founder, Carlo Petrini, organised a campaign in protest against the opening of a McDonald's fast food restaurant in the centre of Rome (Schneider 2008, 385-386). Slow Foodists, however, do not simply argue against fast food; their campaign has a much broader agenda. Petrini claims that he aims to reconstruct the notion of food as a "cultural product" and to link it to ethical problems of sustainability, biodiversity and social justice. Moreover, he believes that these same values should also be applied to other spheres of life, besides eating (Schneider 2008, 385). Petrini strongly believes that food is "tied to national identity and prosperity," and he proposes the notion of food as less of a universal issue, but rather as being more closely connected to a territory, which is understood as a specific geographical location together with its inhabitants, their history, culture, and traditions, from which follows the use of location-specific ingredients, food-production technologies and cooking methods (Schneider 2008, 388-389).

While discussing the numerous ethical questions connected with food, eating, and community, Petrini underlines the role of taste and pleasure in preserving local cultures from homogenisation caused by globalisation (Schneider 2008, 385). Slow Food started as a campaign for the acknowledgement of the pleasure in slowness as a lifestyle, criticising the contemporary consumerist mentality of instant gratification (personified by the fast food chains), and later also engaging in the fight against the food safety and hygiene standards proposed by the European Union, which would result in banning some traditional local foods in member states (A. Leitch 2008, 382). Slow adopted the *lardo di Colonnata* as the key example of an "endangered food," following the attempt by the hygiene authorities to ban the use of marble in curing pork fat on the basis of unified EU standards[1] (387). The *lardo* of Colonnata was chosen because it embodies all of the values which Slow Foodists hold dear in food. It is true to its tradition and is tied to a shared past in a small community, possessing cultural as well as nutritional value for its community. It also possesses a symbolic meaning, as it is limited to a specific region and is connected with rituals of pleasure such as an annual *lardo*-eating festival. Finally, its preparation process is lengthy and relies on traditional methods and excludes the use of chemicals and modern technology. In sum, *lardo* was chosen because to eat it "is to remember and celebrate [a] past of collective history and corporeal memory" (386). Thus, in the understanding of Slow Foodists, a good life is a life led by following the values of community, pleasure, tradition and corporeal history, rather than those of duty, rationality, or over-protective safety.

Like Carlo Petrini of Slow Food, Hercule Poirot, too, refuses to comply with the traditional standards of morality and appropriateness. As was seen in 1.1.3, Poirot defies morality in a Kantian sense to a much greater extent than Miss Marple. Not only does he use tricks, omissions, and lies to solve crimes and extract information from the people around him, but he also often takes it upon himself to decide whether to punish the criminal, let them take the easy way out by committing suicide, or even let them escape unpunished. Moreover, Poirot does not act in compliance with Kantian morality in his attitude to pleasure either. On the contrary, evidence of his hedonism and the strong emphasis he places on eating well and on living pleasurably in general, are scattered throughout the novels.

Poirot's ritual of drinking a cup of hot chocolate each morning (e.g. *Elephants Can Remember* 163), his love of sweets, especially of his signature *sirop de cassis* (e.g. *Three Act Tragedy* 42), his delicate taste in food (e.g. *Death in the Clouds* 85), and even his appearance, more specifically his "pleasantly rounded" stomach (*After the Funeral* 193), all point to the fact that the Belgian detective is a hedonist who enjoys life and food and is not willing to sacrifice all pleasure in the name of duty. However, under the ethical standards of Slow Food, such focus on eating satisfactorily and enjoying a slow pleasurable lifestyle is considered morally superior to that of the self-restricting Miss Marple, who refuses to devote time to food.

Furthermore, not only does Poirot transgress traditional morality through his hedonism, he also transgresses traditional gender roles. This is manifest not only in his approach to food (he prefers sweet, ornamental, and light foods, i.e. foods typically associated with women [see 3.4]), but also in his investigation methods. In addition to relying on domestic knowledge to solve crimes (see 4.1), he also frequently stresses the passive nature of his method. This is strongly emphasised in *The Murder on the Links*, where Poirot works side by side with a specialist from Paris whom he labels "the human foxhound" (81). While the other man busies himself at the scene of crime and engages in various—often physically demanding—activities, Poirot does "not run to and fro, making journeys, and agitating [him]self." Instead, he "lean[s] back in a comfortable chair, and close[s] his eyes," awaiting the others in the "*salon*," as it "is cool there on this hot morning" (99). He expresses a similar sentiment in *Dumb Witness*, where he explains to Hastings: "The false beard, it is *vieux jeu*, and shadowing is only done by the lowest branch of my profession. The Hercule Poirots, my friend, need only to sit back in a chair and think" (67).

Another feminine aspect of Poirot's investigation is the emphasis which he places on feeling and intuition, techniques which are traditionally attributed to female investigators or to women in general (Dzirkalis 2007, 19). While Poirot often explicitly claims that his method is based solely on reason or pure logic, and never on instinct (e.g. *Dumb Witness* 60), in reality the opposite is frequently the case. Poirot has premonitions or observes them in other people and acts on them, such as in *The Murder on the Links*, where he remarks to Hastings: "You are what the Scotch people call 'fey,' Hastings. It presages disaster" (26) and then goes on to claim: "I am afraid.' 'Afraid of what?' 'I do not know. But I have a premonition—a *je ne sais quoi*!' [...] 'I have a feeling,' he said slowly, 'that this is going to be a big affair—long, troublesome problem that will not be easy to work out" (27). Feelings such as 'fey' and other intuitive insights appear regularly throughout Christie's novels, and are experienced both by Poirot and other characters; for example by Mike, the protagonist of *Endless Night* (149, 153). More significantly, these premonitions often lead the character to the correct solution to a problem (e.g. in *The Mystery of the Blue Train* or *Murder on the Orient Express*).

Besides intuition, Poirot also relies on his feelings to judge situations or to find out whether the suspects are lying or telling the truth. After questioning the wife of the deceased in *The Murder on the Links*, he exclaims: "I am an imbecile, my friend! If ever there was love and grief in a woman's voice, I heard it then. My little idea was all wrong. *Eh bien!* I must start again!" (69). Once an intuitive insight comes to Poirot he experiences yet another feeling: that of excitement. And it is excitement, which transforms this mild, chocolate-eating, and *sirop*-drinking eccentric into a dangerous and sharp criminal hunter, a transformation which is symbolised by the green cat-like "tinge in his eye" (e.g. *Dumb Witness* 106, *The Murder on the Links* 22).

All three of the aspects which are characteristic of Poirot's and Marple's (and a number of other Christie's detectives') methods, namely passivity, emotion, and intuition, form part of the abductive method of reasoning (see 1.2.3). Pascual Soler characterises abduction as "a feeling of great intensity on which no rules of logic can be imposed. This does not mean that abduction does not proceed rationally or logically. It posits a scientific hypothesis, and yet it constitutes no science. It seeks a theory, but is no theory" (2009, 9). David Carson (2009) agrees, mentioning that Charles Sanders Pierce himself associated "abduction with those sudden insights (hypotheses) when we, unexpectedly, get an idea which solves, or appears to solve, a problem we had not previously managed to solve" (197); it suggests that intuitive insights or instincts are successful because, according to Pierce (1931-35), "[a]ll human knowledge, up to the highest flights of science, is but the development of our inborn animal instincts" (quoted in Niiniluoto 1999, S448). Pierce went so far as to claim that abductive judgements are not "fully conscious." At the same time he believed that they are the most basic type of reasoning, as "our everyday knowledge about the observational properties of ordinary physical objects [...] involves abduction" (quoted in Niiniluoto 1999, S442). Agassi adds that

> even when working through the finite list of possible solutions, as permitted within the fixed theoretical framework, we do not think

> mechanically; though the conditions permit it in principle, in fact there are too many possibilities to exclude. And then, some think intuitively, like chess players [...]. (1982, 107)

Agassi claims that it is this tension between the two types of reasoning, the logical and the intuitive or abductive, or, as he describes it, between the "ambivalence about the nature of reason," which becomes "both the source and the dynamics of the tension in the problem-solving novel, be that the detective, spy, or science fiction thriller" (107).

Agassi's statement certainly applies in the case of Agatha Christie's detectives. Although they attribute a great deal of their success to the logic, order, and method of their investigation, they are in fact often reliant on abductive insights and what could be labelled as sudden inspiration to lead them to the correct solution, a method explicitly acknowledged by Christie's description of the process as "a triumph of guesswork over logic" (*Murder Is Easy* 238). In *By the Pricking of My Thumbs* Tuppence's investigation procedure consists of aimless gossiping with various ladies in the village, especially her hostess Mrs Copleigh; at the beginning of this process, she is unaware of what questions she wants to ask, but instead hopes that a piece of important information will somehow be uncovered during the course of natural conversation. In Tuppence's own words, her investigation material is a combination of "all old tales and gossip and hearsay and legends, mixed up in the most glorious kind of hasty pudding" (290). It is worth noting that large portions of this investigation take place in Mrs Copleigh's kitchen and that throughout the conversation Tuppence is depicted eating "bacon and eggs and [...] slices of thick bread and butter and [...] blackberry jelly, homemade, her favourite kind," absorbing the food into her body while she tries to "absorb the flood of information" into her brain (140).

Like Tuppence, Miss Marple, too, connects her abductive power to her body, especially to her senses. In *Nemesis* she speaks of her "fine sense of evil" and compares it to a "very keen sense of smell," claiming to have inherited it from an aunt who could recognise the "distinctive odour" of lies and thus "smell" when people were trying to deceive her (131). It is important to note here that Marple does not choose to compare her investigation method to the visual sense, the superior "rational" sense in the Aristotelian system, but rather to the base "bodily" sense of smell. This rejection of vision in favour of the more "bodily" or "primitive" senses of touch, taste, and smell is evident when Marple, after returning to the former house of a murdered girl, examines the scene in the following fashion:

> She sat down in the drawing room, and closed her eyes for a minute, breathing rather fast. She appeared to be somewhat out of breath. [...] she was trying to acquire through her closed eyes what the feeling was she had on coming into this house again. Was something in it sinister? No, not so much sinister as unhappy. Deep unhappiness. So much so it was almost frightening. (*Nemesis,* 210)

Finally, after the case has been solved and Marple is asked how she managed to succeed in untangling it after so many years, she replies that "It wasn't really, you know, logical deduction. It was based on a kind of emotional reaction or susceptibility to—well, I can only call it atmosphere" (239).

In terms of the actual workings of abductive reasoning, Pascual Soler emphasises the need for "a connection with the world" (2009, 9). In other words, the "jolt of guessing" or the sudden insight is "triggered" by an object of the world, however little or insignificant it may be (163). Thus Poirot, the master of noticing the seemingly insignificant, is the only one to point out that there is no dust on the mantlepieces and that all of the magazines are laid out straight on the coffee tables, indicating that the room has already been cleaned that day. This insight later leads him to guess the location of a vital hidden clue (*The Murder on the Links* 52).

However, abduction is not only the ability to connect to and be inspired by objects regardless of their small size, but it can also allow us to connect to the world as a whole. As Stephanie S. Tolan (2006) observes, intuition (a crucial element of abduction) is understood by the members of various "indigenous peoples" as being the basis of "the oneness of being," or the oneness of humans with the world (55). This represents another example of how abduction stands in opposition to rational or logical thinking, which tends to emphasise the exceptional nature of thinking in humans, and the consequent separation of humans from the rest of the world. Abduction, on the contrary, highlights the interconnection between humans and the world, and can be compared to the act of eating, during which humans return at least partly to the natural, universal state of predation (see 4.3). Food, like abduction, "is about instincts, sentiments, sensations, intuitions, feelings and emotions" (Pascual Soler 2009, 24). Furthermore, it is about "undermining the subject/object dichotomy" (Heldke 1992, 218), and it also touches on the conflict between transgression and oneness.

It can be concluded that both abduction and eating represent one's connection with, rather than distance from, the world and that both concepts reside in the body. The connection between cooking, eating, detection, and the bodily nature of abductive thinking is especially visible in culinary mysteries, whose protagonists investigate "with the body," and even if they do not cook, they all the same participate in eating "in the interest of detective research" (Pascual Soler 2009, 24). And although Christie's novels do not belong, strictly speaking, to the genre of culinary mysteries, the interconnections between cooking, eating, and thinking can be observed on numerous occasions, especially in the case of the hedonistic detective Hercule Poirot.

In a number of novels Poirot entertains his witnesses at a set table during meals, or cooks for them before interrogating them (*After the Funeral* 109, for more examples see 4.1). In *The Murder on the Orient Express*, all of the interviews with witnesses are conducted in the dining car of the train (60). Also, when a group of investigators needs to gather together and jointly work out the solution to an especially baffling case, they frequently do so during or after a wholesome meal (84). If the work comes to a halt and a problem seems to be impossible to solve, what Poirot "prescribes" to further the investigation is a "simple but satisfying meal [...]. Let us say *omelette aux champignons. Sole a la Normande*, a cheese of Port Salut. And with it red wine" (142). This exemplifies what Pascual Soler describes as the need of the culinary detective to "remain on the immanent side of thought. Immanence produces pleasure and pleasure does not interrupt detection. No longer do detectives put their forks down nor is cooking separated from detection" (2009, 23). Instead

> [b]y exalting physical pleasure the Belgian detective substitutes epicurism for asceticism. Transcendence is ousted by immanence when he conjoins pleasure with intellectual research because for Poirot the mind is collected in the body, which is obviously feminine (by tradition). (10)

As David Carson states, the abductive detective values "slow time,' that is time to reflect" (2009, 200). The hedonist detective, as a precursor to the Slow Food ethics of Carlo Petrini's, values "slow time" to take her/his pleasure and to enjoy her/his food. And the abductive hedonistic detective, then, values "slow time" to both eat and think, or, more typically, to think through eating.

4.3. Food and Murder[2]

> I don't care in the least what you're reading
> Please don't talk about murder while I'm eating
> (Ben Harper, "Please Don't Talk About Murder While I'm Eating")

Everything here's a weapon:
i pick up a meat fork,
imagine
plunging it in,
(Pat Lowther, "Kitchen Murder", 1974)

The previous chapter has shown that Agatha Christie uses food in her detective novels as an "index to character, an omen of events, a reminder that killers must eat, too, and their victims" (Walker 2001, 41), thereby lending reality to the stories, as well as upsetting a number of notions and beliefs held for granted by the characters (and the readers). This is a tool which is still used today by contemporary culinary crime novels. Sections 4.1 and 4.2 further explore food as a plot-constructing tool and a useful investigation method of the domestic detective. However, as Walker observes, food can take on a much more sinister undertone in crime stories. Crime authors often remind the reader that food can be dangerous: it can conceal the criminal, distract the victim, or it can even become a means of murder itself. Culinary crime author Diane Mott Davidson observes that "[f]ood and mystery stories are so popular because a preoccupation with food lends itself to the traditional domestic mystery that focuses on relationships," [...] "In that genre, you see people pretending to like someone, but serving them food (that is) poisoned" (interview by McCracken 1993, E1).

The more sinister aspects of food and its connections with killing and death tend to be tabooed and ignored in developed Western societies. The act of killing for food often provokes feelings of revulsion in contemporary Westerners (Wrye 2007, 54). Consequently, the cultural practice of cooking together with manifold rituals surrounding the act of eating were developed over time in order to mask the closeness of humans to other animals and their need to destroy and end life in order to maintain their own lives. In other words, eating rituals serve to disguise "our own bestiality" (Symons 1991, quoted in Wrye 2007, 54). Eating is traditionally understood as an act of care, nurturance, and communion rather than as an act of murder. Sarah Sceats (2004) maintains that "[f]ood is a currency of love and desire, a medium of expression and communication." She goes on to mention "the giving of symbolic bread and wine as a token of love and trust" and adds that "food may be an expression of support or an invitation to celebrate; for lovers there is an intimate, sexual subtext, appetite incorporated into sexuality" (11).

Indeed, food in Christie's novels is often connected with safety, peace, and the absence of crime. The opening scenes of her novels, which Cawelti understands as the symbolic embodiment of peace and order soon to be disrupted by crime (1976, 97), are frequently set at the breakfast, lunch, or dinner table. The newspaper, coffee and kippers—the indispensable breakfast props in a middle-class English family—in *A Murder Is Announced*, the unappetising but homely boiled beef in *The Murder at the Vicarage*, or the mid-morning tea served just like any other day at the typists' office in *A Pocket Full of Rye* are all symbolic of the calm and peace of a crime-free household.

Even as the stories proceed and increasingly mysterious and disturbing events unfold, eating and food-preparation rituals serve to give the characters a short moment of consolation and a feeling of normality, however brief that may be. When Canon Pennyfather finds out that he has been kidnapped and drugged, and then abandoned in the streets of London, he decides to stop and have dinner: after all, nine o'clock is dinner-time and it "seemed to him that though he was not quite as hungry as he ought to be, he had better keep his spirits up by having a meal" (*At Bertram's Hotel* 96). Later, after he has fallen unconscious, suffered from a concussion, and has finally been rescued, he muses: "Sausage and mash. The words had a faintly agreeable quality. 'I believe,' he said to himself, 'I'm hungry" (64). Not only food itself, but also kitchen sounds, smells, and sights can have a calming effect on characters who are afraid or under stress (e.g. *Death Comes as the End* 23). Food, and often drink too, can even ease the pain after the death of a beloved person or a family member (*Death Comes as the End* 150, 184; *After the Funeral* 21, etc.).

While the dinner table frequently represents the initial stage of calmness, which is about to be broken by crime, food can also become the means by which peace and calm is restored following a crime. When Poirot stops Rowley from strangling his girlfriend Lynn at the last moment, he sends the agitated man to boil some coffee or tea and the routine actions connected with the preparation of tea help to clear the shock and to diminish the violence of the scene (*Taken at the Flood* 331). Anne, the protagonist of *The Man in the Brown Suit*, often uses food for comfort, either using ice-cream sodas to steady her nerves or "a substantial lunch" to fortify her "for further conflict" (355); she is also comforted by her fiancé Harry in a similar fashion when he serves her a cup of milk and a bowl of soup after rescuing her from a murderer (265).

If a character prepares food for others or eats her/himself, this can serve as proof that she/he is a harmless person who is not associated with danger or crime. In the course of her investigation in *By the Pricking of My Thumbs*, Tuppence is forced to visit a strange house with a haunted, spooky atmosphere inhabited by a witch-like woman. However, Tuppence's tension and feeling of danger is relieved when the old woman serves tea according to the familiar ritual: on a "tea tray" with "a plate of scones, a jar of jam and three cups and saucers" (107). Similarly, when Mike wishes to prove to his anxious young wife that the old village gypsy is not a dangerous sorceress but an ordinary woman, he shows her that she works in the garden "digging up potatoes;" such homely activities are used to show that she cannot be a real menace (*Endless Night* 157). On the contrary, the criminal mastermind Mr Aristides immediately falls under suspicion when he claims that he will not join the company at dinner, because he is on a diet and eats very little (*Destination Unknown* 285).

This kind of dissociation of food from crime is frequent in the novels and it is also consciously maintained by the characters, who refuse even to speak of murder and crime during mealtimes (*Nemesis* 117; *And Then There Were None* 107; etc.). Even serving food in the presence of death can be problematic; for example the manager of a hotel in which a guest has just been murdered feels that it would be inappropriate to serve lunch to other tourists that day (*Evil Under the Sun* 207). In yet another story, Poirot observes that the quarry garden where a murder had once been committed has a haunted feeling. He remarks that no one wants to picnic there because "One would not want for some reason to bring your hard-boiled eggs and your lettuce and your oranges and sit down here and crack jokes and have a jollification" (*Hallowe'en Party* 261). Furthermore, while it is understandably inappropriate to stuff oneself while someone else has become a victim of crime, a number of characters also find it downright disgusting to share a meal with an actual criminal. John Cavendish, the son of the victim in *The Mysterious Affair at Styles* claims emphatically that "one's gorge does rise at sitting down to eat with a possible murderer" (37) and only after the main suspect Mr Inglethorp announces he is leaving the house can the Cavendish family finally enjoy a cheerful breakfast (72).

The conscious distancing of eating from murder reflects the refusal to accept that "the most basic feature of animal existence on planet earth—that we are food and that through death we nourish others," a denial which, according to Val Plumwood (2008), is embedded in contemporary Western worldview. Predation, and especially "predation on humans," the quintessential merging of eating and killing is considered "monstrous" by many Westerners and the "[d]ominant concepts of human identity position humans outside and above the food chain" (324). Moreover, many humans experience feelings of revulsion not only when confronted with the idea of cannibalism or of humans being eaten by animals, but also when considering the idea of killing animals for food (Wrye 2007, 54). This revulsion is so strong that it can drive some people not to eat meat, or even to become vegans who avoid "all products derived from animals, including wool and silk" in order not to cause death.

However, with recent studies suggesting that plants, like animals, "are lively and seek to keep it that way" and that they can even learn, feel, and suffer (Angier 2009), some claim that "[r]ather than just dismissing plant suffering as inevitable, vegans should try to reduce that [plant suffering] as well;" in other words, they must admit their "own shame from harming plants" (Lewis 2007). Noah Lewis (2007) maintains that:

> Plant exploitation parallels animal exploitation. There are factory farms with monocropping, cloning, genetic engineering, pesticides, herbicides (!). Agriculture is a constant battle against the plants, insects and other animals that initially lived on the land. Beyond plants as food, plants are kept in houses as "pets," used for entertainment (Christmas trees, Jack-o-lanterns), people wrap themselves in dead plants, and doctors are always experimenting on one plant or another looking for the next "miracle" drug.

In summary, it is an inevitable condition of humans as a part of nature that they must end the life of another creature to sustain their own life, and can, in turn, become the means for the sustenance of life of others through predation, parasitism, or decay. While this phenomenon is considered a "tragedy" (Angier 2009) or understood as "suffering" (Lewis 2007) by some and, on the contrary, believed to be the essence of life and an embodiment of the eternal cycle of being by others (e.g. Plumwood), it is nevertheless certain that death and food are inseparably connected.

Although Christie exploits the traditional cultural symbolism of food as being representative of safety, peace, and home, she also makes use of this more problematic aspect of eating. Firstly, she depicts the dining ritual as something which is governed by strict laws that cannot be bent in the slightest without terrible consequences. The disrupted or broken food ritual can be something as simple as a bad omen; when a member of the dinner party is late or does not show up, it often signals that he or she is in grave danger (*By the Pricking of My Thumbs* 187-194) or has already been murdered (*Endless Night* 216). In *A Pocket Full of Rye* the careless handling of the teapot, together with the water that refuses to boil, foreshadow the poisoning of one of the characters by taxine administered in his coffee (5-7). When careless servants forget to cut the sandwiches to go with the afternoon tea, the meal is followed by yet another violent death, this time of the lady of the house (*A Pocket Full of Rye* 66). Inaccuracy or carelessness in carrying out tasks connected with food preparation can also become the cause of death. Such is the case of Mrs Inglethorp, who on the eve of her murder was too distraught and nervous to sit down to a proper evening meal, and as a result the poisoner succeeded in killing her with only a small amount of strychnine, which would have been much less harmful had she had a full stomach (*The Mysterious Affair at Styles* 25). Similarly, when Mr Babbington accepts an offered cocktail in spite of the fact that he is unused to drinking alcohol, he fails to notice the bitterness caused by the presence of a foreign substance in the glass; he goes on to drink the liquid and subsequently dies of poisoning (*Three Act Tragedy* 33-34).

The gradual shift from seeing food as soothing and homely to associating it instead with danger, hunting and survival is clearly visible throughout the plot of *And Then There Were None*. Upon the characters' arrival at the mysterious house to which they have been invited, the sight of drinks standing ready in the hall is sufficient to make them "cheer up" and forget their anxieties about having accepted the suspicious invitation (40). However, as the story progresses and the members of the party are killed off one by one by a mysterious murderer, neither the assurance that the "larder is well-stocked" (156), nor the impeccable serving skills of the butler (53, 155) can succeed in restoring the sense of normality. When the number of surviving guests dwindles to just three, mealtimes are no longer seen as a welcome ritual. The party stops gathering for meals around the dining table; in fact, they even stop cooking their meals, and instead eat them all together, standing around the kitchen table, fearing to let each other out of sight for a single moment (227-229, 266). They have all become prey to a hidden hunter and spend every moment in fear for their lives, just like animals in the wilderness. In the end the fear grows so unbearable that all but one refuse to eat altogether, and the one character who still endeavours to take the trip to the kitchen to have his midday meal is killed in the process (268). Thus the story exemplifies how, in Michelis's words an "act of physical as well as symbolic abject violence signifies the collapse of boundaries between the (outside) world of crime and (inside) world of cultured consumption of food" (2010, 147).

In treatments of this kind, Christie points out the impossibility of separating food from death, or, as Jane Jakeman (1993) puts it, she turns the "familiar and nourishing dishes—the secure and cosy snacks and remedies, redolent of nursery nostalgia" into bad omens, criminal ploys or even weapons and "vehicles for poison." The criminals in Christie's novels are often hedonists who enjoy life and always welcome the opportunity to eat well (e.g. Mike in *Endless Night* or Sir Eustace in *The Man in the Brown Suit*); she uses the traditional notion of food and eating as safe, and the inherent goodness of the well-fed and jolly gourmand to mask the criminal and to misdirect the reader's suspicion. Thus a criminal's connection to food can allow her/him to commit crime unsuspected. This deflection of suspicion is so successful that "it seems that the victim often gratefully received the fatal dose in some delicious little dish served up by an attentive murderer" (Jakeman 1993).

The connection of cooking and ill will gains full force in the character of Miss Gilchrist, an unmarried middle-class woman reduced to the position of servant by the economic decline in post-war Britain. Miss Gilchrist dreams of opening her own tea shop and "cooking nice little meals" for her customers (*After the Funeral* 173) and she is known for her obsession with the "correct composition of brioches and chocolate eclairs [and] the proper use of herbs in cooking" (268). At the end of the story it is revealed that she has committed murder in order to gain the financial means of fulfilling this dream. At the same time Miss Gilchrist's close connection to food allows her to appear far removed from crime and violence in the eyes of the other characters in the story—nobody suspects the cake-baking and tea-serving old lady of planning a cold-blooded murder (164). She uses food to mask her true nature and intentions even when visiting the family of the deceased. She engages the old butler in talk of good old times and the meals that used to be shared, creating a feeling of safety and camaraderie, which dispels all suspicion (356). Thus in the character of Miss Gilchrist, Christie was able to depict the paradox inherent in food, cooking, and eating: the inevitable contradiction between the sustaining and terminating of life that it embodies.

In his study of the history of poison, Morton Satin (2007) observes that food has always been a source of fear for the population and that a certain amount of danger is embedded in the act of eating (14). Not only are people afraid of the so-called "foodborne diseases", meaning diseases caused by bacteria or other agents present in foodstuffs (22), but they also fear the deliberate contamination of their food, whether by the careless producer, the cheating tradesman (Beardsworth and Keil 1997, 151), or, more recently, the terrifying bio-terrorist (Satin 2007, 22). In short, food is not only a source of pleasure, but also a source of anxiety. As Satin suggests, eaters worry about food safety, but they are also concerned about food availability and about not being able to "get enough food to remain healthy and active or, for that matter, alive" (Beardsworth and Keil 1997, 150). Moreover, as humans are omnivores, they are faced with what is called "the omnivore's paradox", which

> emerges out of the fact that all omnivores (and this includes, of course, the human omnivore) experience the opposing pulls of neophilia (the inclination to sample novel food items) and neophobia (caution when confronted with novel items, based on the possibility that they may be

> harmful). All omnivores must find ways of coping with this paradoxical juxtaposition of attraction and repulsion. Thus, for the omnivore, eating is a profoundly ambivalent activity. (152)

The omnivore's paradox is not the only ambivalent aspect of food. In fact, three distinct paradoxes arise in the act of eating. Firstly, the human eater is faced with the "pleasure/displeasure paradox," which stems from the fact that "while food can provide gustatory gratification and a welcome sense of fullness and satisfaction, it can also produce sensations and reactions ranging from mildly unpleasant to severely distressing" (152). Even more disturbing is the "health/illness paradox" which is borne out of the fact that while food can contribute to one's health and physical well-being, the same food, when eaten immoderately, in a wrong manner, or when altered, can bring about disease or result in the deterioration of the body (153). Finally there is the ultimate "life/death paradox," which was already discussed at the beginning of this section. This paradox posits that "while the consumption of food is absolutely essential for the maintenance of life, the act of eating usually entails the death and dissolution of other organisms" (153).

This paradoxical nature of food and eating and the danger inherent in the activity have long been recognised and utilised by crime fiction authors. As Glenn Collins (2012) observes, "[f]ood has always been one of the easiest ways to kill someone, as Agatha Christie and the Borgias can attest" (P16) In her article on food and crime, Angelica Michelis (2010) examines this interconnection more closely. She, too, acknowledges the ambivalence inherent in food, stating that:

> [r]epresentations of the preparation as well as the consumption of food are implicated in the construction of binary oppositions: civilisation vs. barbarism; inside vs. outside; pleasurable vs. abject, but at the same time reveal that these apparently separate spheres inhabit each other. Acts of consumption are moments of transgression as well as acts of sustenance. (144)

As ambivalent, symbolic, and meaningful acts, eating rituals

> have often played a role in crime fiction; food and eating are used to indicate specific character traits, to reference class identity and to create the idiosyncratic identity of the detective him/herself. Food can also be implicated in the commission of crime [...] Poison as a means of murder is often concealed in food and drink, drawing attention to the potential for crime in the act of hospitality and to the possibility of death in nourishment. (144)

In Christie's novels food is frequently viewed as a threat or is even directly used as one. In *A Pocket Full of Rye* a mad murderer uses the individual lines of a food-themed nursery rhyme as a theme for a series of murders (90, 120-121, etc.), while in *Death Comes as the End*, the king's new wife Nofret is greeted in the household with an animosity which is expressed with particular vehemence during shared meals; firstly her food is over or under-seasoned on purpose, later a dead mouse is baked in her serving of bread (108). Other food related technique employed by criminals to threaten individuals is the threat of starvation. When the young adventuress Anne falls into captivity, the kidnappers plan on using hunger as an enforcement strategy: "A little starvation will do no harm [...] She will answer questions better if she is hungry" (*The Man in the Brown Suit* 199).

However, Christie's criminals do not stop at using food to threaten their victims. On the contrary, they often resort to the direct use of kitchen tools to accomplish the deed of murder itself. Michelis notes that the "kitchen knife, like a Brechtian prop, is often shown in its ambiguity as a tool in the preparation of food and as a weapon that can kill and violate bodies" (2010, 145) and indeed, Christie's characters contemplate the usefulness of a sharp kitchen knife as a weapon on a number of occasions (*The Murder at the Vicarage* 7; *A Caribbean Mystery* 145-49). Moreover, kitchen utensils or foodstuffs can be used to deflect suspicion, because objects as innocent as a picnic basket or a sliced vegetable seldom connote evil. This is cunningly made use of by a drug smuggling gang who hide heroin in salt and pepper containers (*Evil Under the Sun* 218), or by a South-African guerrilla who uses vegetable vocabulary to denote various items of ammunition (*The Man in the Brown Suit* 313). However, the use of food as a means of crime is at its most sinister in *Hallowe'en Party*, where a large bucket of apples in water is used by a maniac to silence a child who has witnessed him committing a crime (31, 35).

One aspect of food consumption which invariably connotes death and murder is meat-eating. Unpleasant persons or criminals are characterised as "carnivorous," and this carnivorous nature renders them both sinister and dangerous. For example, in *At Bertram's Hotel* the hotel owner and a mafia member Mr Robinson is described in the following manner: "Mr Robinson smiled. He was a fat man and very well dressed. He had a yellow face, his eyes were dark and sad-looking and his mouth was large and generous. He frequently smiled to display over-large teeth. 'The better to eat you with,' thought Chielf Inspector Davy" (195). In *The Murder at the Vicarage*, the sinister atmosphere of the vicarage household is enhanced by a story of a missionary who was eaten by a cannibal tribe

(27-31). Meat and death are explicitly placed side by side in the first chapter of *Evil under the Sun*, during Poirot's macabre description of the leisurely sunbathers lying on the hotel beach, eliciting shocked disapproval from his female companion:

> He waved a hand towards the recumbent figures. "That reminds me very much of the Morgue in Paris."
> "Poirot!" Mrs Gardener was scandalized.
> "Bodies—arranged on slabs—like butcher's meat!" (8)

Finally, probably the most frequent and also the most immediately visible merger of food and death is embodied in the motif of poisoning. Timothy Taylor (n.d.) observes that "[f]ood is married to crime through the poisoner." From the birth of the detective genre "plenty of fictional poisoning went on. Agatha Christie is littered with corpses whose last breaths smelled oddly sweet, or bitter, or of almonds." And although accidental poisoning by old fish or meat (*A Pocket Full of Rye* 27) or by unsanitary exotic foods (*A Caribbean Mystery* 40) is mentioned occasionally, most of the poisoning present on the pages of Christie's novels is carried out with deliberate harmful intent. Christie's characters are well aware of the possibility of being poisoned and acknowledge that food can easily be turned into a means of killing. In *By the Pricking of My Thumbs*, the inhabitants of a home for the aged speculate whether they are slowly being poisoned by the staff so that their organs could be used for medical research. One of them goes as far as to claim that she has been given poisonous mushrooms in her stew (36).

The perception of food as a threat is heightened every time a crime takes place. Thus in *Death Comes as the End* the characters grow more and more suspicious of their servants and of each other after every death. In the end the matron Esa has a servant taste all of her food and drinks in front of her eyes before she dares to eat and drink them herself (287). Following the death of Mrs Horton in *Murder Is Easy*, some of the characters begin to suspect her hen-pecked husband of having poisoned her with arsenic, as he was seen administering "a soothing cup of beef-tea or gruel" to her while she was sick (197, 203). In the same novel, Lord Whitfield's keen interest in the "Greater Fitness Campaign" and his desire to inspect calories, vitamins, germs, cultures, and bacteria in a museum in London arouse feelings of suspicion in his family members and friends, who cannot help but suspect that the purpose of all of this research is to discover effective methods of poisoning through food (211).

The act of killing through the poisoning of food is one of the most menacing motifs in Agatha Christie's novels, as by employing it she is once again able to make use of the method of distancing, and to turn the homely and familiar into the uncanny and dangerous. As stressed on numerous occasions in the novels (*The Mysterious Affair at Styles* 83; *Three Act Tragedy* 99; *Evil under the Sun* 121; etc.) poison is considered a woman's weapon. As such it is doubly dangerous, because a woman is traditionally expected to be sensitive, calm, and caring, not aggressive and dangerous.

Paradoxically, it is exactly the caring and nurturing nature of food, which is exploited by the poisoner and the crime of poisoning frequently displays a personal or even loving character (however twisted that love may be). When Miss Waynflete tries to poison Bridget in *Murder Is Easy* she says she is going to get her a nice cup of tea, because that is what she needs to calm her after the upsetting events (285); similarly, when Miss Marple is hospitably offered a cup of warm milk to help her sleep well, she is in fact being poisoned by her hostess (*Nemesis* 226). In *By the Pricking of My Thumbs* the characters mention a number of cases of carers who are revealed to be psychopathic murderers, poisoning their charges through lovingly prepared meals or cups of cocoa (284 or 339). Similarly, in *At Bertram's Hotel* a poisoner makes their act of murder even more perversely caring and personal when they send a young girl Elvira a box of chocolates, in which the poison was added only to one type of candies: those with violet cream which the poisoner knows are Elvira's favourite (241-42). In *Nemesis*, again, Clotilde loves and cares for her charge so much that she prefers to poison her "painlessly" with an overdose of sleeping pills dissolved in a drink rather than let her marry a disreputable man (231). Thus in the figure of the female poisoner the two contradictory aspects of food—the nurturing and the lethal—are brought together and made one.

Notes

[1] *Lardo* is an Italian word denoting cured pork fat. The *lardo* of Colonnata is a type of *lardo* traditionally consumed and produced in the region of Carrara, famous for its marble production. In the past, *lardo* was a source of fast energy for quarry workers. In its traditional production method local marble is used: the fat is placed in "rectangular, marble troughs," stored in damp cellars, covered in herbs, rock salt, and slices of bacon, and then pickled for six to nine months. However, in the late 1990s new standardised European Union food safety legislation outlawed the use of any porous materials (including marble) in food production. As a result, in 1996 local health authorities collected the pickling troughs and placed them in quarantine. This provoked a controversy over how much control the EU should

have over local food production and it fired up campaigns for the protection of traditional and local foods in Italy. (A. Leitch 2008, 381-399)

[2] An earlier version of this section was published in *Prague Journal of English Studies* 3 (1), 2014: 35-46.

CHAPTER FIVE

FOOD AND SETTING

After the preceding discussion of characters and plot in the previous two chapters, the last chapter will address the issue of setting. As was explained in section 1.3, setting plays a paradoxical role in crime fiction. On the one hand it needs to be as realistic as possible in order to ensure reader identification with the text; on the other hand it must be as ahistorical and imaginary as possible to grant the detective story the required ritualistic, general, and archetypal qualities, thereby allowing the readers to experience a cathartic purging of suppressed guilt (see sections 1.1 and 1.3).

This chapter aims to prove that it is very often references to food and drink that help Agatha Christie to construct such contradictory settings. It is argued that this stems from the fact that although our experience with food is very realistic and palpable, it is at the same time also unstructured, non-verbalised, and fleeting, being as it is processed primarily through the "irrational," largely unconscious senses of smell and taste. Thus our eating and drinking experiences can conjure images of places and experiences which seem precise and exact, but which are also uncertain, indescribable, and unfixed.

The two sections of this chapter examine how food references function in the portrayal of two aspects of setting. Section 5.1 focuses on place, listing the functions of place in Christie's novels and focusing largely on the role of foodscapes. It further explores the role of domestic eating spaces in the construction of Christie's stories. Section 5.2 then turns its attention to time. The issue which proved to be crucial in this section was that of memory and nostalgia, and therefore this section also expands the discussion of nationality which was begun in chapter three. However, what brings these two sections together is their focus on the unconscious and ritualistic aspects of the setting, and of crime fiction in general, which are reflected in the ritualistic nature of human (and the characters') eating habits.

5.1. Food and Place

As shown in chapter one, setting in general, and location or place in particular belong (together with characters and plot) among the three most crucial elements of a detective story. In fact, the success of any type of "fiction depends for its life on place. Location is the crossroads of circumstance, the proving ground of 'What Happened?" (Welty [1955] 1998, 783). In a crime story, place serves a variety of functions. It

> can transport one into the story, rendering the characters and plot more vivid. Further, the geography and, in some cases, the changing geography over which the story transpires, can be important to the plot, often playing a role in the solution of the mystery. Characters must "fit" the place in which the action takes place. The physical landscape can create an atmosphere to enhance and enliven a story with great effect. (Demko 2006)

Detective stories have been set in a great variety of settings. To quote only the example of Agatha Christie, her plots have taken place almost everywhere, in the little village of St. Mary's Mead (e.g. *The Murder at the Vicarage*), a London foreign students' residence (*Hickory Dickory Dock*), a deserted island (*And Then There Were None*), a Dover seaside hotel (*Evil under the Sun*), the French Riviera (*The Mystery of the Blue Train*), a Caribbean holiday resort (*A Caribbean Mystery*), and even the High Atlas mountains in Morocco (*Destination Unknown*). Nevertheless in a majority of cases the location of a crime story, however exotic or remote it may be, remains strictly delimited. This is in line with the requirements of the classical detective formula: it enables the author to enclose all of her/his suspects within one neat finite space. Furthermore, the setting is also closed in terms of class, with the majority of characters belonging to the upper or upper-middle classes of society (see 1.3.1).

One of the crucial roles of setting, as was discussed in section 1.3.1, is its contribution to the realism of the story. The plot's location is used to explore local colour and to achieve verisimilitude. Thus "Conan Doyle tempts us to the foggy, foul alleys of London and the evil moors of the exurbs." Other authors even give their detectives the ability to "solve crimes with geographic knowledge of the setting" (Demko 2006). Christie, too, often used actual place names or even made her characters dine in real-life restaurants or cafes in order to achieve the semblance of reality. The first chapter of *At Bertram's Hotel* begins with directions including street names, which, although vague enough not to actually reveal the location of the imaginary hotel, are supposed to help readers localise it in central London. In *The Secret Adversary*, the detective duo Tommy and

Tuppence "chew a bun" together at Lyons' (13-14), dream about dining at the Savoy or the Ritz (42), and meet for lunch at a grillroom at Piccadilly Circus (42). Similarly, in *Why Didn't They Ask Evans?* The protagonist Frances describes her typical night out on town, providing the reader with the names of the restaurants and entertainment venues she usually visits with her posh London circle of friends: the Savoy, the Marionette, or the Bullring (28).

While a number of Christie's stories share Sir Arthur Conan Doyle's favoured setting of the urban landscape of London, most of her stories also show evidence of the new trend adopted by Golden Age crime authors: the gradual move away from the urban settings which had previously been associated with the genre. While pre-Golden Age authors explored the juxtaposition between the dangerous and violent city streets versus the calm and comforting interiors of houses, detectives' studies, or homes; Golden Age writers chose to focus on rural and domestic settings as sources of evil (see 1.3.1).[1] By choosing such settings as the locus for their plots filled with murder, passion, and violence, authors began to deconstruct the traditional image of home as a safe haven and the idealised vision of rural life as pure, innocent, and, as a result, crime-free. The quintessential symbols of this idealised rurality, the nostalgic manor house and the cosy little village where everyone knows everyone else, were turned into haunted places filled with dark secrets and passions lurking under the hedgerows.

Agatha Christie indeed embraced the possibilities offered by setting her stories in the manor house. The motif of the haunted house is a driving force behind a number of her stories (e.g. *Nemesis*, *Postern of Fate*, or *Sleeping Murder*). Moreover, by exploiting the idea of haunting, or of atmosphere in general, Christie is at the same time able to introduce the use of intuition, feeling, and susceptibility as detection methods (see 4.2). Frequently, characters who enter these mysterious houses experience premonitions or sudden insights. In *Sad Cypress* this happens to both the future murder victim and the chief suspect:

> Elinor turned the handle of the side door. She passed from the warm sunlight into the shadow of the house. She shivered. It felt cold in here, dark, sinister. It was as though Something was there, waiting for her, in the house ... She walked along the hall and pushed the baize door that led into the butler's pantry. It smelled slightly musty. She pushed up the window, opening it wide. (85)

> The three of them walked up the drive to the house. Elinor had left the front door open. They passed inside into the cool of the hall. Mary shivered a little. Elinor looked at her sharply. She said, "What is it?"
>
> Mary said, "Oh, nothing - just a shiver. It was coming in—out of the sun."
>
> Elinor said in a low voice, "That's queer. That's what I felt this morning." Nurse Hopkins said in a loud, cheerful voice and with a laugh, "Come, now, you'll be pretending there are ghosts in the house next. I didn't feel anything!" (89-90)

In *Sleeping Murder*, the atmosphere of the house and the unconscious memories evoked by it are the only clues which lead the protagonist on her investigation of an unsolved and unreported murder from the past. Similarly, in *Peril at End House*, the violent events unfold in an old aristocratic home:

> Our way led out of the front gate of the hotel and up a sharp hill to the right. At the top of it was a small lane with a notice on the wall: "TO END HOUSE ONLY." We followed it and after a few hundred yards the lane gave an abrupt turn and ended in a pair of dilapidated entrance gates, which would have been the better for a coat of paint. [...] The house itself was large and rather dreary looking. It was shut in by trees, the branches of which actually touched the roof. It was clearly in bad repair. Poirot swept it with an appraising glance before ringing the bell-an old-fashioned bell that needed a Herculean pull to produce any effect and which once started, echoed mournfully on and on. (32-33)

Even the house's owner, Miss Buckley, is described as having a "haunting and arresting" air about her and "an elfin look" (19). By defamiliarising the familiar and cosy in this way, Christie is able to create a pervasive sense of danger and insecurity. She uses the same technique when depicting her other signature setting, the small English village (e.g. *A Murder Is Announced, The Murder at the Vicarage*, etc.). In Christie's novels, places usually associated with calmness, peace, and stability are revealed to be sites of danger and death. This intrusion of the sinister is symbolically framed by the opening and closing scenes, which are frequently set at the table in the dining room, or in another similar area of the home (see 1.3.1). The intrusion of a particular murder into the orderly daily life of the characters then parallels the intrusion of crime in general into what at first glance might appear to be an idyllic and traditional way of life.

It is important to note that Christie frequently employed food-connected settings (restaurant, dining room, coffee room, or kitchen) as places of calmness at risk of being invaded by crime. This appears to indicate that foodspace somehow connotes order, and it is indeed assumed that Christie made use of this connotation throughout her stories. The following paragraphs therefore aim to examine the connection of food and place in general, and subsequently the more specific connection of foodspace and order.

5.1.1. Kitchen Crime: Foodspace as Setting in Crime Fiction

All food-connected activities such as shopping, cooking, and eating are necessarily set in a certain space. However, this space is not limited to the physical place in which the activities occur. On the contrary, it includes "complex physical, social and cultural contexts" (Mikkelsen 2011, 210). A number of food scholars display "a growing interest in studying the influence of our food environment" and thus attempt "to understand how people, spaces and food *interact* and how this interaction *influences* our food behaviour" (ibid., original emphasis). It is believed that the space in which people eat their food can reveal a lot about the "social organisation of eating" in general (Chaney 2001). This complex understanding of foodspace led to the coining of the term "foodscape," which refers to the whole context—physical and abstract—in which people encounter food. Gisèle Yasmeen (2008) defines foodscape, a term derived from "landscape," as "a process of viewing place in which food is used as lens to bring into focus selected human relations." Foodscapes represent "the spatialization of foodways," including the "interconnection between people, food, and places" (525).

There is considerable debate over the scope and specific meaning of the term "foodscape." Some understand it as "all opportunities to obtain food within a given region" (Burgoine 2010, quoted in Mikkelsen 2011, 210), as "the ways in which food is produced, purchased or obtained, prepared, and consumed, and the relationship between food and the individuals of the community" (M. C. King 2009, quoted in Mikkelsen 2011, 211), or as " the multiplicity of sites where food is displayed for purchase, and where it may also be consumed" (Winson 2004, 301). Some understand foodscapes on a micro-level, as pertaining to "the family meal at home, emphasizing the physical appearance of foods, the plates they are served from, the table at which it is eaten, as well as the room in which it is served" (Sobal and Wansink 2007, quoted in Mikkelsen 2011, 212). Others point to the ethical dimensions of buying and eating food coming from various locations or to the power struggle inherent in the contact of various groups of consumers/producers in a given community (Mikkelsen 2011, 211). However, all of these approaches are united by their understanding of place as a pivotal context in both food production and consumption. In other words, the above-mentioned scholars acknowledge that the "preparation and consumption of food are spatially defined and defining activities" (Yasmeen 2008, 524).

As this suggests, foodspace or foodscapes can be studied on a number of different levels. On the macro level, food-related behaviour is often influenced by the opposition of local versus foreign, or, in other words, of "at home" versus "away," or "abroad." This approach allows us to explore concepts such as traditional and/or local food on the one hand, and ethnic cuisines and exotic food on the other. In Britain, the local and traditional has historically had the upper hand, and changes to food habits or foreign cuisines have generally taken a long time to be accepted. John Burnett observes that although French restaurants were the ones to set the style for English public eating in eighteen- and nineteen-century Great Britain, "the tastes of most English people of whatever rank except, perhaps, the very highest, remained stubbornly attached to roast meats, game, poultry and fish, with simple dressings and no elaborate sauces" (2004, 11).

Today, despite the wide selection of various imported foods and the unending list of "ethnic" eateries, the British, especially in rural regions, still place a strong emphasis on eating locally, although understandings of what "local" means tend to differ. Some view it strictly in terms of "food miles" or geographical locations, while others associate it with ethical values or traditional methods of production. In general, however, local is understood as being synonymous with safe, high-quality, and tasty, a view which has been prompted by the "increasing disquiet about the state of the environment, the high profile of food scares, and concerns for local economies" (Blake et al. 2010, 410). Governments, food activists such as the Local food movement (see 2.3), and consumers themselves "have increased concerns over the quality and provenance of the foods they eat" (Blake et al. 2010, 410). Despite the wide range of possible interpretations, all understandings of local share the association

> with trust, shared norms and values, heritage, quality, stewardship, familiarity, simplicity, artisanal and community, which construct an alternative to the industrialized food systems that have been blamed for breaches in consumer safety, animal cruelty, "Frankenstein foods," cultural homogenization, and the undermining of farmers in both the global north and south. (411)

In other words, what is local and homely is also considered trustworthy and safe, an attitude which is shared by contemporary Britons and the characters of Christie's novels; Christie's characters clearly voice their preference of traditional British fare and often show mistrust or even dislike of foreign cuisines (see 3.5).

This connection between homeliness and safety is not only evident when people choose locally produced goods over imported ones, but is also manifest in the division of foodspaces into private and public, and in the various connotations attached both to eating at home and to eating out. Janet A. Flammang (2009) claims that there is a sharp division between the two spheres of eating, and of life in general; the domestic/private/ feminine sphere is placed in opposition to the political/public/masculine one. She observes that revolution-era USA witnessed the cultivation of an idealised image of the middle-class home, which was identified with the "virtues of charity and hospitability" (40). In contrast to the dangerous outside space primarily represented by the city, the home was viewed as a moral and safe place (42). In Victorian Britain, a similar understanding of the opposed and gendered private and public spaces was also prevalent. Victorian society "put emphasis on gender-based divisions of labour, especially amongst its upper and middle classes. The woman's role was to stay at home and look after the children, whilst the burden of providing for the family fell squarely on the man's shoulders" (Dube 2006, quoted in Muwati and Gambahaya 2012, 103). The home and "the kitchen as the 'main staging' arena" in particular became the primary elements of this feminine private space (102).

This "ideologically constructed" gendered understanding of public and private spaces has permeated Western society until the present day (Yasmeen 2008, 524-25) and it is also reflected in the division of foodspaces. The kitchen, dining room, or breakfast room at home stand in opposition to pubs, cafés, and restaurants. Burnett points out that public eating was not always as commonplace and taken-for-granted as it is in contemporary society. In England, the first cafés, called "Pleasure Gardens" or "Tea Gardens," begun to emerge only in the seventeenth century. They were situated in the parks of London, a location which was perfectly suited to offer refuge for city dwellers, and these establishments specialised in the new exotic drinks of the time: tea and coffee (2004, 3). The connection of exotic or foreign food with the public eating space (as opposed to local traditional food served at home) was already visible in these first cafés. Later in the seventeenth century, the first coffee houses opened their doors. At that time, women were not permitted to enter these establishments, as coffee was regarded as a public rather than a domestic drink and coffee drinking itself was considered "a social activity, associated with lively discussion, the dissemination of news and ideas," especially among academics and businesspeople (4). Tea, a feminine equivalent of coffee, was "predominantly a domestic drink" and only with the opening of first teashops did women acquire a public space where they could meet over food and drinks (5).

By the eighteenth century, thanks to the rapid economic growth brought about by imperialism and the Industrial Revolution, the demand for luxury goods and leisure activities in Britain was on the rise. Eating was slowly establishing itself as a popular free-time activity. "Gastronomy was becoming recognised as a fine art" and what, how, and where one ate started to become indicative of an individual's social status. This resulted in two phenomena: a "remarkable proliferation of cookery books" and the introduction of the modern French concept of the restaurant to Britain (5). "By 1830 a hierarchy of eating-places existed, catering for a range of needs and incomes—from humble cook-shops and 'ordinaries,' to better-class inns, chop-houses and dining rooms, up to a few renowned taverns and hotels" (9). Simultaneously, a new class of restaurants was established. These venues "deliberately provided a refined atmosphere which attracted a discerning clientele" and therefore became associated with social status and wealth.

In the twentieth century public eating was more popular than ever before. The beginning of the century saw the invention of "the first hamburger sandwich," as well as "the rapid growth of all kinds of catering," and "the establishment of regional and national chains, and the development of franchising" (Flammang 2009, 53). Not only did public eating and convenience foods offer a possible solution for working wives and mothers (54), but eating out also "became an increasingly popular leisure activity of middle- and working-class people," and restaurants (unlike food stalls or convenience food chains) were "associated with pleasure rather than work" (53). Eating out on the one hand reflected "the urban industrial values of speed and efficiency," but on the other hand it represented a "way to escape from the tangle of emotions and relations of household food:" once food was transformed into a product destined for sale, it stopped being "entangled in the unpleasantness of intense family memories and smothering obligations" (52). In addition, restaurant dining or eating out also became associated with celebratory meals or meals for special occasion (Edwards 2013).

Today, "[e]ating out is generally regarded as a social activity" (Edwards 2013), not only in that it involves a number of people engaging in interaction, meaning the members of the diner party, the staff, and the diners at different tables, but also in that it helps to build social relationships and construct identity. As was shown above, by as early as the nineteenth century, the choice of restaurant had become seen not only as a marker of personal taste in food, but also as a sign of one's status, and this continues to be the case today. John S.A. Edwards (2013) observes that the status-creating nature of the restaurant environment is evident even in its spatial layout; it "can be symbolic and used to indicate status, define personal space and to regulate privacy and interaction." In other words, eating out is "a form of individual self-expression," as well as "a mark of refinement and education," especially when one chooses to dine at "exclusive, high priced restaurants" (Morgan et al. 2008,114).

It is important to point out that the social function of the restaurant as a place of interaction and the creation of interpersonal relationships can stand in conflict with its other social function, that of status-creation. Eating at upper-class venues can impede the interaction between the members of a lunch or dinner party. According to Joanne Finkelstein, "eating in trendy restaurants" is characterised by "an uncivilized[2] sociality," rather than by sincerity and genuine respect for one another (Finkelstein 1989, quoted in Flammang 2009, 55). As a result, communication is limited to exchanges conducted in an environment of "artifice and pretense of supercilious waiters, power tables, and eating to be seen" (55).

Thus the experience of eating out is transformed into a type of performance enacted in front of an attentive audience. Indeed,

> [f]oodservice has always contained elements of theatrical performance, from the rituals of the Jewish Passover meal or the early-Christian Agape, through the pageantry of court banquets and the formality of silver-service waiting to the spectacles of contemporary themed restaurants with singing waiters or exploding volcanoes. (Morgan et al. 2008, 111)

The space of the restaurant itself is turned into a stage and the individual elements: "the seating arrangements, lighting, décor and odours" (Edwards 2013) work in synergy to create a specific desired atmosphere (Morgan et al. 2008, 112). The restaurant, as a site of special occasion meals and "extraordinary experiences," becomes a "sacred space" which is "set apart from everyday life." Eating in such a space is "conducted according to rules that allow the participants and audience to explore activities and feelings outside their normal experience" (114). The effect of such staging on eaters is so powerful that "identical food is rated differently in different dining settings" (Edwards 2013).

Yasmeen sees the effect of the staged restaurant space as being closely connected with nostalgia, as many upper class eating establishments exploit pseudo-historical, traditional, or aristocratic themes. Thus the restaurant settings often become what she calls "depthless images" or "simulacra," or "fanciful 're-creations' of a past that never *really* existed" (2008, 532, original emphasis). "The postmodern experience" encountered within these foodspaces "is framed by the use of *pastiche*, or exaggerated representations that mock the original form being alluded to" (532, original emphasis). The pseudo-historical images which constitute the restaurant space are "void of function and content." Instead, they serve "to add symbolic capital" to the restaurants,[3] and, in turn, to the customers who dine in them (533).

Yasmeen cites Thai food gardens with their artificial ponds and fish-filled water canals, staged folk-dance performances, and pseudo-historical architecture (2008, 532) as an example of this type of theatrical foodspace and setting for staged nostalgia. However, similar instances can also be found in Christie's novels, reflecting the fact that the genre of the crime novel depicts society as being "bereft of reality" and populated not by people, but merely by "insubstantial marionettes" (Kracauer 1999, 290). Such is the case in *Sparkling Cyanide*, where the luxurious surroundings of the Luxembourg, a popular upper-class restaurant, are turned into a stage not once, but twice: firstly as the scene of a murder by poisoning, and later, in a post-modern twist, as a stage for the re-enactment of the fateful dinner from many years ago. Similarly, in *At Bertram's Hotel*, the old-fashioned and comfortable hotel is revealed to be no more than a stage to amuse the audience of guests, a cover which a crime syndicate uses to carry out their operations. In both of these cases, the nostalgic or theatrical quality is achieved through the interplay of the elements of space, time and memory, a technique which is discussed in greater detail in section 5.2.

In addition to employing the restaurant, the hotel lobby, or café as a theatre stage, Christie also made use of the stereotypical opposition between the private, understood as the homely, comforting, and safe, and the public, which is depicted as hostile or, at least, indifferent. This hostility is embodied in the figure of the unwilling waitress/waiter and in the inferior quality of the food and drinks being served. This motive reappears in a number of novels, such as in *Why Didn't They Ask Evans*, where "tepid coffee" is served by a "listless" waitress in the Orient Café, a coffee house whose "somewhat grand name [is] not borne out by the interior decoration" (343). A similar theme is found in *The Man in the Brown Suit*, where Sir Eustace is repeatedly mistreated by the serving staff, being served a "poisonous breakfast," bad fish (174), hard peaches

(185), or "stale cake" and "lukewarm tea" (252). Significantly, as the restaurant facilities are located in Johannesburg during a local uprising, there is always the possibility that "[w]hen the food gives out," the customers will be "flung on the mat" (311).

In sharp contrast to these unsatisfactory public eateries stands the home, the shabby family house in the country with its roaring fires in the winter, and the happy children whose obliging butler sneaks them treats when no one is looking (*Evil under the Sun* 30; *After the Funeral* 11, 37). The interiors of such houses are traditional and the most important rooms are the decorative dining room, the drawing room, and the cosy morning room: all places for sharing meals and talking over a cup of tea or coffee. The prototype of such a space is depicted for instance in *Three Act Tragedy*, where Mr Satterthwaite visits an acquaintance and is admitted in a "tiny sitting room with its faded chintzes and its well-polished pieces of old furniture." He describes it not only as "a lady's room," that is domestic, comfortable, and feminine, but also as "a Victorian room;" a room preserved from the past (51).

5.1.2. The Dining Ritual: From Order to Menace

The sense of safety and peace connected with traditional private eating spaces is not only due to their location in the home, but it is also a result of their ritualised usage. According to Flammang, "[t]able rituals reassure people that they can find order, safety, familiarity and comfort both in everyday and in new and unexpected settings" (2009, 103). When people seated together in a dining room handle "the same foodstuffs," they can more quickly acquire "the impression that it is possible to handle any topic of conversation" (110). The ritualised nature of eating serves to reinforce this impression.

According to Flammang, rituals "promote togetherness, reinforce social bonds, and foster a sense of belonging" (2009, 100). Food rituals represent "powerful and universal organizers and stabilizers of family life," reinforcing the sense of order and facilitating interpersonal communication (102). Food rituals are closely tied to eating spaces within the home, especially to the dining room and the dinner table. All aspects of the dining experience, from the "dinner table conversation" (112) to the seating and position at the table of the members of opposite sexes (102) are to a greater or lesser degree dictated by unspoken conventions. Flammang maintains that this type of ritualised eating is especially prominent in non-family households and settings where eating together is necessary for the creation of a sense of social bonds and stability (2009, 45). This can be observed for example in *Hickory Dickory Dock*, where the entire community life of a group of students living in a residential home, including the crime investigation, happens in the common dining room. The ritualised and fixed nature of seating around the dinner table is referred to in *Elephants Can Remember*, where Mrs Oliver is worried about who her neighbour will be at lunch, as she will be forced to speak to this person for the whole duration of the meal (15). The subsequent coffee drinking then provides guests with the opportunity to choose their talking partner, as after lunch it is acceptable for guests to leave their chairs, intermingle, and have intimate conversations in "confidential corners," sitting at coffee tables (19).

Not only do conventions dictate the table placings of the diners (Flammang 2009, 103), they also establish which food-connected actions are performed in which rooms of the house. The dining room represents the most prominent of these foodspaces. It is the "key space, one that is central for social interaction" (Frankowski et al. 2011, 41) during meals, and it also serves as the "locus of ritual" (42). Other rooms dedicated to clearly defined food-preparation and food-consumption tasks appearing throughout Christie's stories include the scullery, larder, pantry, kitchen, breakfast/morning room, drawing room, bedroom, coffee room, and lounge. This fixed separation of space is especially prominent in the Victorian mansion, the typical setting of Christie's novels. Not only does the stereotypical setting highlight the ritualistic nature of characters' eating and domestic habits, but it also heightens the sense of nostalgia (see above). The environments of Christie's private homes are as staged as those of her restaurants. An example of this is given in *Dumb Witness*, when Poirot and Hastings set to investigate the home of a rich deceased lady, Miss Arundell. The two investigators are shown around the house by the housekeeper and all of the representative spaces are displayed, complete with props: antiques, chintzes, portraits, ready to be turned into a stage on which a pseudo-Victorian fantasy comes to life:

> "This is the morning-room, sir." [...] A pleasant room with its long windows giving on the street. It was furnished with good, solid, old-fashioned furniture, mostly Victorian, but there was a Chippendale bookcase and a set of attractive Hepplewhite chairs. [...]The maid conducted us across the hall and into the corresponding room on the other side. This was much larger.
>
> "The dining-room, sir."
>
> This room was definitely Victorian. A heavy mahogany dining-table, a massive sideboard of almost purplish mahogany with great clusters of

> carved fruit, solid leather-covered dining-room chairs. On the wall hung what were obviously family portraits.
>
> […] She flung open another door. "The drawing-room, sir."
>
> The drawing-room conjured up memories of the past. A faint fragrance of potpourri hung about it. The chintzes were worn, their pattern faded garlands of roses. […]
>
> The atmosphere of a bygone day, a day of leisure, of refinement, of "ladies and gentlemen," closed round me. This was indeed a "withdrawing-room." Here ladies sat and did their fancy-work, and if a cigarette was ever smoked by a favoured member of the male sex, what a shaking out of curtains and general airing of the room there would be afterwards! (90-93)

Christie also uses foodspace in her novels to highlight class and gender boundaries, and, even more importantly, to transgress them. Firstly, the foodspaces in the homes of her characters are divided sharply into the servants' space (kitchen, pantry, larder) and the owners' space (dining room, coffee room, lounge). These borders are normally not crossed. The serving staff work in the kitchen but also eat their own meals there (*After the Funeral* 14) and many of them, especially the cooking staff, never leave the assigned areas of the house. The detective seems to be the sole transgressive figure who is allowed access to both the drawing room and the kitchen (*After the Funeral* 221, see also 3.2).

Gender boundaries are demarcated by the eating-place too, most specifically when eating takes place in the context of the bedroom. Eating in the bedroom, or even in one's bed, is an action associated with women, while men as the stronger sex are expected to eat downstairs and sitting up, unless they are suffering from an illness (*Evil under the Sun* 77, 108; After the Funeral 41). Here yet again Poirot becomes the unconventional figure, transgressing gender boundaries by choosing to take his breakfast in his room (*Evil under the Sun* 79; see also 3.4).

Gender associations also rule foodspaces beyond the four walls of the house. The kitchen garden, an indispensable part of a traditional Victorian household (*Nemesis* 92), is traditionally viewed as a woman's domain (Flammang 2009, 230). This stereotypical notion is given a new significance by Miss Marple, who uses her garden as a place of investigation, or even surveillance, and thus transforms it from a harmless feminine space into a place which is feared by her not-always-moral neighbours. This is visible in *The Murder at the Vicarage*, where Marple's garden is described by the other characters as "a smoke screen" behind which Marple hides and thus "always sees everything" (11). Marple acknowledges the value of her garden as an aid in investigation herself, claiming that "it makes a very useful excuse for talk" both with acquaintances and strangers passing by (126).

Marple's garden is not the only foodspace in Christie's novels which is used as a venue of investigation and questioning. In fact, Christie's detectives frequently turn kitchens, pubs, dining rooms, and restaurants alike into examination rooms. In *Dumb Witness*, for example, Poirot bribes the waiter at the local restaurant with a "substantial tip" in order to make him more willing to part with confidential information about other customers and village inhabitants (85). Female investigators enjoy even more power, as their gender gives them access to the backstage of food preparation normally hidden from the sight and influence of men—the kitchen. Thus Tuppence is able to infiltrate the apartment of the wealthy Mrs Vandemeyer disguised as a parlour maid, thereby gaining access to vital clues and allowing her to eavesdrop on secret conversations conducted at the dinner table (*The Secret Adversary* 116).

By turning foodspaces, especially the domestic areas of the kitchen and kitchen garden, from places of comfort into places of investigation, interrogation, and surveillance, Christie continued the theme of questioning and upsetting the traditional association of home and food with safety, comfort, and order. Christie was not the only one to appreciate the more sinister aspects of foodspaces. In fact, Janet A. Flammang claims that eating rituals were initially created out of a need to control the behaviour of people in the most dangerous of settings; the dining room, where death is immediately present in the form of sharp knives or in the possibility of poisoning (2009, 101). She observes that while rituals of hospitality have an ostentatious function of showing generosity and friendship, they also have another function, that of placating and preventing hostility. The two concepts of hospitality and hostility seem to be inherently connected; both derive from the same Latin base "*hostis*," meaning stranger (103) and as hospitality is indeed exactly that, a standardised way of dealing safely with strangers, the threat of possible hostility "might always lurk in the background" (104).

Schivelbusch points to the fact that gift giving, drinking, and eating rituals have always been instances of power struggles of strangers meeting in a single foodspace and being forced to co-exist and cooperate (1993, 171-73). The ancient taboos and patterns of behaviour connected to giving, receiving, sharing food, and reciprocating survive even today in the form of pub rituals and drinking contests (173), or in the social conventions concerning dinner invitations and exchanging gifts. The latter stands out as the most conspicuous occasion for the establishment of relations of sub/super-ordination, as the giver is always in the position of power over the receiver, who becomes gratitude-bound and is expected to reciprocate (176).

Indeed, the kitchen, the dining room, and the picnic garden are frequently depicted as sites of hostility, struggle, and violence in Christie's novels. In *Hallowe'en Party* the drawing room of an old house romantically named "Apple Trees" becomes the site of a horrible murder of a child (16). Similarly, in *A Caribbean Mystery* the dining room takes on a sinister bent when one of the servant girls is found stabbed with a kitchen knife (150). The conversion of a comforting foodspace into a place of terror is complete in *A Murder Is Announced*, where the criminal, Leticia, turns her kitchen into a lethal trap by attempting to drown her maid Mitzi in a sink filled with dishwater (318).

The above examples demonstrate how Christie's treatments of setting, especially of domestic and food-connected spaces, contribute to a theme which permeates the whole body of her work, that of the omnipresence of crime. This theme is developed symbolically through the process of defamiliarisation, defined here as the transformation of the familiar into the uncanny. Foodspaces play a central role in the defamiliarising of setting. They are depicted as being haunted and twisted, or leading to or aiding crime, and as soaked with violent emotions, dormant family conflicts, and hatred; a portrayal which is far from the safety and order traditionally associated with them. This treatment of setting enabled Christie to question the ideal of the cosy, comfortable, feminine home, to de-idealise the private space, and to make the threat of crime even more acute by locating it in the home in general and in the dining room and the kitchen in particular.

5.2. Food and Time

As was demonstrated in section 1.3.2, the concept of time in a detective novel is by no means straightforward. On the contrary, the genre tends to problematise the traditional linear understanding of time on a number of levels. Firstly, while the categories of past, present, and future are normally clearly separated, in a detective novel they become intermingled, each merging with the other until it becomes impossible to tell what has happened or is happening now, what has taken place in the past, and what is yet to happen. Moreover, the detective story breaks the boundaries between fiction and reality so frequently that the reader is no longer able to differentiate between fictional time and real time, as imaginary adventures of the sleuth are placed side by side with both current and historical events. Section 1.3.2 reached the conclusion that nostalgic time is the most common of the non-traditional forms of time employed in crime fiction. The term "nostalgic time" refers to a remembered period which is considered to be better, purer, of a higher standard, more moral, and more harmonious than the present. However, no such period has ever existed, and nostalgic time ultimately remains purely imaginary. This section aims to prove that the concept of nostalgic or imaginary time is closely connected with food; that it is through food that Agatha Christie constructed this form of time in her novels. However, first it is necessary to establish whether time is of any importance when talking about food, and if so, how the two concepts are related.

5.2.1. Time to Eat: The Milk-Train, the Five o'Clock, and the Food Ritual

Like all human activity, food preparation and consumption are affected by time on a number of different levels. The "activities of shopping and meal preparation, [...] can be viewed in terms of the time they take (a chronological/durational perspective) or as significant events (a successional/event perspective)" (Davies 1997). In addition, the act of eating itself also takes up a certain amount of time, whether it is compressed into the shortest period possible, as in the case of fast food, or deliberately prolonged, such as is the practice of Slow Foodists or hedonists. A number of scholars (e.g. Mintz or Schivelbusch, see 2.2) have dealt with how food practices change in history, paying particular attention to how changing times change what people eat. However, one other focus has been on the specific times at which particular meals are eaten, and their significance.

Sherrie McMillan (2001) observes that the "names of meals and their general times were once quite standard. Everyone in medieval England knew that you ate breakfast first thing in the morning, dinner in the middle of the day, and supper not long before you went to bed, around sundown." McMillan goes on to specify the exact hours at which individual meals were eaten in England at different points in history, claiming that these eating "rituals" were "followed with iron-clad discipline" (2001).

Such disciplined adherence to prescribed mealtimes is also evident in Christie's novels. The fact that certain meals are eaten at certain times is accepted unquestioningly not only by the more conservative and traditional of the characters such as the elderly aristocrat Miss Arundel in *Dumb Witness*, who will have breakfast cleared away at half-past ten, regardless of whether the rest of the household have eaten or not (24), but the routine is also maintained by the young and rebellious; even the wild parties attended by the New Woman Frances and her group of friends are strictly timed, starting “at half-past eight,” waiting up for latecomers until “a quarter-past nine,” and subsequently having dinner at ten (*Why Didn’t They Ask Evans* 28). Public eateries, too, insist that customers arrive on time to consume their meals. When Mike is waiting for his wife Ellie at the restaurant where he has reserved a table for them for lunch, the waitress informs him that if he does not start the meal alone, the table will be given over to other guests (*Endless Night* 216). Similarly, the visitors at a local inn in *Taken at the Flood* must respect that “the only time coffee was served there was [...] for breakfast” and that “The Windsor Soup, Vienna Steak and Potatoes, and Steamed Pudding which comprised Dinner would be obtainable in the COFFEE-ROOM at seven sharp.” If any of the guests wandered into the restaurant at a different hour, they would find it silent and unstaffed (258).

It is unthinkable for characters to break these ritualised mealtimes, and they are adhered to in the most ridiculous circumstances. Upon realising it is nine o’clock, Canon Pennyfather decides to go and have curry for dinner even though he is not hungry at all (*At Bertram’s Hotel* 95-96). A regular one o’clock lunch is provided to Tommy even when he is being held captive by a group of criminals (*The Secret Adversary* 237). A late arrival for a meal is either considered rude and offending (*Hickory Dickory Dock* 83) or it is a bad sign, indicating that the said person is in grave danger (*At Bertram’s Hotel* 125; *By the Pricking of My Thumbs* 194); it could even mean that they are dead (*Endless Night* 216, see also 4.3). Moreover, to intrude upon a household at the time of a meal is impossible in polite society. On several occasions, Poirot beaks off his questionings of witnesses or suspects as soon as he realises that it is the time of lunch or dinner (e.g. *Hallowe’en Party* 287-88). This is also the case in *Dumb Witness*, when Poirot’s interview with one of the witnesses is interrupted by her children demanding their midday meal:

> Poirot looked at his watch and gave an exclamation.
>
> "A thousand pardons! I delay your lunch hour."
>
> Glancing at her husband, Mrs Tanios said uncertainly: "Perhaps we can offer you—"
>
> Poirot said quickly: "You are most amiable, madame, but I have a luncheon engagement for which I am already late." (236)

Mealtimes in larger households are typically announced by sounding a bell or a gong to ensure that everyone will be at the table punctually (*And Then There Were None* 41; *Passenger to Frankfurt* 174; etc.). Individual meals are held so unerringly at the assigned times that the characters often use food references to establish alibis, or they name a meal instead of the exact hour to place events in time. In other words, when asked "When was that?" the characters frequently reply with a meal reference, for example:

> "When was the last time you saw Celia Austin?"
> "At dinner yesterday evening."
> (*Hickory Dickory Dock* 120)

> "his demise occurred quite suddenly at the end of dinner"
> (*Three Act Tragedy* 67)

or

> "So you passed close by the deceased's seat?"
> "No—at least—well, yes, I must have done so. But this was long before anything could have happened. I'd only just drunk my soup."
> (*Death in the Clouds* 47)

As a result, food language is often employed to speak about time, such as in phrases like "Good-bye till tea-time." (*Sparkling Cyanide* 129), or the information that Suzanne "is not the type that gets excited before breakfast" (*The Man in the Brown Suit* 184), and that Miss Marple's nap extended "until dinnertime" (*Nemesis* 108). Even regular train services are sometimes referred to not by the hour at which they depart, but by the meal which is being prepared or consumed at the moment, for example the "breakfast train" (*After the Funeral* 106) or the "milk train" (*Taken at the Flood* 343). Conversely, time language is used to denote meals such as "elevenses," a mid-morning snack eaten at eleven o'clock (*Hickory Dickory Dock* 150), or the "five o'clock," another name for afternoon tea (*At Bertram's Hotel* 178).

The reasons behind this generally strict adherence to mealtimes, a habit which persists until today, are twofold. Firstly, the need to eat at fixed intervals follows from the dictates of the so-called circadian clock, i.e. "an internal biological clock that ensures all the activities of our cells and organs follow a 24-hour cycle" (Bailey 2012). The circadian clock

> dictates what time of the day or night we feed, when we metabolise food into energy, and when we are active and when we rest. It's responsible for the surge of cortisol that forces us up in the morning, the surge of melatonin that gets us ready for bed at night, and the cycles of hunger, thirst and energy we experience throughout the day. (Bailey 2012)

Any irregularity in our habits, including changes in the timing of meals, sleep, or other physical activities, has a harmful effect on the body; it "throws our cellular rhythms out, putting stress on our bodies over time. Our metabolism gets confused, so we produce less insulin and our blood sugar levels go up, predisposing us to diabetes and obesity" (Bailey 2012). There are also cultural reasons for this strict adherence to set mealtimes. As McMillan observes, if two people consume their food at different mealtimes, it suggests that they are of different social status. While eighteenth-century peasants were still "eating on the medieval schedule," which meant taking a break "after six or seven hours of work in the morning to have dinner around noon," aristocrats and other members of the upper classes, who enjoyed a leisurely lifestyle, were gradually postponing the time of dinner until "by 1770 their dinner hour in London was four or five" (2001).

The connection between mealtimes and identity is also visible in Christie's novels. While working class characters adapt their eating habits to their jobs, such as the office workers in *Passenger to Frankfurt* who are allocated only a short break for lunch in the middle of the workday (71), the rich indulge in late breakfasts and even later dinners. The hotel in *A Caribbean Mystery* starts serving dinner only at eight thirty, a time when Miss Marple is already in bed, but at which the evenings of party-loving youth are only beginning (149, 245). Similarly, at eleven o'clock the chambermaid in *Evil under the Sun* is already having her mid-morning snack, while the rich hotel guest Arlena is only finishing her breakfast (190, 96). In addition to marking class, mealtimes can also indicate a character's nationality. As Poirot observes in *Evil under the Sun*, eating lunch at one o'clock is very English (273), as is having tea at five p.m. In *Dumb Witness* Poirot has the following exchange with Hastings:

> "Tea, Hastings? What an idea! Regard the time."
>
> "I have regarded it - looked at it, I mean. It's half-past five. Tea is clearly indicated."
>
> Poirot sighed.
>
> "Always the afternoon tea with you English! No, mon ami, no tea for us. In a book of etiquette I read the other day that one must not make the afternoon call after six o'clock. To do so is to commit the solecism. We have, therefore, but half an hour in which to accomplish our purpose." (147)

The adherence to strictly fixed mealtimes such as those mentioned above represents one of the main elements which contribute to the ritualistic nature of eating. As Robin Fox (n.d.) notes, the centrality of food in human life means that it is "a perfect vehicle for ritual, and food rituals become central to most religions" (18). Various food taboos function as "marker[s] of social boundaries." Numerous special events, such as weddings, graduations, funerals, and others are celebrated by feasts which not only "serve a practical purpose in feeding the guests," but "also serve the ritual purpose of uniting the celebrants in the common act of eating, with all its rich, symbolic associations" (19).

However, it is not only food which is eaten at feasts and special occasions which has a ritualistic nature. On the contrary, all food is routine, conventional, and therefore ritualised, as it is generally "regulated by a series of unspoken rules" (Marshall 2005, 69). The "frequent, diurnal nature of [food] consumption practice implies routine and often unreflexive (un)conscious decisions" (Marshall 2005, 69-70). The unconscious nature of eating stems from the various conventions attached to it, "regulating the sequence and order of dishes and provid[ing] guidelines on appropriateness and comportment in certain situations" (72). Such a ritualistic understanding of meals or "eating events" "acknowledges [...] the fact that consumption is located throughout different parts of the day, week, and year marking the passing of time" (75).

Furthermore, eating rituals are not simply a consciously followed practice, but rather a form of sensual experience, interconnecting unconscious sensory perceptions with emotional and rational operations (Marshall 2005, 79). This irrational, emotional aspect of food rituals is manifest in the way in which people tend to carry out established habits in spite of their impractical or even harmful nature. One example of this kind of behaviour was noted by Charlotte Balcomb Lane. She observed the breakfast ritual of working Americans, who "crawl" every morning "through drive-throughs and scramble through doors at fast-food restaurants" (Balcomb Lane 1994) in order to buy their daily fast-food breakfast, even though it would be much healthier, faster, and cheaper to have breakfast at home. There are two reasons behind this seemingly illogical behaviour. Firstly, the adherence to routine actions eliminates the need to be "innovative" and to decide what and where to eat; the ritual offers a certain degree of safety, familiarity, and comfort. Secondly, thanks to the ritualistic nature of the breakfast, more or less the same group of people meet at the same time every day, and as a result the meal becomes a forum in which they can socialise and build relationships, and enjoy the "the coffee-shop camaraderie they share with employees and other customers" (ibid.).

5.2.2. Culinary Memory

A significant phenomenon testifying to the emotional nature of food rituals is the nostalgia connected with habitually eaten meals or foods. In "The Ritual of Tea: Crisis Requires Steady Hand on Kettle" (1992) Pattie Moran recounts an anecdote about a recent visit to an upper-class restaurant. During the meal her sister was horrified by the waiters' providing tea bags instead of loose leaves, wondering "Whatever happened to the proper cup of tea?" This lead the author to reminisce about the teas she used to drink as a child and the many ornamental actions connected with the preparation and consumption of this beverage. In her conclusion Moran admits that over the course of time she has come to enjoy the ritual, or the idea of tea, "more so than the drink itself" (1992, D1).

Food and nostalgia, or food and memory in general, frequently go hand in hand. Chef and culinary author Nigel Slater (2006) claims that he is probably "not the only one for whom many of life's most intimate details come flooding back at the sight, smell and taste of particular foods." He notes that a number of his acquaintances are able to identify "a favourite or, in some cases, a most hated dish with which they can recall particular moments of their lives." An important element which all such food-induced memories have in common is that the senses which play a primary role in such recollections are smell and taste rather than vision or hearing (i.e. the "superior" senses, see 2.3). These two "primal" senses are "capable of painting a picture with richer, deeper brush strokes than any snapshot in [a] photograph album." As Slater observes:

> It is curious that, while I struggle to remember my mobile phone number or grapple helplessly to recall the closest of friends' names when I am required to introduce them to someone, the merest sniff of chocolate ice cream has been known to bring back memories from 20, 30, 40 years ago with frightening clarity. (2006)

Many characters in Christie's novels also find that specific memories can be evoked through this mnemonic quality of food. Captain Hastings is able to remember a certain summer morning in vivid detail thanks to the—to him—revolting cup of morning chocolate drunk by Poirot on the occasion (*Dumb Witness* 53). In *Taken at the Flood*, the protagonist Lynn associates her memories of foreign adventures with various sensory experiences, but especially with the "smell of hot dust, and paraffin, and garlic" (60). In *Sparkling Cyanide*, too, the protagonist's memories of her childhood are interlaced with food references in what seems to be unconscious "glimpses of the past [coming] back—brief flashes—short scenes" of her "as a small child eating bread and milk, and Rosemary, important in pig tails, 'doing lessons' at a table" (9).

The interconnection of smell, taste, and memory is by no means coincidental. On the contrary, from the physiological point of view, smell, and consequently taste (as "smell may account for more than 90 percent of the sense we call taste" [Hirsch, interview by Rice 2001]) are closely linked to both memory and emotion. All of these impulses and feelings are regulated by a part of the human brain called the hippocampus. "The hippocampus is particularly important for forming long-term, declarative memories—those that can be consciously recalled" and also "for spatial memories," hence the vividness of a majority of smell-induced recollections (Allen 2012). And as John S. Allen notes, "[f]inding food is so important to survival that it is clear that the hippocampus is primed to form memories about and around food" (2012).

The sense of smell also plays a role in triggering emotions; in fact it is believed that it "has a more powerful impact upon the emotions than any of the other senses." Furthermore, the emotional reaction to smell is experienced "even before we have identified the source of the odor" (Hirsch, interview by Rice 2001). Thanks to this mutual interconnection, "[f]ood is an effective trigger of deeper memories of feelings and emotions, internal states of the mind and body" (Allen 2012), or memories which are "immediate, and undiluted by language, thought or translation" (Ackerman, interview by Rice 2001).

In his book titled *Remembrance of Repasts: An Anthropology of Food and Memory* (2001), David E. Sutton studies issues of senses, emotions, food and memory from a cultural, rather than biological point of view. He too, recognises the centrality of taste and smell in forming and recalling memories and argues for adopting a "less visualist approach to memory." He proposes moving "away from understanding memory, and culture itself, in terms of written, or textual models," which have until recently been pushing all other aspects to the background (11). Sutton believes that memories triggered by food are "images of past sustained by ritual performance" and that they are "embodied" rather than "verbal or textual" (12). In order to study them successfully it is necessary to avoid the mind/body dualism and overcome the prejudiced view of vision as the superior sense. Instead Sutton proposes the idea of the mindful body. This term refers to the oneness of the rational and physical and to a unity of all senses (13), a "synesthesia" understood as a "synthesis or crossing of experiences from different sensory registers" (17).

In *Sparkling Cyanide* it is precisely this immediateness and wholeness of food memories which leads Mr Barton to the idea of staging a reconstruction of the dinner at which his wife was poisoned in order to uncover which of the invited guests was the murderer. Barton hopes that a "synesthetic" dinner reconstruction will affect those present to such a degree, and bring back such vivid memories, that the criminal will lose their nerve and give themselves away under the emotional strain of the situation. For this reason he carefully plans the whole event with the headwaiter—the same man who served dinner on the fatal night years ago:

> Charles, the notorious and popular head waiter, came towards him, bending his stately head and smiling in welcome.
> "Good morning, Mr Barton."
> "Good morning, Charles. Everything all right for tonight?"
> "I think you will be satisfied, sir."
> "The same table?"
> "The middle one in the alcove, that is right, is it not?"
> "Yes—and you understand about the extra place?"
> "It is all arranged."
> "And you've got the—the rosemary?"
> "Yes, Mr Barton. I am afraid it won't be very decorative. You wouldn't like some red berries incorporated—or say a few chrysanthemums?"
> "No, no, only the rosemary." "Very good, sir. You would like to see the menu. Giuseppe."
> With a flick of the thumb Charles produced a smiling little middle-aged Italian.
> "The menu for Mr Barton."
> It was produced.
> Oysters, Clear Soup, Sole Luxembourg, Grouse, Poires Helene, Chicken Livers in Bacon. (163-164)

Every little detail, from the location of the table to the scent of rosemary to the food on the menu is intended to be identical to the night of the murder; all of the guests' senses are to be engaged. And indeed, the plan seems to work, and individual invitees start to feel nervous and tense even upon receiving the invitations. A similar technique is employed by a shrewd writer who wishes to confirm the identity of the murderer in *Three Act Tragedy* by finding out if he was left- or right-handed. As the murderer was pretending to work as a butler when she met him, she tricks him into replaying the scene of serving her food:

> "The mark on the butler's right wrist? No, I won't forget."
> "Well, good-bye—half a sec—did you say right wrist? You said left just now."

"Did I? How stupid of me." "Well, which was it?" Miss Wills frowned and half closed her eyes.

"Let me see. I was sitting so—and he—would you mind, Sir Charles, handing me that brass plate as though it was a vegetable dish. Left side."

Sir Charles presented the beaten brass atrocity as directed. "Cabbage, madam?"

"Thank you," said Miss Wills. "I'm quite sure now. It was the left wrist, as I said first. Stupid of me."

"No, no," said Sir Charles. "Left and right are always puzzling." (245)

Again, various spatial and culinary cues are combined to reconstruct an immediate recollection of the past.

As was mentioned above, food memories are not only conveyed by "exotic," rare or festive foods. On the contrary, "[a]ny meal could potentially be the object" with the ability to trigger memories. It is exactly the repetitive nature of everyday eating rituals, which, according to Sutton, makes the special-occasion meals appear so memorable (2001, 2). Sutton turns to the structuralist analysis of meals carried out by Mary Douglas in order to support this argument. Douglas understood meals as "a system of repeated analogies" (Sutton 2001, 7) in which each meal "must recall the basic structure of other meals" (8) in order to be recognised as a meal. Everyday meals tend to be associated with particular times (105) and they are repeated at regular intervals, either daily, weekly or yearly, or they "stretch out over the life-course" (8) to create a rhythm. Such "repetition works both at the level of meal, and at the discursive level (linguistic repetition) to make certain types of meals memorable in certain cultural contexts" (103). Although everyday meals are not individually memorable, they function as "default values" according to which the meal structure is re-established after it has been broken on special occasions by means of the introduction of rare food items, elaborate cooking methods, or some other diversion from the usual formula. In other words, "ritual and everyday contexts of eating echo and mutually reinforce each other" (16).

It follows from the above that food memory is based on a system of similarities and differences between meals, with the differences triggering specific mnemonic reactions. However, once created, "memories are not simply stored images drawn out of the brain at appropriate intervals, but are very much formed as an interaction between the past and the present." This would suggest that memories can be altered, "condensed," or "recontextualized" (9). In the words of Frederic Bartlett, remembering is "an imaginative reconstruction, or construction, built out of the relation of our attitude towards a whole active mass of organiased past reactions or experience" (1932). This means that memory can be used as a tool in creating individual or group identity, or even in building nationalism (Sutton 2001, 4, 6). In this context, food can become a "culturally constructed memory site" similar to "landscapes" or "ceremonial or personal objects" (10-11). Group memory can be created by means of a "common cuisine," which is defined by Sidney Mintz as a community of people who eat similar foods "with sufficient frequency to consider themselves experts on it. They all believe, and *care* that they believe, that they know what it consists of, how it is made, and how it should taste" (1996, 96, original emphasis).

Group food memory is transmitted and reinforced through what Sutton calls "table talk," the discussion of various food experiences of the group's members. Like memory itself, table talk "works largely by analogy," by comparing and simultaneously evaluating a set of given food experiences (Sutton 2001, 109). This approach would suggest that there are two distinct types of memorable food events: the first is a regular meal in which there is some kind of difference which renders that specific event memorable; the second is a meal whose repetition is "savoured" because the meal in itself is festive or special, for example Christmas dinner. While in the first case it is the difference or exception which is most valued, in the second case the most positively remembered experiences are those which follow the formula or template as closely as possible (109).

Listing, especially the "retrospective listing of the everyday" is another important feature of food talk or food discourse (110). Many food lists are characterised by "attention to detail that goes beyond any informational function." The consumed food is described vividly, often to the point of redundancy. These redundant descriptions can be accounted for by the phatic function of food talk, meaning that it serves not only "to communicate new information," but also to "maintain and to build social relations" (111). When used in literary texts, food lists can either be created for the "sheer joy of naming" (112), when the sole mentioning of dishes and foodstuffs gives the reader/listener pleasure (such as in the case of food porn, see 2.4.1), or they can serve to achieve verisimilitude (Sutton 2001, 112).

The genre which combines all of these functions of food talk with the function of evoking memory itself is the food memoir. Barbara Frey Waxman (2008) claims that food memoirs are so popular exactly because the genre succeeds in connecting pleasure, emotions, and memory, the three qualities which operate biologically side by side in the human body. She believes that "[f]ood memoirists intuitively grasp these important links among smells, tastes, strong emotions, and keen memories" (363). A meal is an extremely memorable occurrence "because of the pleasure it has given us and also because eating is connected in a primal way with our continued survival" (364). Describing memories in food terms is a manner which seems most natural to us.

Moreover, as Janet Theophano (2002) observes, not only memoirs, but cookbooks or single recipes themselves also have the ability to transmit thoughts, memories and life stories (1). She claims that cookbooks feature such "timeless" themes as "life and death, youth and age, faithfulness and betrayal, memory and forgetfulness" (6) and they often serve "as a place for readers to remember a way of life no longer in existence or to enter a nostalgic re-creation of a past culture that persists mostly in memory" (49). There is, according to Sutton, an "obvious link of food and nostalgia" (2001, 70), which is a longing not for the past, but "for an idealized state, a sanitized impression of the past . . . with all negative emotions filtered out" (Hirsch, interview with Rice 2001). However, like the nationalist nostalgia discussed in 1.3.2, food-induced nostalgia, too, "is a 'bittersweet' emotion because it represents a return to a past that 'never truly existed" (Rice 2001).

As was shown in 1.3.2, Golden Age detective novels are permeated by feelings of nostalgia, and Agatha Christie's stories are no exception to this. Furthermore, Christie frequently constructs the nostalgic reminiscences of her characters as miniature food memoirs, focusing on what the individual character used to eat, taste, smell, and feel, or what she/he believed people have eaten, tasted, smelled, and felt in the imagined past. Nostalgia often appears in the form of a longing for one's youth or childhood, such as in *Passenger to Frankfurt*, when the protagonist's aunt longs for the times when groceries were not bought in supermarkets "all rebuilt" with "baskets and wine trays to carry round and try to fill up with things you don't want," but rather at the local grocer's who had "good taste" and was also familiar with the tastes of his customers (54). In *After the Funeral*, the butler Lanscombe remembers how he used to allow children of the house to creep into the pantry during dinner parties and give them "jelly and Charlotte Russe" (11), and in *Endless Night* Major Philpott's childhood memory of gypsies is embodied by the "tin mug of gypsy stew" he used to eat with them as a schoolboy. The same longing for lost childhood is expressed by Elinor, the protagonist of *Sad Cypress*, in the following reminiscence:

> Dear Hunterbury... In the years before her parents died, when they had been in India, she had come here for holidays. She had played in the woods, rambled by the stream, picket sweet peas in great flowering armloads, eaten fat green gooseberries and dark red luscious raspberries.

> Later, there had been apples. There had been places, secret lairs, where she had curled up with a book and read for hours. (120)

However, Christie did not limit herself to depicting these brief instances of nostalgia for the long gone days of youth. Instead, she suggested that there is a much more sinister aspect to dwelling in the imagined past, and that nostalgia often masks or even causes crime. The theme of nostalgia as a means of hiding sinister secrets drives the plot in both *Nemesis* and *At Bertram's Hotel*. In *Nemesis* the manor house inhabited by three spinster sisters is surrounded by an old vineyard and a dilapidated greenhouse, which the sisters refuse to sell, rebuild, or pull down because of the memories of better times which they associate with it. The now overgrown Cherry Pie shrubs symbolise a past time when everything was in order, and when the memory of the murder of their favourite niece did not yet haunt the house and the gardens. The youngest of the sisters lovingly recounts her memories of a "Black Hamburg and one of those small white grapes, very sweet, you know. And a third one of beautiful muscats" (93), and frequently mentions hothouses filled with ripe peaches (106). However, at the end of the story it is revealed that the overgrown garden is not only left standing in memory of the dead girl, but that the girl's corpse is in fact hidden among the weeds. Moreover, it is proved that the person who murdered the girl and hid her there is one of the sisters, who now holds the dead girl in twisted loving memory.

A similar motif can be found in *At Bertram's Hotel*, where the hotel manager has reconstructed the atmosphere of a nostalgic past so perfectly that on entering the hotel "you felt, almost with alarm, that you had reentered a vanished world. Time had gone back. You were in Edwardian England once more" (8). The main element in this constructed past is the ritual of the five o'clock tea, which is also the main attraction of the hotel to rich foreign tourists wishing to experience England "as it once used to be." Every day, at

> tea hour, the lounge hall was full. [...] the big entrance lounge was the favourite place for the afternoon tea drinking. The elderly ladies enjoyed seeing who came in and out, recognising old friends, and commenting unfavourably on how these had aged. There were also American visitors fascinated by seeing the titled English really getting down to their traditional afternoon tea. For afternoon tea was quite a feature of Bertram's. It was nothing less than splendid. Presiding over the ritual was Henry, a large and magnificent figure, a ripe fifty, avuncular, sympathetic, and with the courtly manners of that long vanished species: the perfect butler. [...] There were large crested silver trays, and Georgian silver teapots. The china, if not actually Rockingham and Davenport, looked like

> it. The Blind Earl services were particular favourites. The tea was the best Indian, Ceylon, Darjeeling, Lapsang, etc. As for eatables, you could ask for anything you liked—and get it! (10-11)

Nevertheless, in this story Christie shatters these warm and pleasant feelings of nostalgia yet again. The hotel, with its idyllic atmosphere and its perfect tea rituals, is revealed to be nothing more than a cover for the illegal proceedings of a nation-wide criminal organisation.

The danger inherent in nostalgia is depicted in its most sinister form in *After the Funeral*. In this novel, the elderly Miss Gilchrist's affectionate remembrances of a tea shop she used to own before the Second World War left her bankrupt and forced her to find different employment (56) become a maniac obsession. Miss Gilchrist's nostalgia, fuelled by a memory which is "almost wholly culinary" (164) is in fact an obsession, rendering her unable to stop thinking about the cakes and scones she used to serve (56). In the end this obsession becomes the motive for her murder of her rich employer and her attempt to claim her estate. In all of these stories Christie's message is the same: although the tasty and sweet-smelling food remembrances may make the past seem idyllic, such uncritical nostalgia can have disastrous consequences. Or, in the words of Mrs Glynne, one of the three sisters: "one must not remember the past too much" (*Nemesis* 164).

Notes

[1] While the audiences of early crime authors, including Sir Arthur Conan Doyle, came mainly from London (Scaggs 2005, 48), Golden Age authors target their novels at the upper-middle and upper classes in general. In the 1920s and 30s, the members of these classes were hit economically by post-war depression. Therefore, according to John Scaggs (2005) the "ideological motivation" of Golden Age crime novels aims "to recover, or return to, a previous period characterised by stability and order." The setting of these novels, the pseudo-Edwardian country manor, becomes a symbolic representation of what is seen as the better past (47). However, while Golden Age authors on the one hand depict the English countryside as an idealised or nostalgic setting, on the other hand they acknowledge "the central fear articulated in Golden Age fiction: that the threat of social disruption comes from within" (46). Thus the Golden Age rural setting, which was originally born from the wish to recover a seemingly harmonious past, ended up challenging the very existence of such past.

The development of crime fiction, including the setting, took a completely different course in the USA. While British Golden Age authors explored rurality, domesticity, and the upper classes, American authors moved towards the so-called hard-boiled crime novel. The hard-boiled mode was a direct reaction to Golden Age fiction. American authors in the middle of the twentieth century rejected the focus on upper-middle classes as not reflective of the reality of contemporary American society. Instead, they attempted to incorporate more social strata into their stories, in order to make them closer to the "common reader" (Browne and Browne 2001, 562). To reflect the urban way of life of modern Americans, these authors substituted the village for the industrial metropolis and the country house for the dark street, which are now considered the standard setting of American hard-boiled mysteries (363).

[2] Finkelstein understands the term "civility" as denoting "exchanges between people who [are] equally self-conscious and attentive to one another and who [avoid] power and prestige differentials" (Flammang 2009, 55). In this context "uncivilised" does not refer to something that is "natural" or "authentic," but rather it is understood as a moral term, describing behaviour that does not comply with the social norms and standards set by "civilised" society.

[3] Symbolic capital is a term employed by Pierre Bourdieu in his sociological discussion of class. In this discussion Bourdieu extends the meaning of the term "capital" to refer not only to a person's financial means (economic capital), but also to the "immaterial" means they have accumulated (i.e. cultural and social capital) (Bourdieu 1997, 46-47). The term "symbolic capital" then denotes "the legitimated, recognized form of the other capitals"—economic, cultural, and social (Lawler 2011, 1418). As with art or language, food can also become one of the elements contributing to a person's cultural or symbolic capital, a point which Bourdieu himself acknowledged (Johnston and Baumann 2007, 166). Where and what one eats can affect their social status to a great degree (165). Thus, if one eats the correct foodstuffs in a correct setting, they can gain what Peter Naccarato and Kathleen LeBesco (2012) label "culinary capital;" they can improve their status through their dietary choices.

CONCLUSION

The introduction to this book posed, among others, a very general question: Does food have any function in fiction, and, if so, what is this function? This general question emerged as the driving force behind the analysis I present in this book. It was the aim of the analysis to find the answer in a specific field, that of the Golden Age detective novels of Agatha Christie. However, while reading the literature pertaining to that field, it became clear that food has much broader implications than those of a literary trope; it permeates the lives of individuals on various levels, and as such is worthy of discussion within any number of scholarly disciplines. Food production and consumption influence the economies and political ideologies of countries around the globe. Food can serve to define nationality, but it can also overcome differences between nations, social classes, or genders; it plays a major role in women's oppression, as well as in their liberation. Food choice and taste are powerful agents in the construction of individual or collective identities, and also give rise to a wide range of ethical and philosophical issues. Food and the body are central to family, community, memory, and nostalgia, but they also serve as a means of transgressing traditionally assigned boundaries.

Food is an everyday presence. It is something which plays a vital part in the lives of organisms all over planet Earth. It is therefore not surprising that it has attracted a great amount of both popular and academic interest. However, a number of food scholars (e.g. Belasco, Counihan, Watson and Caldwell, etc.) have noticed that this interest in food is a relatively recent phenomenon. Food studies as a discipline is a young field which "moved from the margins to the centre of intellectual discourse in the English-speaking world" (Watson and Caldwell 2005, 1) only as late as the 1990s. In the Central European academic environment, in which this book was written, food studies have not been widely recognised as a separate field even to date.

The paradoxical situation, in which food is at the same time both omnipresent and invisible, can be ascribed to the fact that mainstream academic thought has been informed to a significant extent by the mind/body dichotomy, and a majority of thinkers from the time of Plato onwards have granted the privileged position to the mind. Thus, in traditional Western patriarchal thought, the rational, metaphysical, and masculine qualities were strictly separated from the emotional, physical, and feminine. The former were considered superior and therefore more worthy of academic interest. Food, thanks to its direct connection to the body and to domesticity, pertains to the latter domain, and thus it was denied the status of a scholarly subject for a long time (see 2.1 and 2.3).

However, the superiority of the mind and, by extension, the Western tradition of thought as such has been questioned by a number of dissident thinkers ever since it gained its ascendency (see e.g. Epicurus in 2.3). Alternative philosophies have found their strongest and most widespread expression to date in the ideologies of feminism and post-colonialism, which have given voice to previously overlooked groups and communities, thereby allowing critical discussion of formerly undervalued topics, including food. Current food scholars agree that the seemingly homely, personal, and individual nature of food belies the fact that eating is an act which is loaded with major political ramifications. Regardless of whether one chooses to eat home-made chicken soup, ramen noodles, a vegan risotto, or a Big Mac menu, this decision is affected by factors as diverse as one's social status, the ideology of the society or community they live in, the current government's policy, and the previous summer's weather. Furthermore, this individual choice can have effects of varying degree on the future eating habits of the community or society, the living and working conditions of food-production labourers, as well as the environment and the well-being of various plants and animals. It seems that not only in relation to female oppression, as observed by Carol Hanisch,[1] but also in relation to food, the personal problems and choices of an individual are indeed strongly political.

It has therefore been the aim of this book to show that food is something far more significant than a mere biological fact or as the necessary fuel which enables humans to perform "higher" rational tasks. The intention has been to show that food is a subject which is filled with cultural (and literary) significance. When analysing references to food and eating in Agatha Christie's novels, I was informed by the structuralist notion that food can function as a cultural sign bearing symbolic meaning which is far removed from its practical function as a source of nourishment (see 2.1). In this book, food is understood as a powerful literary device which serves a number of functions in detective novels, but which can also be seen as a bearer of cultural meanings, and as a means of constructing and deconstructing identities, value systems, and memories. In order to justify the analysis of food in the specific case of detective fiction, I have suggested some connections between food and the crime novel. These include the shared formulaic nature of both cooking and mystery writing (as understood by critics in the structuralist tradition, especially by John G. Cawelti), and the intermingling of pleasure and death (see 2.4 or the introduction).

Cawelti's approach, in which crime fiction is defined as a formula, was adopted as the theoretical framework of this book. In line with this framework, each chapter of the analytical section focused on one of the three underlying elements of a classical detective formula: the characters (especially the detective), the plot (crime and investigation), and the setting (place and time). All three of the analytical chapters were intended to prove the hypothesis that food is a tool which is deliberately used by Agatha Christie as a literary device to help her construct her stories, but which is also used as a means of social commentary by depicting, mocking, or even criticising the norms and values of contemporary Britain and contemporary understandings of Englishness. Moreover, throughout all of the chapters of this book, I have attempted to demonstrate that references to food and cooking were a handy tool that enabled Christie to feminise the detective novel, which had hitherto been a largely masculine genre of fiction.

Although each of the chapters tackled the problem of food from a different angle, focusing on a number of its aspects, all of the chapters demonstrated that references to food and eating occur throughout Christie's novels and are repeatedly employed by the author in specific ways. Firstly, each of the analytical chapters observed how food is turned into a literary device, which Christie used to achieve different ends. Chapter three demonstrated how food can help sketch a character. It was proven that the food which the characters in the novels eat and the times at which and ways how they eat it shows what kind of people they are, from the fussy and pedantic Poirot with his elaborate menus and sandwiches cut in right angles, and the hedonists Ariadne Oliver and Tuppence with their love of fruits and rich meals, to the ascetic Miss Marple, whose ignorance of food is just as significant as the other characters' indulgence.

Chapter four turned its focus to the second element of the classical detective formula and examined how food aided Christie in the construction of her plots. Here again, a number of interesting functions of food references were discovered. Not only is domestic and food-related investigation the method most frequently applied by both Poirot and Miss Marple, but poisoned food or drink is also the preferred form of murder weapon for a large number of Christie's criminals. In addition, meals are cooked and served by many of the characters to others in order to facilitate questioning, a method of which Poirot is particularly fond. Finally, the tension between the safety of a set breakfast or dinner table, and the murderous potential of steak knives and concealed poison represents the driving force behind a number of Christie's plots.

The final chapter concentrated on how Christie used food to construct her signature crime scene: the nostalgic cosy world of rural England. On the one hand, descriptions of meals create a sense of reality and make the places and people described seem more physical, but on the other hand they are used to enclose the stories within an ahistorical imaginary timeframe. This imaginary time is created by ritualising the plots and the genre, but it is also achieved by conjuring a nostalgic sense of a past which is largely imagined and essentially untrue. Food references serve to summon up memories of the childhoods of the characters or to paint the picture of an idealised traditional way of life, which has presumably been lost a long time ago. The same goal is accomplished by references to foodspaces, such as fancy dining rooms, cosy cafés, and chintz-adorned tearooms. These places, too, evoke the traditional stereotypical image of Englishness, which serves as the backdrop to the majority of Christie's stories. Furthermore, Christie often emphasised the ritualistic nature of eating, describing in detail the strict observance of mealtimes and the proper use of ingredients and props (dinner gongs, china, silverware etc.), which parallels the ritualistic form of the puzzle mystery genre and highlights the ritualistic nature of murder and evil.

In addition to concentrating on these specific uses of food references, all three analytical chapters have worked together to illustrate two more general points: firstly that Christie used food as one of the tools in altering the rigid rules of the Golden Age detective formula, and secondly that food helped her to mock, satirise, and eventually transgress the norms and values of the society she depicted in her novels. Christie frequently constructed stereotypical characters, as these types of characters are expected by readers in a classical detective novel. However, she transformed these characters from simple stock types into caricatures poking fun at English people and Englishness. This is particularly visible in the character of Captain Hastings, who, as his name suggests, occupies the place of the slow-witted helper who is never able to surpass his continental counterpart, Hercule Poirot. In each of the novels in which Hastings features, we see him trying and failing to arrive at the correct conclusion and all of these comical failures are accentuated by references to his extremely English character, be it his love of the five o'clock tea or his gentlemanliness and knight-in-shining-armour sense of honour.

Methods such as those described above are aimed at transgressing the boundaries of the crime genre as they had existed since the time of Sir

Arthur Conan Doyle's Sherlock Holmes mysteries. Instead of the masculinist rational universe of Holmes, Christie proposed a feminised alternative for the detective novel. The feminisation of the formula is visible in all of its elements: the detectives, in the forms of the effeminate Poirot, the spinster Miss Marple, and the crime author Ariadne Oliver; the plots and crimes; murders and crimes of passion, but in most cases private, family crimes; or the setting of the home or the cosy village, as opposed to Holmes's hostile city streets. Even the process of detection itself is feminised, with detectives relying on domestic knowledge and intuitive insights rather than on mathematical logic and the latest scientific discoveries. Food plays an important role in creating this new feminine universe of crime. Feeding is an inseparable element of the home and of the cosy atmosphere around which Christie centred her novels. The kitchen is a vital source of domestic information and gossip to Christie's detectives, and poison represents the ultimate women's weapon.

Although the functions of food and the feminisation of the crime genre observed in Christie's novels are characteristic of the Golden Age writing, they can also be found in the works of contemporary authors writing in the culinary mystery genre. These novels, and those of similar genres such as the culinary romance or culinary memoir, are a product of the increasing interest in food in popular culture, a rise which is paralleled by the same growing interest within academia. Consequently, a number of scholars have begun to address the topic of food in literature, and a couple of them devote their full focus to the issue of food in crime fiction (see 2.4.1). These authors acknowledge the interconnection between food and crime and the strong potential of food as a literary device.

Nevertheless, despite the effort of a number of such authors (Michelis, Rippetoe, Pascual Soler or Saylor), there is still a relative lack of research into the topic of food in crime fiction in particular, and even on food in literature in general.[2] While the lack of available literature has been an advantage in that this book has hopefully been able to cover a previously undiscussed subject and offer a novel way of analysing the classical detective novels by Christie, at the same time it has represented a possible limitation, as it has led to the reliance on a very eclectic selection of sources covering various scholarly fields and also non-scholarly resources such as popular literature and online journalism. However, while such handling of secondary sources could perhaps be understood as diminishing the credibility of the bibliography, there are undoubtedly many advantages to this approach. Non-academic sources and non-mainstream or online journalism (e.g. *Gastronomica*) can serve as a venue for the presentation of alternative or new opinions and insights, and can allow us the opportunity to discuss subjects not considered of value or interest by mainstream academia. Until recently, food was exactly this kind of subject, and therefore it is assumed that the inclusion of non-academic sources has contributed to a broader understanding of the field, and thereby added a multiplicity of voices to my research.

As food in Agatha Christie's work has not, to the author's knowledge, been discussed as a separate topic before, this book was constructed as a comprehensive overview of the uses and functions of food in all of her novels. However, in the course of the analysis a number of further questions have arisen, offering various possibilities for expanding the present research or for conducting similar research in other fields. Section 3.3 and 3.4 on gender and food focused especially on the gender transgressions of the two detectives, Miss Marple and Hercule Poirot. However, the texts offer numerous other examples of stereotypical and transgressive eating habits of minor characters. The recurring stereotypes of the matron and the New Woman, both briefly mentioned in section 3.4, invite further analysis. Issues such as dieting and asceticism, or, on the contrary, indulgence in sweets and comfort foods or overeating all appear in the novels and would merit closer attention.

Another aspect that could be addressed in greater detail is the connection of food and rurality, as opposed to food and urbanity. The Golden Age crime novel features a significant shift from urban to rural settings. Such a shift, however, did not occur in American hard-boiled novels which are as a rule set in big cities (Cawelti 1976, 140; Knight 2004, 110). It might prove interesting to observe if the mechanisms of this shift and the reasons behind the American authors' return to the urban setting formerly popularised by Doyle, are connected with food, and, if so, how this process took effect. Although the presence of food in the hard-boiled tradition has already been analysed (e.g. by Saylor or Rippetoe), it is a field which invites further research. Such research might concentrate for example on the contradictions between the gradually feminised classical formula and its successor, the cosy mystery (see the introduction); similarly, another focus may be on the contradictions between this feminised formula and the masculinist hard-boiled tradition. Such research might attempt to uncover the role played by food in creating, sustaining, or subverting these contradictions.

Morality is yet another question which is repeatedly addressed in crime fiction and the morality of eating, or food ethics, is a field that has gained prominence in contemporary food philosophy (see 2.3). The issues of hedonism versus asceticism, of the morality of the body versus that of the mind, and of pleasure versus duty have been introduced, especially in connection with the role of the detective as provider of justice and the ultimately moral figure; however, this topic contains a number of complex problems which would merit closer attention. It might also prove of interest to explore Poirot's hedonism as a method, as well as the use of the body and the senses (both Poirot's and Marple's), rather than the mind as venues of the thinking process.[3] In fact, Christie's novels feature a number of transgressions, not only pertaining to the norms of reasoning, but also to gender (see above), all marked to a certain extent by the characters' food preferences. Reading the stories through these transgressions, whether related to food or not, might lead to new insights into and interpretations of the texts.

Finally, in a number of instances throughout the text, references were made to food-related language. Food language and food idioms are used frequently and in various contexts, either to describe characters, to refer to methods of research, to clues, to place, or to denote time. Although these examples were not given much space within the framework of the present research, they certainly provide fertile ground for further analysis.

The suggestions listed above are just a handful of possible directions that future research might take up; indeed, the interdisciplinary nature of the field of food studies offers almost limitless possibilities. However, the body of analysis presented here serves to answer the question stated at the very beginning of the introduction. There is indeed food in fiction in general, and there is plenty of food in crime fiction. Furthermore, when that food is not taken for granted and the reader asks her/himself why it is there, it can lead to a different and possibly surprising understanding of the analysed text. Just as in society, eating in literature is not mere refuelling. Instead, it is an action ripe with significance, which, when critically examined, can open up alternative meanings of one's own culture.

Notes

1 Hanish, Carol. 1969. "The Personal Is Political." <http://www.carolhanisch.org/CHwritings/PIP.html>

2 For a brief literature overview see Section 2.4.

3 This topic has already been discussed in relation to contemporary culinary mysteries by Nieves Pascual Soler (2009).

APPENDIX A

ANALYSED NOVELS IN CHRONOLOGICAL ORDER

1920	*The Mysterious Affair at Styles*
1922	*The Secret Adversary*
1923	*Murder on the Links*
1924	*The Man in the Brown Suit*
1925	*The Secret of Chimneys*
1926	*The Murder of Roger Ackroyd*
1927	*The Big Four*
1928	*The Mystery of the Blue Train*
1929	*The Seven Dials Mystery*
1930	*The Murder at the Vicarage*
1931	*The Sittaford Mystery*
1932	*Peril at End House*
1933	*Lord Edgware Dies*
1934	*Murder on the Orient Express*
1934	*Three-Act Tragedy*
1934	*Why Didn't They Ask Evans*
1935	*Death in the Clouds*
1936	*The ABC Murders*
1936	*Murder in Mesopotamia*
1936	*Cards on the Table*
1937	*Dumb Witness*
1937	*Death on the Nile*
1938	*Appointment with Death*
1938	*Hercule Poirot's Christmas*
1939	*Murder Is Easy*
1939	*And Then There Were None*
1940	*Sad Cypress*
1940	*One, Two, Buckle My Shoe*
1941	*Evil Under the Sun*
1941	*N or M?*

1942 *The Body in the Library*
1942 *Five Little Pigs*
1942 *The Moving Finger*
1944 *Towards Zero*
1944 *Death Comes as the End*
1945 *Sparking Cyanide*
1946 *The Hollow*
1948 *Taken at the Flood*
1949 *Crooked House*
1950 *A Murder Is Announced*
1951 *They Came to Baghdad*
1952 *Mrs McGinty's Dead*
1952 *They Do It with Mirrors*
1953 *After the Funeral*
1953 *A Pocket Full of Rye*
1954 *Destination Unknown*
1955 *Hickory Dickory Dock*
1956 *Dead Man's Folly*
1957 *4.50 from Paddington*
1958 *Ordeal by Innocence*
1959 *Cat Among the Pigeons*
1961 *The Pale Horse*
1962 *The Mirror Crack'd from Side to Side*
1963 *The Clocks*
1964 *A Caribbean Mystery*
1965 *At Bertram's Hotel*
1966 *Third Girl*
1967 *Endless Night*
1968 *By the Pricking of My Thumbs*
1969 *Hallowe'en Party*
1970 *Passenger to Frankfurt*
1971 *Nemesis*
1972 *Elephants Can Remember*
1973 *Postern of Fate*
1975 *Curtain*
1976 *Sleeping Murder*
1998 *Black Coffee* (originally produced as a theatre play in 1930)

APPENDIX B

PLOT SUMMARIES OF ANALYSED NOVELS

4.50 From Paddington

When Miss Marple's friend Elspeth becomes a witness to a murder committed in a train carriage, Miss Marple understands that this is a case for her. But her health is no longer what it used to be, so she asks young and intelligent Lucy Eylesbarrow to become her spy in Rutherford Hall, where the corpse is supposedly hidden.

The ABC Murders

A serial killer threatens a number of seaside towns in the south of England. Before each of his murders, he sends a letter to Poirot informing him about the place of his next crime. The mysterious murderer seems to have no motive: he chooses his victims based on the first letters of their names.

After the Funeral

At her brother Richard's funeral, Mrs Cora Lansquenet informs the shocked attendees that he did not die of natural causes, but was murdered. Although most of the guests dismiss this piece of information as just another example of Cora's flippant manner, the family lawyer Mr Entwhistle decides to investigate into the matter and asks detective Hercule Poirot to help.

And Then There Were None

Mr Amis, the owner of a luxurious mansion on a deserted island off the coast of Devon, decides to organise a house party to which he invites a diverse group of ten. The individual invitees do not know each other and the host himself is missing. When bad weather cxuts the island off from the mainland, an unknown murderer starts killing the members of the party one after another.

Appointment with Death
The story is set in a hotel in Jerusalem and in the ancient city of Petra. One night at dinner Poirot overhears a conversation about a planned murder. When Mrs Boynton, a tyrannical mother of four is found dead the following night, her children become chief suspects. However, Poirot is not satisfied with this solution and decides to find out what has really happened.

At Bertram's Hotel
In this story, Miss Marple decides to revisit the famous Bertram's Hotel, a place of which she has fond memories from her youth. Bertram's is well known for its nostalgic atmosphere, first-class service, and old-timer inhabitants. But soon after Miss Marple's arrival, the hotel's reputation is damaged by the disappearance of one of the guests and the murder of one of the employees. Both Scotland Yard and Miss Marple begin to investigate the case.

The Big Four
In this story, Hercule Poirot and Captain Hastings become involved in a case of espionage. When Hastings returns from his journey to South America and visits Poirot, he finds out that Poirot was offered a job in Rio and plans to leave London soon. Their meeting is interrupted by the appearance of an unknown man, who seems to be drugged or injured. The only things he is able to say are Poirot's name, the words Li Chang Yen, and the number four. A couple of moments later the man dies. Chief Inspector Japp is summoned and he reveals that the dead man was a former secret service agent. Poirot realises that his job offer in Rio was only a trick to lead him away from the case of the Big Four.

Black Coffee
When physicist Sir Claude Amory discovers that one of his guests has stolen the formula for a deadly explosive he has recently invented, he turns off the lights in the whole house in order to allow the guilty person to return the formula unobserved. However, the criminal takes advantage of the darkness and murders Sir Amory. Captain Hastings and detective Hercule Poirot have also been invited to the house party and Poirot immediately starts to investigate. This book is Charles Osborne's novelisation of Christie's theatre play by the same title.

The Body in the Library

When a dead body of an unknown blonde woman is found in the library of Mr and Mrs Bantry's home, the inhabitants of St. Mary's Mead start gossiping about possible suspects. A number of people have motives. The police have started an investigation, but Mrs Bantry decides to ask her old friend Miss Marple to help.

By the Pricking of my Thumbs

Tommy and Tuppence decide to visit Tommy's ageing Aunt Ada in the Sunny Ridge nursing home. While Tuppence is waiting in the sitting room, Mrs Lancaster, one of the inhabitants of the home, approaches her with a bizarre comment about a child hidden behind a fireplace. After this encounter, Tuppence experiences an uneasy feeling and when Aunt Ada dies and a picture of Mrs Lancster's cottage is found among her possessions, Tuppence decides to visit the place and learn more about the old woman.

Cards on the Table

Hercule Poirot is invited to play a game of bridge at the house of the eccentric Mr Shaitana. The bridge party is composed of four people who committed murder in the past, but managed to escape unpunished, and of four sleuths: Poirot, Mrs Ariadne Oliver, Superintendent Battle of Scotland Yard, and Colonel Race of the secret service. In the course of the evening, Mr Shaitana is murdered and the four investigators attempt to discover which of the four criminals was the murderer in this case.

A Caribbean Mystery

Miss Marple's nephew Raymond West treats her to a luxurious holiday in the Caribbean. When one of the other inhabitants of the hotel, elderly Major Palgrave, dies, Miss Marple refuses to believe that his death was due to his old age and decides to investigate into the matter. She is assisted by the disabled but shrewd millionaire Mr Jason Rafiel.

Cat Among the Pigeons

Meadowbank is a girls' boarding school directed by the strict headmistress Miss Bulstrode. One night two teachers find the dead body of the games mistress in the sports pavilion. Soon afterwards, another death ensues and parents start taking their daughters home. One of the students, Julia Updike, summons Hercule Poirot to help her to solve the case.

The Clocks

When Sheila Webb arrives at the house of Miss Millicent Pebmarsh, who hired her for a typing job, she is immediately struck by the extraordinary number of clocks displayed in the living room. Four of the clocks have stopped at 4:13. When Sheila inspects the room closer, she discovers a man's corpse. At that moment Miss Pebmarsh enters the room and Sheila realises that the woman is blind. Sheila runs out of the house and she accidentally meets agent Colin Lamb. When she describes what she has witnessed, Colin together with Inspector Hardcastle start an investigation.

Crooked House

This novel is set in a mansion on the outskirts of London, which houses the extended family of Mr Aristid Leonides, a wealthy Greek immigrant. When Mr Leonides dies under unusual circumstances, all of his family members become possible suspects, as each of them benefits from the death of their rich relative. Charles Hayward, the fiancé of Mr Leonides's granddaughter, begins an insider investigation of the case.

Curtain: Poirot's Final Case

In the last Hercule Poirot mystery the detective returns to the Styles manor, the setting of the first novel of the Poirot series. Styles has been turned into a guest hotel. Poirot has collected a number of newspaper articles about seemingly unconnected murders, and he becomes convinced that all of the crimes have been committed by the same murderer, one of the guests at Styles.

Dead Man's Folly

The mystery writer Ariadne Oliver is in charge of organising a treasure hunt in George Stubbs's mansion. While she is preparing the event, she experiences an overwhelming feeling of imminent danger. Mrs Oliver's instinct proves to be correct. The girl assigned the role of victim in the treasure hunt is murdered during the game. When the corpse is discovered, Mrs Oliver asks Poirot for help with the investigation.

Death Comes as the End

This story takes place in ancient Egypt about four thousand years ago. When the mortuary priest Imhotep brings home his young concubine Nofret, the members of his family strongly disapprove. Nofret becomes the target of their threats and harassment. As a result, she complains to her husband. To punish his family, Imhotep decides to disinherit everyone except for Nofret. Soon after his message is delivered, someone murders Nofret.

Death in the Clouds
Hercule Poirot is taking the plane from Paris back to England. During the flight, the stewards notice that one of the passengers, the wealthy Madame Giselle, has been poisoned. It is certain that one of the other passengers is the culprit and after the plane lands in Croydon, Poirot together with the police begin an investigation.

Death on the Nile
Newlyweds Linnet Ridgeway and Simon Doyle are spending their honeymoon in Egypt. They are joined by Simon's jealous ex-fiancée Jackie who still hopes to win back Simon's favour. The three of them embark on a sailing trip on the Nile, where they meet the famous detective Hercule Poirot. When Linnet is found shot in her cabin, Jackie becomes the chief suspect.

Destination Unknown
This thriller centres on a series of mysterious disappearances of renowned scientists. British secret agent Jessop is assigned the task of finding the missing women and men. He hires Hilary Craven as a spy. Hilary, masked as the wife of one of the scientists, travels to a research centre in the Atlas mountains, where she discovers the headquarters of an international crime syndicate.

Dumb Witness
Emily Arundel is very wealthy, but also strict and frugal. Each of her relatives has financial problems and each would welcome financial help from their rich aunt. Thus, when the elderly Miss Arundell dies, none of her family members investigates the cause of her death. However, before her demise Miss Arundell was able to send a letter to Hercule Poirot informing him about her suspicion that someone is planning her murder.

Elephants Can Remember
In this novel Ariadne Oliver is invited to a literary luncheon where she becomes acquainted with Mrs Burton-Cox. Mrs Burton-Cox insists that Mrs Oliver take up the investigation into a suicide case that took place ten years ago. As the victims in the case were the parents of one of Mrs Oliver's goddaughters, she decides to look into the case. As with the rest of her investigations, she asks her friend Hercule Poirot to assist her.

Endless Night

Contrary to the wishes of her family, rich heiress Ellie Guteman marries her working class boyfriend Michael Rogers. The young couple hire a famous architect to build them a modern home. Soon afterwards Ellie's secretary Greta is invited to stay at the house with the newlyweds. The relationship between Michael and Greta is fraught with hostility; moreover, Ellie gets into a conflict with a gypsy living in the neighbourhood. One day Ellie has gone missing and a couple of hours later her dead body is discovered.

Evil Under the Sun

Hercule Poirot is spending his vacation in a seaside resort at the Devon coast. One day a corpse of a woman is found at Pixy Cove near Poirot's hotel. The murdered woman is the well-known actress Arlena Stuart. Poirot soon discovers that all of the hotel guests are connected to Arlena in various ways. However, each of them also has an alibi for the time of the murder.

Five Little Pigs

Miss Carla Lemarchant visits Hercule Poirot to offer him a job. She wants him to investigate the murder of her father. The case is complicated by the fact that the murder happened sixteen years ago and the purported culprit, Carla's mother, has been found guilty and sentenced to life imprisonment. Nevertheless, before her death, Carla's mother left behind a letter, in which she professed her innocence. Poirot decides to attempt to reconstruct the case.

Hallowe'en Party

During a Halloween party, one of the invited children, Joyce Reynolds brags about being a witness to a murder. Later that night her murdered corpse is discovered. Joyce has been drowned in a bucket of water prepared for an apple-bobbing contest. Mrs Oliver, who was present at the scene of the crime, travels to London to consult detective Hercule Poirot.

Hercule Poirot's Christmas

This story is set on Christmas Day. All of the relatives of the rich patriarch Simon Lee have been unexpectedly invited to spend the holidays in his mansion. However, Mr Lee is found murdered the following morning. As each member of the house party will benefit from the elderly man's death, all of them become suspects.

Hickory Dickory Dock

After a series of petty thefts take place at a students' hostel in Hickory Road, London, the warden Mrs Hubbard asks Poirot to help her to discover the offender. Soon afterwards, one of the residents of the hostel is found poisoned with an overdose of morphine. Poirot attempts to solve the second crime, as well, but the suspicious owner of the hostel, Mrs Nicoletis hinders his progress.

The Hollow

Poirot has been invited to have Sunday lunch at the house of the eccentric Lady Angkatell. When he arrives, he witnesses a shocking scene: Gerda Christow, one of the house guests, is holding a gun in her hand and on the floor next to her lies the dead body of her husband John. However, despite the fact that Gerda was holding the weapon, Poirot realises that a number of the other members of the household had equal opportunity of committing the crime.

Lord Edgware Dies

Hercule Poirot and Captain Hastings attend a theatre performance where they meet the American actress Jane Wilkinson. Later that night, Jane asks Poirot to help her to persuade her husband, Lord Edgware to file for a divorce. Poirot agrees to help, however when he discusses the matter with Edgware, the man claims he has already taken the necessary legal steps. Soon after his conversation with Poirot, Lord Edgware is found stabbed to death.

The Man in the Brown Suit

The protagonist, Anne Bedingfield witnesses an accident in one of the stations of the London underground: a passer-by falls down onto the rails and dies of electric shock. A man wearing a brown suit announces that he is a doctor. He inspects the deceased, confirms his death, and disappears. However, he loses a scrap of paper. When Anne picks it up, she realises that the sentence written on it contains a coded message, and she decides to decipher it.

The Mirror Crack'd from Side to Side

In this story the peaceful atmosphere of St. Mary's Mead has been destroyed by real estate development. Miss Marple decides to explore the new suburbs and meets the annoying Heather Badcock. Soon afterwards Marple hears surprising news: Heather died after drinking a poisoned cocktail at a high society party. As the crime seems extremely unlikely, Miss Marple decides to begin an investigation into the case.

The Moving Finger

The inhabitants of the rural town of Lymstock receive a series of threatening anonymous letters. The threats force Mrs Symmington, one of the receivers, to commit suicide. Although there is no evidence of foul play, Miss Marple believes that something is amiss. When the murdered body of Agnes the maid is discovered in the Symmingtons' house, the police, as well as Miss Marple, begin to investigate into both of the cases.

Mrs McGinty's Dead

When Mrs McGinty is murdered, her lodger James Bentley is the only suspect. However, Superintendent Spense is convinced of Bentley's innocence. He calls Hercule Poirot to help him investigate the case. However, none of the villagers are willing to assist in the investigation. After Poirot comes across a newspaper clipping about a long-forgotten murder among the possessions of the deceased, he realises that the case might have far-reaching implications.

The Murder at the Vicarage

St. Mary's Mead is a stereotypical calm English village. However, one day the murdered body of Colonel Protheroe is found in the vicar's study. Protheroe was generally disliked by the villagers. Each of them has a motive, and two of them even confess to having committed the crime. The police are unable to gain any information from the suspicious and secretive locals, which makes them realise that they will need an insider's help in order to solve the crime.

Murder In Mesopotamia

This story is set at an archaeological site in Hassanieh, Iraq. Nurse Amy Leatheran, who arrives at the archaeological camp to take care of Louise Leidner, the wife of the head archaeologist, immediately notices the hostility between the individual inhabitants of the camp. A week later Mrs Leidner is found murdered. All of the members of the dig are possible suspects and detective Hercule Poirot is summoned to discover which one of them is the murderer.

A Murder Is Announced

When a newspaper advertisement announces that a murder will be committed on Friday, October 29, in Miss Blackock's house, the inhabitants of the rural town of Chipping Cleghorn believe that the announcement is a prank. However, when the announced murder really takes place, the police are called to investigate the case. As they seem to be unable to solve the mystery, Miss Marple decides to help.

Murder Is Easy
After years spent in India, Luke Fitzwilliam returns to England. During his train journey to London he meets an elderly lady who confides in him that she is headed to the offices of the Scotland Yard to inform them about the crimes that have been happening in her hometown of Wychwood. When Luke learns that the lady accidentally died before she was able to talk to the police, he decides that he must investigate the case.

The Murder of Roger Ackroyd
When Mrs Ferrars dies, all evidence suggests that her death was a suicide. However, none of the inhabitants of King's Abbot understands why she decided to take her life before her impending wedding to the wealthy Roger Ackroyd. The following day Mr Ackroyd invites the local doctor and imparts Mrs Ferrars's secret to him. But as soon as the doctor leaves the manor, Mr Ackroyd is found dead.

The Murder on the Links
Hercule Poirot receives an urgent letter from the South American millionaire Mr Renauld, who claims to be in imminent danger of death. Poirot sets off for Mr Renauld's estate immediately. In spite of his hurry, he arrives too late. Mr Renauld has been stabbed to death. Poirot starts to investigate. Soon afterwards another stabbed corpse is discovered on the estate.

Murder on the Orient Express
The Orient Express sets on its three-day journey across Europe. It is forced to stop in the middle of the night, because the railway is blocked by a snowdrift. In the morning the passengers find out that one of them has been stabbed to death in his sleep. Hercule Poirot, who happens to be on board the train, takes up the investigation of the case.

The Mysterious Affair at Styles
Mrs Cavendish, the owner of the Styles manor, is poisoned by strychnine added to her coffee. A number of the members of her family had a motive to commit the crime. However, only after the intervention of Hercule Poirot, an eccentric Belgian refugee who lives on the premises is the true

identity of the criminal uncovered. This is the first title in the Hercule Poirot series, which later proved to be Christie's most popular one.

The Mystery of the Blue Train
The luxurious Blue Train transports wealthy passengers from Calais to the French Riviera. Among the passengers is Ruth Kettering, the owner of the most valuable ruby in the world. A day after the beginning of the train journey, Ruth's murdered corpse is discovered and the invaluable stone is missing. Ruth's father, an American millionaire, asks Hercule Poirot to find the stolen gem and to catch her daughter's murderer.

N or M?
It is World War Two and Tommy has been hired by the secret service to search for undercover criminals. This time he travels to the seaside town of Leahampton where two German spies working under the code names "M" and "N" are purportedly hidden. Although Tuppence was not hired to participate, she decides to join Tommy on his mission.

Nemesis
Miss Marple is reading her daily papers and she notices an obituary announcing the death of an acquaintance, Mr Rafiel. A couple of days later Marple receives a letter with an unusual offer: Mr Rafiel left her twenty thousand pounds, which she can collect on condition that she solves an unspecified crime case. Although Miss Marple is given almost no clues and very few instructions, she decides to take up the task.

One, Two, Buckle my Shoe
Hercule Poirot has arranged an appointment with his dentist, Dr Morley. Only a couple of hours later, Inspector Japp informs Poirot that Dr Morley was found shot in his office. While the police classify the death as suicide, Inspector Japp believes that the dentist was murdered, and he decides to consult with Poirot.

Ordeal by Innocence
Mr and Mrs Argyl, a childless couple, decided to adopt five immigrant children, including Jacko. Now an adult, Jacko asks his foster mother to lend him money. She refuses and a heated argument ensues. Soon afterwards Mrs Argyl is murdered and Jacko is arrested and sentences to life imprisonment. However, a year and a half later a new witness is discovered and investigation has to be resumed.

The Pale Horse
An elderly priest is called to a woman's deathbed. After he has heard the dying woman's confession, she hands him a piece of paper with a list of names written on it. On his way home, the priest is murdered. When the protagonist Mark Easterbrook learns that the list was found in one of the priest's shoes, he decides to discover what the people featured on it had in common.

Passenger to Frankfurt
In this spy novel Sir Stafford Nye is approached by an unknown woman at Frankfurt airport. The woman claims that unless he exchanges passports with her, she will be in imminent danger of death on her flight to London. Nye agrees to help her. However, as a result he becomes an unwilling participant in a case of global espionage.

Peril at End House
During his vacation in Cornwall, Hercule Poirot meets the young heiress and owner of the End House, Nick Buckley. Nick has been a victim of a number of attempted murders. In order to ensure Nick's safety, Poirot arranges for her to be sent to a hospital, where she is forbidden from seeing any visitors. However, during her hospital stay Nick becomes the victim of yet another murder attempt, when someone sends her a box of poisoned chocolates.

A Pocket Full of Rye
In this novel, the criminal chooses a nursery rhyme as the theme for the seemingly unconnected murders of businessman Rex Fortescue and Gladys the maid. In the course of her investigation into these two deaths, Miss Marple uncovers a number of crimes from the past. All of them have a connection to Mr Fortescue's gold-mining business in Africa.

Postern of Fate
Tommy and Tuppence are now retired and they purchase an old house in the country. When they move in, they discover an encoded message which describes a crime that took place sixty years ago. Tommy and Tuppence decide to investigate into the matter, and with the help of the secret service they are eventually able to solve a spying case.

Sad Cypress
Elinor Carlisle has been accused of and is tried for the murder of Mary Gerrard, the protégée of Elinor's rich aunt. Elinor is the only person who

has a motive and there is a large amount of evidence against her. However, doctor Peter Lord, who is secretly in love with Elinor, believes in her innocence and persuades Hercule Poirot to attempt to discover the truth about the case.

The Secret Adversary
Tommy Beresford and Prudence Cowley, nicknamed Tuppence, have just returned from their First World War service. In order to earn money, they decide to establish a detective agency, which they name "The Young Adventurers, Ltd." When they publish an advertisement in the newspaper, they are hired to find a missing American, Jane Finn, who allegedly possesses an important diplomatic document.

The Secret of Chimneys
Anthony Cade works as a tour guide in Africa. When he is asked to impersonate a friend and deliver a manuscript to London instead of him, he accepts the offer, hoping to experience some excitement. However, after his arrival in England, he unintentionally becomes involved in a murder. In order to prove his innocence, Anthony decides to find the criminal.

The Seven Dials Mystery
This story is also set in the Chimneys mansion. Sir Oswald Coote and his wife have invited a couple of young men and women to a house party. One of them, Gerry Wade, is notorious for being a late riser. His friends decide to play a prank on him: they set eight alarm clocks to go off the following morning in Gerry's bedroom. When the clocks fail to wake Gerry up, his friends enter his room to see what the matter is, and they discover that Gerry has been murdered.

The Sittaford Mystery
A group of six people are confined in their home in the secluded village of Sittaford during a snowstorm. They decide to pass the time summoning spirits of the dead. One of the ghosts informs the gathering that their friend, Captain Trevelyan, has been killed. Soon the friends discover that the ghost's message was true. The only suspect in the case is Trevelyan's nephew Jim. However, Jim's fiancée Emily is convinced of his innocence. She conducts an unofficial investigation with the aim of uncovering the real murderer.

Sleeping Murder

When Gwenda Reed returns to England after years in New Zealand, she unwittingly buys the house in which she used to live as a small child. However, when Gwenda moves in, she is haunted by vague memories of a crime she witnessed in her childhood. She asks Miss Marple to help find out the truth about the long-forgotten case.

Sparkling Cyanide

Rosemary, the wife of George Barton died in the Luxembourg restaurant during her birthday party. All of her family are convinced that she committed suicide. However, a year later George receives an anonymous letter informing him that Rosemary was murdered. In an attempt to uncover the murderer, George decides to re-enact the fateful birthday party.

Taken at the Flood

Until his death, Gordon Cloade had always provided financial support and security for his family. However, Mr Cloade's will established that his young wife Rosaleen should become the sole heiress to his estate. The rest of the family are dissatisfied with this decision. They insist that Rosaleen should provide them with financial support, but Rosaleen's brother David forbids her from doing so. One day a man who claims to have evidence that Rosaleen's marriage to Gordon Cloade was void attempts to blackmail David. Soon afterwards, the blackmailer's murdered corpse is discovered and Hercule Poirot arrives in order to investigate the case.

They Came to Baghdad

A secret meeting of the representatives of world powers is held in Baghdad. However, the meeting is jeopardised by an international terrorist organisation. At the same time, Victoria Jones travels to Baghdad to find the man with whom she has fallen in love. As the story proceeds, Victoria accidentally gets involved in an international conspiracy.

They Do It with Mirrors

Miss Marple decides to visit Ruth van Rydock, a friend from her youth. Ruth tells Miss Marple that her sister's husband has decided to turn the family estate into a home for juvenile delinquents. Ruth is worried about the safety of her sister and asks Miss Marple to pay her a visit and make sure that everything is in order.

Third Girl

Norma Restarick visits Hercule Poirot in order to confess that she might have committed a murder. However, before Poirot is able to ask for any details, the young woman changes her mind about the confession and leaves his office. When Poirot attempts to find her and talk to her, he learns that the she has gone missing.

Three Act Tragedy

The famous theatre actor Sir Charles Cartwright is hosting a dinner party. During the event, Reverend Babbington, one of the invitees, dies after drinking a cocktail. When the cocktail glass is analysed, no traces of poison are discovered, therefore it is ruled that the elderly Reverend Babbington died of natural causes. However, a few weeks later another man dies in the same manner. Detective Hercule Poirot is summoned to help to shed light on the case.

Towards Zero

Lady Tressilian invites a diverse house party to her seaside mansion each summer. This year the famous tennis player Nevile Strange is one of the invitees. However, there are a number of unresolved conflicts among the houseguests. Thc tension culminates in the murder of the hostess. Although the evidence indicates that Strange is the culprit, Superintendent Battle does not believe him guilty and decides to conduct further investigation.

Why Didn't They Ask Evans?

During a game of golf in the seaside town of Marchbolt, Bobby James discovers a badly injured man lying unconscious near the links. His golf partner, Doctor Thomas runs to call help. Unfortunately, the injured man dies before the doctor is able to return, and Bobby is the only one to hear his last words: "Why didn't they ask Evans?"

BIBLIOGRAPHY

Analysed Novels

Christie, Agatha [1957] 2002. *4.50 from Paddington*. London: HarperCollins.

—. [1936] 2007. *The ABC Murders*. London: HarperCollins.

—. [1953] 2001. *After the Funeral*. London: HarperCollins.

—. [1939] 2007. *And Then There Were None*. London: HarperCollins.

—. [1938] 2001. *Appointment with Death*. London: HarperCollins.

—. [1965] 2002. *At Bertram's Hotel*. London: HarperCollins.

—. [1927] 2002. *The Big Four*. London: HarperCollins.

—. [1942] 2007. *The Body in the Library*. London: HarperCollins.

—. [1968] 2001. *By the Pricking of My Thumbs*. London: HarperCollins.

—. [1936] 2008. *Cards on the Table*. London: HarperCollins.

—. [1964] 2002. *A Caribbean Mystery*. London: HarperCollins.

—. [1959] 2002. *Cat Among the Pigeons*. London: HarperCollins.

—. [1963] 2002. *The Clocks*. London: HarperCollins.

—. [1949] 2002. *Crooked House*. London: HarperCollins.

—. [1975] 2002. *Curtain: Poirot's Last Case*. London: HarperCollins.

—. [1956] 2008. *Dead Man's Folly*. London: HarperCollins.

—. [1945] 2001. *Death Comes as the End*. London: HarperCollins.

—. [1935] 2001. *Death in the Clouds*. London: HarperCollins.

—. [1937] 2007. *Death on the Nile*. London: HarperCollins.

—. [1954] 2003. *Destination Unknown*. London: HarperCollins.

—. [1937] 2002. *Dumb Witness*. London: HarperCollins.

—. [1972] 2002. *Elephants Can Remember*. London: HarperCollins.

—. [1967] 2007. *Endless Night*. London: HarperCollins.

—. [1941] 2001. *Evil Under the Sun*. London: HarperCollins.

—. [1943] 2001. *Five Little Pigs*. London: HarperCollins.

—. [1969] 2001. *Hallowe'en Party*. London: HarperCollins.

—. [1938] 2001. *Hercule Poirot's Christmas*. London: HarperCollins.

—. [1955] 2002. *Hickory Dickory Dock*. London: HarperCollins.

—. [1946] 2011. *The Hollow*. New York: HarperCollins.

—. [1933] 2007. *Lord Edgware Dies*. London: HarperCollins.

—. [1924] 2002. *The Man in the Brown Suit*. London: HarperCollins.

—. [1962] 2002. *The Mirror Crack'd from Side to Side*. London: HarperCollins.
—. [1943] 2002. *The Moving Finger*. London: HarperCollins.
—. [1952] 2002. *Mrs McGinty's Dead*. London: HarperCollins.
—. [1930] 2002. *The Murder at the Vicarage*. London: HarperCollins.
—. [1936] 2001. *Murder in Mesopotamia*. London: HarperCollins.
—. [1950] 2002. *A Murder Is Announced*. London: HarperCollins.
—. [1939] 2002. *Murder Is Easy*. London: HarperCollins.
—. [1926] 2007. *The Murder of Roger Ackroyd*. London: HarperCollins.
—. [1923] 2001. *Murder on the Links*. London: HarperCollins.
—. [1934] 2001. *Murder on the Orient Express*. London: HarperCollins.
—. [1920] 2002. *The Mysterious Affair at Styles: Hercule Poirot's First Case*. Norwood: Deodand Publishing.
—. [1928] 2001. *The Mystery of the Blue Train*. London: HarperCollins.
—. [1941] 2001. *N or M?*. London: HarperCollins.
—. [1971] 2006. *Nemesis*. London: HarperCollins.
—. [1940] 2002. *One, Two, Buckle My Shoe*. London: HarperCollins.
—. [1961] 2011. *The Pale Horse*. London: HarperCollins.
—. [1970] 2003. *Passenger to Frankfurt*. London: HarperCollins.
—. [1932] 2001. *Peril at End House*. London: HarperCollins.
—. [1953] 1985. *A Pocket Full of Rye*. Glasgow: Fontana Collins.
—. [1973] 2001. *Postern of Fate*. London: HarperCollins.
—. [1940] 2001. *Sad Cypress*. London: HarperCollins.
—. [1922] 2001. *The Secret Adversary*. London: HarperCollins.
—. [1925] 2001. *The Secret of Chimneys*. London: HarperCollins.
—. [1929] 2001. *The Seven Dials Mystery*. London: HarperCollins.
—. [1931] 2002. *The Sittaford Mystery*. London: HarperCollins.
—. [1976] 2002. *Sleeping Murder*. London: HarperCollins.
—. [1945] 2002. *Sparkling Cyanide*. London: HarperCollins.
—. [1948] 2002. *Taken at the Flood*. London: HarperCollins.
—. [1951] 2003. *They Came to Baghdad*. London: HarperCollins.
—. [1952] 2002. *They Do It with Mirrors*. London: HarperCollins.
—. [1966] 2002. *Third Girl*. London: HarperCollins.
—. [1935] 2002. *Three Act Tragedy*. London: HarperCollins.
—. [1944] 2008. *Towards Zero*. London: HarperCollins.
—. [1934] 2001. *Why Didn't They Ask Evans?* London: HarperCollins.

Works Cited

Acocella, Joan. 2010. "Queen Of Crime." *New Yorker* 86 (24): 82-88. *Academic Search Complete, EBSCOhost.*

Adolph, Andrea. 2009. *Food and Femininity in Twentieth-Century British Women's Fiction.* Farnham: Ashgate.

Agassi, Joseph. 1982. "The Detective Novel and Scientific Method." *Poetics Today* 3 (1, *Types of the Novel Semiotics of Social Discourse*): 99-108.

Akers-Jordan, Cathy. 1998: "Ellery Queen: Forgotten Master Detective." PhD Diss. U of Michigan-Flint.

Akersten, Teresa. 2010. "The Mystery Of Agatha Christie." *Read* 59 (13): 14-16. *MasterFILE Premier*, EBSCO*host*.

Allen, Dick and David Chacko, eds. 1974. *Detective Fiction: Crime and Compromise.* San Diego: Harcourt Brace Jovanovich.

Allen, John S. 2012. "Food and Memory." *Harvard UP Blog*, May 18. <http://harvardpress.typepad.com/hup_publicity/2012/05/food-and-memory-john-allen.html>

Allhoff, Fritz and Dave Monroe, eds. 2007. *Food and Philosophy: Eat Think and Be Merry.* Malden: Blackwell Publishing Ltd.

Anderson, Benedict. [1983] 2006. *Imagined Communities: Reflections on the Origin and Spread of Nationalism.* Revised ed. London: Verso.

Angier, Natalie. 2009. "Sorry, Vegans: Brussels Sprouts Like to Live, Too." *The New York Times*, December 21. <http://www.nytimes.com/2009/12/22/science/22angi.html?_r=0>

Aquinas, Thomas. [1265-1274] 2000. *Summa Theologica.* 5 vols. Raleigh: Hayes Barton P.

Archibald, Diana Christine. 1998. "Constructing Home Sweet Home: Domesticity and Emigration in the Victorian Novel." PhD Diss. Washington State U.

Aristotle. [350 BC] 2009. *Nicomachean Ethics.* Translated by W.D. Ross. <http://classics.mit.edu/Aristotle/nicomachaen.html>

Ashley, Bob, Joanne Hollows, Steve Jones and Ben Taylor. 2004. *Food and Cultural Studies.* Oxon and New York: Routledge.

Atkins, Peter J, Peter Lummel and Derek J Oddy, eds. 2008. *Food and the City in Europe Since 1800.* Abingdon, Oxon: Ashgate Publishing.

Auden, Wystan Hugh. 1948. "The Guilty Vicarage: Notes on the Detective Story, by an Addict." *Harper's Magazine*, May.

Aydelotte, William. 1967. "The Detective Story as a Historical Source." In *The Popular Arts: A Critical Reader*, edited by Irving Deer and Harriet Deer, 132-154. New York: Scribner's.

Bailey, Penny. 2012. “Feature: Keeping Time—Circadian Clocks.” *Wellcome Trust*, November 2. <http://blog.wellcome.ac.uk/2012/11/12/feature-keeping-time-circadian-clocks/>

Bakhtin, Mikhail. [1965] 1984. *Rabelais and His World*. Translated by Hélène Iswolsky. Bloomington: Indiana UP.

Balcomb Lane, Charlotte. 1994. “Fast Break: Breakfast at the Drive-Through, It’s Quick, Cheap and There’s No Dishes to Wash, Who Cares What It Tastes Like?” *Sun Sentinel*, April 14. <http://search.proquest.com/docview/388696833?accountid=16775>

Bartlett, Frederic. "A Theory of Remembering." In *Remembering: A Study in Experimental and Social Psychology*. Cambridge: Cambridge UP. e-book. <http://www.bartlett.psychol.cam.ac.uk/TheoryOfRemembering.htm>

Barthes, Roland. [1957] 2001. *Mythologies*. Translated by Annette Lavers. New York: Hill and Wang.

—. 1974. *S/Z*. Translated by Richard Miller. Malden: Blackwell Publishing.

—. [1961] 2008. “Toward a Psychosociology of Contemporary Food Consumption.” In *Food and Culture: A Reader*. 2nd ed., edited by Carole M. Counihan and Penny van Esterik, 28-35. New York: Routledge.

Beardsworth, Alan, Alan Brynan, Teresa Keil, Jackie Goode, Cheryl Haslam and Emma Lancashire. 2002. “Women, Men and Food: The Significance of Gender for Nutritional Attitudes and Choices.” *British Food Journal* 104 (7): 470-491.

Beardsworth, Alan and Teresa Keil. 1997. *Sociology on the Menu: An Invitation to the Study of Food and Society*. London and New York: Routledge.

Belasco, Warren J. 2008. *Food: The Key Concepts*. Oxford and New York: Berg.

—. 2006. *Meals to Come: A History of the Future of Food*. Berkeley and Los Angeles: U of California P.

Bentley, Amy. 1994. “American Gastro-Anomie.” Review. of *Paradox of Plenty. A Social History of Eating in Modern America*, by Harvey Levenstein. *Reviews in American History* 22 (3): 523-529.

Bevan, David, ed. 1988. *Literary Gastronomy*. Amsterdam: Rodopi B.V.

Blake, Megan K., Jody Mellor and Lucy Crane. 2010. "Buying Local Food: Shopping Practices, Place, And Consumption Networks In Defining Food As ‘Local." *Annals Of The Association Of American*

Geographers 100 (2): 409-426. *Academic Search Complete, EBSCOhost.*

Bosman, Julie. 2008. "Tapes Offer New Clues to a Master of Mystery." *The New York Times*, September 14. <http://www.nytimes.com/2008/09/15/books/15agatha.html?_r=0>

Bourdeau, Louis. [1894] 2005. *Histoire de l'alimentation.* Adamant Media Corporation, Elibron Classics. PDF e-book.

Bourdieu, Pierre. [1979] 1984. *Distinction: A Social Critique of the Judgement of Taste.* Translated by Richard Nice. Cambridge, Massachusetts: Harvard UP.

—. 1997. "The Forms of Capital." In *Education, Culture, Economy, Society*, edited by A.H. Halsey, Hugh Lauder, Phillip Brown and Amy Stuart Wells, 46-58. Oxford: Oxford UP.

Briganti, Chiara and Kathy Mezei. 2006. *Domestic Modernism, the Interwar Novel, and E. H. Young.* Aldershot: Ashgate.

Brown, James W. 1984. Fictional Meals and Their Function in the French Novel, 1789-1848. Toronto: U of Toronto P.

Brown, Matthew. 2007. "Picky Eating Is a Moral Failing." In *Food and Philosophy: Eat, Think and Be Merry*, edited by Fritz Allhoff and Dave Monroe, 192-207. Malden: Blackwell Publishing.

Browne, Ray B and Pat Browne, eds. 2001. *The Guide to United States Popular Culture.* Madison: The U of Wisconsin P.

Burgoine Thomas. 2010. "Collecting accurate secondary foodscape data: A reflection on the trials and tribulations." *Appetite* 55: 522–27.

Burnett, John. 2004. *England Eats Out: 1830-Present.* Harlow: Pearson Education Limited.

Burton Smith, Kevin. 2010. "Murder on the Menu." *Mystery Scene* 116. <http://www.mysteryscenemag.com/index.php?option=com_content&view=article&id=2754:murder-on-the-menu&catid=20:articles&Itemid=191>

Cargill, Kima. 2007. "Desire, Ritual, and Cuisine." *Psychoanalytic Review* 94 (2): 315-332.

Carnegie, Charles V. 2002. *Postnationalism Prefigured: Caribbean Borderlands.* Piscataway: Rutgers UP.

Carson, David. 2009. "The Abduction Of Sherlock Holmes." *International Journal of Police Science and Management* 11 (2): 193-202. *Academic Search Complete*, EBSCO*host*.

Carter, Ronald and John McRae. 2001. *The Routledge History of Literature in English.* 2nd ed. Oxon: Routledge.

Carvajal, Doreen. 1997. "Be Thankful This Isn't a Story about Cannibalism." *The New York Times*, November 16..

<http://www.nytimes.com/1997/11/16/weekinreview/be-thankful-this-isn-t-a-story-about-cannibalism.html>

Cawelti, John G. 1976. *Adventure, Mystery, and Romance: Formula Stories as Art and Popular Culture.* Chicago: U of Chicago P.

Chandler, Raymond. 1950. "The Simple Art of Murder." In *The American Literature Archive*, edited by Brian A. Bremen. Accessed April 25, 2015. <http://www.en.utexas.edu/amlit/amlitprivate/scans/chandlerart.html>

Chaney, David. 2001. Review of *Eating Out: Social Differentiation, Consumption and Pleasure*, by Alan Warde and Lydia Martens. *Canadian Journal of Sociology* 26 (3): 525-7. <http://search.proquest.com/docview/220532673?accountid=16775>

Chesterton, G. K. [1901] 1974. "A Defence of Detective Stories." In *Detective Fiction: Crime and Compromise*, edited by Dick Allen and David Chacko, 384-386. San Diego: Harcourt Brace Jovanovich.

Christie, Agatha. 2011. *An Autobiography.* New York: HarperCollins.

—. 2012. *The Mousetrap and Other Plays.* Reprinted. New York: HarperCollins.

—. [1932] 2002. *The Thirteen Problems.* London: HarperCollins.

—. [1948] 2012. *The Witness for the Prosecution and Other Stories.* New York: HarperCollins.

—. 2012. "Why I Got Fed Up with Poirot." 1945. *The Guardian*, September 28. <http://www.guardian.co.uk/books/2012/sep/28/agatha-christie-why-i-got-fed-up-with-poirot>

—. 2010. "Why They Wanted to Take 20 Years off Poirot (and Give Him a Girlfriend!)." *Mail on Sunday*, July 11. *Newspaper Source, EBSCOhost.*

Coe, Andrew. 2009. *Chop Suey: A Cultural History of Chinese Food in the United States*. Oxford: Oxford UP.

Collins, Glenn. 2012. "Creating a Page Turner With Murder and Mealtime." *The New York Times*, July 16. <http://www.nytimes.com/2012/07/18/dining/mystery-writers-combine-murder-and-mealtime.html?_r=0>

Counihan, Carole M. 1999. *The Anthropology of Food and Body: Gender, Meaning, and Power.* New York and London: Routledge.

Counihan, Carole M. and Penny Van Esterik, eds. 2008. *Food and Culture: A Reader.* 2nd ed New York: Routledge.

Craig, Patricia. 2009. "Clues to Christie's mind." *Irish Times*, September 26. *Newspaper Source*, EBSCO*host.*

Crisp, Roger. 2006. "Hedonism Reconsidered." *Philosophy and Phenomenological Research* 73 (3): 619-645.

Curran, John. 2011. *Agatha Christie's Secret Notebooks: Fifty Years of Mysteries in the Making.* New York: HarperCollins.

Curtin, Deane W and Lisa Maree Heldke, eds. 1992. *Cooking, Eating, Thinking: Transformative Philosophies of Food.* Bloomington: Indiana UP.

Dalby, Andrew. 2000. *Dangerous Tastes: The Story of Spices.* Berkeley and Los Angeles: U of California P.

"Dame Agatha Christie." 2013. *Columbia Electronic Encyclopedia.* 6th ed. *MasterFILE Premier, EBSCOhost.*

Davidson, Alan. 2006. *The Oxford Companion to Food.* 2nd ed Oxford: Oxford UP.

Davidson, Edward H. 1957. *Poe: A Critical Study.* Cambridge, MA: Belknap-Harvard UP.

Davies, Gary. 1997. "Time, Food Shopping and Food Preparation: Some Attitudinal Linkages." *British Food Journal* 99 (3): n. pag. *<http://search.proquest.com/docview/225145512?accountid=16775>*

DeLucia, Matt. 2006. "Thomas Keller: The Evolution of the Modern Chef." *Restaurant Insider* 2 (1). <http://www.nyrestaurantinsider.com/jan2006_keller.asp>

Demko, George J. 2006. "Criminous Places: The Geography of Mysteries." *G. J. Demko's Landscapes of Crime.* <http://www.dartmouth.edu/~gjdemko/criminous_places.htm>

Deutsch, Tracey. 2010. *Building a Housewife's Paradise: Gender, Politics, and American Grocery Stores in the Twentieth Century.* Chapel Hill: The U of North Caroline P.

Dixey, Rachael. 1996. "Gender Perspectives on Food and Cooking Skills." *British Food Journal* 98 (10): n. pag. <http://search.proquest.com/docview/225139886?accountid=16775>

Dorn, Jennifer. 1997. "The Literary World Of Agatha Christie." *British Heritage* 18 (5): 50. *MasterFILE Premier, EBSCOhost.*

Douglas, Mary. [1966] 2002. *Purity and Danger: An Analysis of Concepts of Pollution and Taboo.* Abingdon, Oxon: Routledge Classics.

Du Bois, Christine M, Chee-Beng Tan and Sidney W Mintz, eds. 2008. *The World of Soy.* Singapore: National U of Singapore P.

Dube, B. 2006. "(Dis)empowering Women: The Gaze in Barbara Makhalisa's Selected Works." In *African Womanhood in Zimbabwean Literature: New Critical Perspectives on Women's Literature in African Languages*, edited by Zifikile Mguni, Munashe Furusa and Ruby Magosvongwe, 24-41. Harare: College P.

Dzirkalis, Anna M. 2007. "Investigating the Female Detective: Gender Paradoxes in Popular British Mystery Fiction, 1864--1930." PhD Diss. Ohio University.

Edge, John T. 2011. "Picnic in the Democratic Forest." *Creative Nonfiction* 41: n. pag. <https://www.creativenonfiction.org/online-reading/picnic-democratic-forest>

Edwards, John S.A. 2013. "The foodservice industry: Eating out is more than just a meal." *Food Quality and Preference* 27 (2): n.pag. *Academic Search Complete, EBSCOhost.*

Epstein, Rebecca L. 2005. "Crime and Nourishment." PhD diss. U of California, Los Angeles.

Erdmann, Eva. 2009. "Nationality International: Detective Fiction in the Late Twentieth Century." In *Investigating Identities: Questions of Identity in Contemporary International Crime Fiction*, edited by Marieke Krajenbrink and Kate M. Quinn, 11-26. Amsterdam: Rodopi.

Feldman, Fred. 2002. "The Good Life: A Defense of Attitudinal Hedonism." *Philosophy and Phenomenological Research* 65 (3): 604-628.

Field, Michele. 2007. "Making Food History." *Gastronomica* 7 (1): 20-24.

Finkelstein, Joanne. 1989. *Dining Out: A Sociology of Modern Manners.* New York, New York UP.

Fitzpatrick, Joan, ed. 2010. *Renaissance Food from Rabelais to Shakespeare: Culinary Readings and Culinary Histories.* Farnham, Surrey: Ashgate Publishing.

Flammang, Janet A. 2009. *The Taste for Civilization: Food Politics and Civil Society.* Baltimore: U of Illinois Press.

Flandrin, Jean Louis and Massimo Montanari, eds. 1999. *Food: A Culinary History from Antiquity to the Present.* New York: Columbia UP.

The Floating Admiral. [1931] 2011. London: HarperCollins.

Forth, Christopher E. 2008. "Nobody Loves a Fat Man: Masculinity and Food in Film Noir." Lecture at the U of Kansas, October 29. <http://www.academia.edu/404395/_Nobody_Loves_a_Fat_Man_Masculinity_and_Food_in_Film_Noir_Men_and_Masculinities_special_issue_on_Fat_Masculinities_forthcoming>

Fox, Robin. n.d. "Food and Eating: An Anthropological Perspective." *Social Issues Research Centre*. Accessed May 1, 2014. <http://www.sirc.org/publik/foxfood.pdf>

Frankowski, Ann Christine, Erin G. Roth, J. Kevin Eckert and Brandy Harris-Wallace. 2011. "The Dining Room as the Locus of Ritual in

Assisted Living." *Generations* 35 (3): 41. *MasterFILE Premier, EBSCOhost.*

Gabrenya, William K. Jr. 2003. "Culture and Social Class." *Research Skills for Psychology Majors: Everything You Need to Know to Get Started.* Melbourne, Florida: Florida Institute of Technology. <http://my.fit.edu/~gabrenya/social/readings/ses.pdf>

Giddey, Ernest. 1990. *Crime et detection: Essai sur les structures du roman policier de langue anglaise.* Berne: Peter Lang.

Goffman, Erving. 1956. *The Presentation of Self in Everyday Life.* Edinburgh: U of Edinburgh Social Sciences Researcg Centre. e-book.

Goody, Jack. 1982. *Cooking Cuisine and Class: A Study in Comparative Sociology.* Cambridge: Cambridge UP.

Gopnik, Adam. 2005. "Dining Out: The Food Critic at Table." *The New Yorker*, April 4. <http://www.newyorker.com/archive/2005/04/04/050404crbo_books>

Grella, George. 1970. "Murder and Manners: The Formal Detective Novel." *NOVEL: A Forum on Fiction* 4 (1): 30-48.

Grew, Raymond, ed. 1999. *Food in Global History.* Boulder: Westview P.

Hack, Richard. 2009. *Duchess of Death: The Unauthorized Biography of Agatha Christie.* Beverly Hills: Phoenix Books.

Hager, Lisa. 2012. "I Believe in Sherlock Holmes: Sherlockian Fandom Then and Now." *Journal of Victorian Culture Online*, April 30. <http://myblogs.informa.com/jvc/2012/04/30/i-believe-in-sherlock-holmes-fandom/>

Hampsten, Katherine. n.d. "Serving Family, Serving Country: Visual Images of Cold War Domesticity in Seventeen Magazine." *Women and Language.* Accessed March 12, 2013. <http://www.womenandlanguage.org/WomenColdWar/index.html>

Hanson, Gillian Mary. 2004. *City and Shore: The Function of Setting in the British Mystery.* Jefferson, North Carolina: McFarland and Co, Inc.

Harris, Marvin.[1985] 1998. *Good to Eat: Riddles of Food and Culture.* Long Grove: Waveland P.

Heldke, Lisa Maree. 2003. *Exotic Appetites: Ruminations of a Food Adventurer.* New York and London: Routledge.

—. 1992. "Foodmaking as a Thoughtful Practice." In *Cooking, Eating, Thinking: Transformative Philosophies of Food*, edited by Deane W. Curtin and Lisa M. Heldke, 203-229. Bloomington: Indiana UP.

Hodgson, John A. 1992. "The Recoil of 'The Speckled Band:' Detective Story and Discourse." *Poetics Today* 13 (2): 309-324.

Hoffmann, Michael. 1999. "Problems with Pierce's Concept of Abduction." *Foundations of Science* 4 (3): 271-305.

Hoverd, William James, and Chris G. Sibley. 2007. "Immoral Bodies: The Implicit Association between Moral Discourse and the Body." *Journal for the Scientific Study of Religion* 46 (3): 391-403. *Humanities International Complete*, EBSCO*host*.

Humble, Nicola. 2001. *The Feminine Middlebrow Novel, 1920s to 1950s: Class, Domesticity and Bohemianism.* Oxford: Oxford UP.

Iannolo, Jennifer. 2012. "Thomas Keller: A Philosophy of Respect." *The Gilded Fork.* <http://gildedfork.com/thomas-keller/>

Iannolo, Jennifer and Mark Tafoya. 2012. "Our Food Philosophy." *The Gilded Fork.* <http://gildedfork.com/our-food-philosophy/>

Iggers, Jeremy. 2007. "Who Needs a Critic? The Standard of Taste and the Power of Branding." In *Food and Philosophy: Eat, Think and Be Merry*, edited by Fritz Allhoff and Dave Monroe, 88-101. Malden: Blackwell Publishing.

Jackson, Cristina A. 2002. *Myth and Ritual in Women's Detective Fiction.* Jefferson, North Carolina: McFarland and Co, Inc.

Jakeman, Jane. 1993. "Food and Drink: Murder most tasteless. Dying for a good meal, Jane Jakeman finds, is not the sort of phrase that would have been used lightly in Victorian kitchens." *The Guardian,* June 5.

James, P D. 2010. *Talking About Detective Fiction.* London: Faber and Faber.

Johnston, Josée and Shyon Baumann. 2007. "Democracy versus Distinction: A Study of Omnivorousness in Gourmet Food Writing." *American Journal of Sociology* 113 (1): 165-204.

Jung, Joachim. 1998. "Twin Authors: How to Write Novels in Tandem." *Journal of Applied Philosophy* 15 (3): 241-250.

Kant, Immanuel. [1785] 2008. *Groundwork for the Metaphysic of Morals.* Edited by Jonathan Bennett. <http://www.earlymoderntexts.com/f_kant.html>

Kaplan, David M. 2012. *The Philosophy of Food.* Berkeley and Los Angeles: U of California P.

Keating, H.R.F. n.d. "Agatha Christie at the Detection Club. Memories of Detection Club Meetings." *MysteryNet: The Online Mystery Network.* Accessed 15 June 2013. <http://www.mysterynet.com/books/testimony/club/>

Keeling, Kara K and Scott T Pollard, eds. 2009. *Critical Approaches to Food in Children's Literature.* New York: Routledge.

Kiell, Norman. 1995. *Food and Drink in Literature: A Selectively Annotated Bibliography.* Lanham: Scarecrow P.

King, M. C. (2009). *Sustainable foodscapes: Obtaining food within resilient communities.* PhD diss. University of Waterloo (Canada).

<http://search.proquest.com/docview/305146309?accountid=16775>

King, Roger J. H. 2007. "Eating Well: Thinking Ethically About Food." In *Food and Philosophy: Eat, Think and Be Merry*, edited by Fritz Allhoff and Dave Monroe, 177-191. Malden: Blackwell Publishing.

Kiple, Kenneth F and Kriemhild Coneè Ornelas, eds. 2000. *The Cambridge World History of Food.* Cambridge: Cambridge UP.

Knepper, Marty S. 2005. "The Curtain Falls: Agatha Christie's Last Novels." *Clues: A Journal Of Detection (Heldref Publications)* 23 (4): 69-84. *Humanities International Complete*, EBSCO*host.*

Knight, Stephen. 2004. *Crime Fiction, 1800-2000: Detection, Death, Diversity.* Basingstoke: Palgrave MacMillan.

Konieczna, Magda. 2005. "Cookbooks aren't literature? The notion gets some boiling; Elora woman fights to improve reputation of culinary writing." *The Guelph Mercury*, September 26.

Korsmeyer, Carolyn. 2007. "Delightful, Delicious, Disgusting." In *Food and Philosophy: Eat, Think and Be Merry*, edited by Fritz Allhoff and Dave Monroe, 145-161. Malden: Blackwell Publishing.

—. 2002. *Making Sense of Taste: Food and Philosophy.* Ithaca: Cornell UP.

Kracauer, Siegfried. 1999. "The Hotel Lobby." *Postcolonial Studies* 2 (3): 289-297. *Humanities International Complete, EBSCOhost.*

Krajenbrink, Marieke and Kate M Quinn, eds. 2009. *Investigating Identities: Questions of Identity in Contemporary International Crime Fiction.* Amsterdam and New York: Rodopi.

Kraus, Michael W., Paul K. Piff and Dacher Keltner. 2011. "Social Class as Culture: The Convergence of Resources and Rank in the Social Realm." *Current Directions in Psychological Science* 20 (4): 246-250.

Kristeva, Julia. 1982. *Powers of Horror: An Essay on Abjection.* Translated by Leon S Roudiez. New York: Columbia UP.

Lafleur, Laurence J. 1956. "In Defense of Ethical Hedonism." *Philosophy and Phenomenological Research* 16 (4): 547-550.

Lawler, Steph. 2011. "Symbolic Capital." In *Encyclopedia of Consumer Culture*, edited by Dale Southerton, 1418-21. Thousand Oaks, CA: SAGE Publications, Inc., SAGE Knowledge.

Lehman, David. 2000. *The Perfect Murder: A Study in Detection.* Ann Arbor: U of Michigan P.

Leitch, Alison. 2008. "Slow Food and the Politics of Pork Fat: Italian Food and European Identity." In *Food and Culture: A Reader.* 2nd ed., edited by Carole M. Counihan and Penny Van Esterik, 381-399. New York: Routledge.

Leitch, Thomas. 2002. *Crime Films.* Cambridge: Cambridge UP.

LeMay, Eric. "In Defense of Food Writing: A Reader's Manifesto." *Alimentum* 11 (2): n. pag. <http://ericlemay.org/indefenseoffoodwriting.html>

Leon, Donna. 2011. *Venetian Verite: Donna Leon's Gritty Italian Mystery.* Interview. *NPR.org,* April 16. <http://www.npr.org/2011/04/17/135441896/venetian-verite-donna-leons-gritty-italian-mystery>

Leve, Lauren. 2011. "Identity." *Current Anthropology* 52 (4): 513-535.

Levenstein, Harvey A. 1993. *Paradox of Plenty: A Social History of Eating in Modern America.* New York: Oxford UP.

Lévi-Strauss, Claude. [1958, vol. 1, and 1973, vol. 2] 2000. *Štrukturálna antropológia.* 2 vols. Translated by Martin Kanovský. Bratislava: Kalligram.

—. [1966] 2008. "The Culinary Triangle." In *Food and Culture: A Reader.* 2nd ed., edited by Carole M. Counihan and Penny van Esterik, 36-43. New York: Routledge.

Levin, Sala. 2012. "The Food of Great Fiction." *Moment Magazine* 37 (3): 72-73.

Lewis, Noah. 2007. "Broccoli vs. Animals." *Vegetus*, August 17. <http://www.vegetus.org/index.htm>

Light, Alison. 1991. *Forever England: Femininity, Literature and Conservatism between the Wars.* Abingdon, Oxon: Routledge Classics.

Lintott, Sheila. 2007. "Sublime Hunger: A Consideration of Eating Disorders Beyond Beauty." In *Food and Philosophy: Eat, Think and Be Merry*, edited by Fritz Allhoff and Dave Monroe, 58-70. Malden: Blackwell Publishing.

Lowther, Pat. 1974. "Kitchen Murder." *boundary 2*, 3 (1): 26.

Lupton, Deborah. 1996. *Food, the Body and the Self.* London: Sage Publications.

Lyons, Antonia C. and Sara A. Willott. 2008. "Alcohol Consumption, Gender Identities and Women's Changing Social Position." *Sex Roles* 58: 694-712.

Lyotard, Jean-François. 1991. "Domus and the Megalopolis." In *The Inhuman: Reflections on Time,* 191-204. Stanford: Stanford UP.

Majors, Kerri. 2012. "Out of the Frying Pan: Food in Fiction." *Midwest Quarterly* 54 (1): 67-81.

Malcolm, David and Cheryl Alexander Malcolm, eds. 2008. *A Companion to the British and Irish Short Story.* Chichester: Blackwell Publishing Ltd.

Mannur, Anita. 2010. *Culinary Fictions: Food in South Asian Diasporic Culture.* Philadelphia: Temple UP.

Marin, Louis. 1989. *Food for Thought.* Translated by Mette Hjort. Baltimore: The Johns Hopkins UP.

Marshall, David. 2005. "Food as Ritual, Routine or Convention." *Consumption, Markets and Culture* 8 (1): 69-85.

McCaw, Neil. 2010. *Adapting Detective Fiction: Crime, Englishness and the TV Detectives.* London: Continuum International Publishing.

McClintock, Anne. 1993. "Family Feuds: Gender, Nationalism and the Family." *Feminist Review* 44 (*Nationalisms and National Identities*): 61-80.

McCracken, Lin. 1993. "Authors Find Food Feeds Novel Ideas: Murder, Chocolate Fuel for Sleuths." *Colorado Springs Gazette—Telegraph*, January 30. <http://search.proquest.com/docview/268052262?accountid=16775>

McMillan, Sherrie. 2001. "What Time is Dinner?" *History Magazine*, October/November. <http://www.history-magazine.com/dinner2.html>

Mead, Margaret. [1943] 2008. "The Problem of Changing Food Habits." In *Food and Culture: A Reader* 2nd ed., edited by Carole M. Counihan and Penny van Esterik, 17-27. New York: Routledge.

Melville, Caspar. 2007. "Atheism à la Mode." *New Humanist* 122 (4): 26-28.

Mezei, Kathy. 2007. "Spinsters, Surveillance and Speed: The Case of Miss Marple, Miss Mole, and Miss Jekyll." *Journal of Modern Literature* 30 (2): 103-120.

Michelis, Angelica. 2010. "Food and Crime: What's Eating the Crime Novel?" *European Journal of English Studies* 14 (2): 143-157.

Mills, Selina, and Rosie Waites. 2008. "Dusty Clues to Christie Unearthed." *BBC Radio 4*, September 15. <http://news.bbc.co.uk/today/hi/today/newsid_7612000/7612534.stm>

Mikkelsen, Bent Egberg. 2011. "Images of Foodscapes: Introduction to Foodscape Studies and their Application in the Study of Healthy Eating Out-of-Home Environments." *Perspectives in Public Health* 131 (5): 209-16. <http://search.proquest.com/docview/902629902?accountid=16775>

Mintz, Sidney W. 1986. *Sweetness and Power: The Place of Sugar in Modern History.* New York: Penguin Books.

—. 1996. *Tasting Food, Tasting Freedom: Excursions into Eating, Power, and the Past.* Boston: Beacon P.

Mintz, Sidney W. and Christine M. Du Bois. 2002. "The Anthropology of Food and Eating." *Annual Review of Anthropology* 31: 99-119.

Monroe, Dave. 2007. "Can Food Be Art? The Problem of Consumption." In *Food and Philosophy: Eat, Think and Be Merry*, edited by Fritz Allhoff and Dave Monroe, 133-144. Malden: Blackwell Publishing.

Montanari, Massimo. 2010. *Cheese, Pears, and History in a Proverb.* New York: Columbia UP.

—. 2006. *Food Is Culture.* Translated by Albert Sonnenfeld. New York: Columbia UP.

Moran, Pattie. 1992. "The Ritual of Tea: Crisis Requires Steady Hand on Kettle." *Kitchener—Waterloo Record*, 3. <http://search.proquest.com/docview/275358095?accountid=16775>

Morgan, Michael, Pamela Watson and Nigel Hemmington. 2008. "Drama in the Dining Room: Theatrical Perspectives on the Foodservice Encounter." *Journal of Foodservice* 19 (2): 111-118. *Business Source Premier*, EBSCO*host.*

Moss, Jessica. 2006. "Pleasure and Illusion in Plato." *Philosophy and Phenomenological Research* 72 (3): 503-535.

Mullen, Anne and Emer O'Beirne, eds. 2000. *Crime Scenes: Detective Narratives in European Culture Since 1945.* Amsterdam: Rodopi.

Murcott, Anne. 1996. "Food as an Expression of Idenity." In *The Future of the Nation-State: Essays on Cultural Pluralism and Political Integration*, edited by Sverker Gustavsson and Leif Lewin, 49-78. Abingdon, Oxon: Routledge.

Muwati, Itai and Zifikile Gambahaya. 2012. "The Private/Public Space Dichotomy: An Africana Womanist Analysis of the Gendering of Space and Power." *Western Journal of Black Studies* 36 (2): 100-107. *Humanities International Complete*, EBSCO*host*.

Nabhan, Gary Paul. 2002. *Coming Home to Eat: The Pleasures and Politics of Local Foods.* New York: W. W. Norton and Company, Inc.

Naccarato, Peter and Kathleen LeBesco. 2012. *Culinary Capital.* New York: Berg.

Niiniluoto, Ilkka. 1999. "Defending Abduction." *Philosophy of Science* 66 (3): S436-S451. *Humanities International Complete*, EBSCO*host.*

Ochs, Elinor, Ruth Smith and Carolyn Taylor. 1989. "Detective Stories at Dinnertime: Problem-solving through Co-narration." *Cultural Dynamics* 2 (2): 238-257.

Onfray, Michel. 2006. *La puissance d'exister: Manifeste hédoniste.* Paris: Grasset & Fasquelle.

Osborne, Charles. [1998] 2002. *Black Coffee.* London: HarperCollins.

Paavola, Sami. 2005. "Peircean Abduction: Instinct or Inference?" *Semiotica* 153 (1/4): 131-154.

<http://www.helsinki.fi/science/commens/papers/instinctorinference.pdf>

Panek, LeRoy Lad. 1987. *An Introduction to the Detective Story.* Bowling Green, Ohio: Bowling Green State U Popular P.

Parasecoli, Fabio. 2008. *Bite Me: Food in Popular Culture.* Oxford: Berg.

Parkhurst Ferguson, Priscilla. 2004. *Accouxnting for Taste: The Triumph of French Cuisine.* Chicago: U of Chicago P.

—. 2010. "Culinary Nationalism." *Gastronomica: The Journal of Food and Culture* 10 (1): 102-109.

—. 1998. "A Cultural Field in the Making: Gastronomy in 19th-Century France." *American Journal of Sociology* 104 (3): 597-641.

Pascual Soler, Nieves. 2009. *A Critical Study of Female Culinary Detective Stories: Murder by Cookbook.* Lewiston: The Edwin Mellen P.

Peirce, Charles Sanders. 1931-35. *Collected Papers.* Vol. 1-5. Edited by C. Hartshorne and P. Weiss. Cambridge, MA: Harvard UP.

Pence, Gregory E, ed. 2002. *The Ethics of Food: A Reader for the Twenty-First Century.* Lanham: Rowman and Littlefield Publishers.

Petrini, Carlo. 2001. *Slow Food: The Case for Taste.* Translated by William McCuaig. New York: Columbia UP.

Plumwood, Val. 2008. "Tasteless: Towards a Food-Based Approach to Death." *Environmental Values* 17 (3): 323-330.

Prchal, Timothy R. 1997. "An Ideal Helpmate: The Detective Character as (Fictional) Object and Ideal Imago." In *Theory and Practice of Classic Detective Fiction*, edited by Jerome A. Delamater and Ruth Prigozy, 29-38. Westport: Greenwood P.

Rebora, Giovanni. 2001. *Culture of the Fork: A Brief History of Food in Europe.* Translated by Albert Sonnenfeld. New York: Columbia UP.

Reed, Christopher. 1996. *Not at Home: The Suppression of Domesticity in Modern Art and Architecture*. London: Thames & Hudson.

Rice, William. 2001. "Food and Memory: Physics and Psychology Explain the Vivid Remembrances Prompted by Fragrances Past." *Chicago Tribune*, June 6. <http://search.proquest.com/docview/419393731?accountid=16775>

Rippetoe, Rita Elizabeth. 2004. *Booze and the Private Eye: Alcohol in the Hard-Boiled Novel.* Jefferson: McFarland and Co, Inc.

Risman, Barbara J. 2004. "Gender as a Social Structure. Theory Wrestling with Activism." *Gender and Society* 18 (4): 429-450.

Rosenbaum, Judy. 2009. Review of *Critical Approaches to Food in Children's Literature*, by Kara K. Keeling and Scott T. Pollard. *Children's Literature Association Quarterly* 34 (3): 297-299.

Ross, Eric B. 1987. "Theoretical Overview." In *Food and Human Evolution*, edited by Marvin Harris and Eric B. Ross, 7-55. Philadelphia: Temple UP.

Rössner, Stephan. 2007. "Anthelme Brillat-Savarin (1755-1826)." *Obesity Reviews* 8 (6): 531-532.

Rousseau, Signe. 2012. *Food Media: Celebrity Chefs and the Politics of Everyday Interference.* London: Berg.

Rowland, Susan. 2001. *From Agatha Christie to Ruth Rendell: British Women Writers in Detective and Crime Fiction.* Houndmills, Basingstoke: Palgrave.

Rzepka, Charles J. 2005. *Detective Fiction: Cultural History of Literature.* Cambridge: Polity P.

Satin, Morton. 2007. *Death in the Pot.* Amherst: Prometheus Books.

Sayers, Dorothy L. [1929] 1974. "The Omnibus of Crime." In *Detective Fiction: Crime and Compromise*, edited by Dick Allen and David Chacko, 351-383. San Diego: Harcourt Brace Jovanovich.

Saylor, V. Louise. 1984. "The Private Eye and His Victuals." *Clues* 5 (2): 111–118.

Scaggs, John. 2005. *Crime Fiction: The New Critical Idiom.* Oxon: Routledge.

Sceats, Sarah. 2004. *Food, Consumption and the Body in Contemporary Women's Fiction.* Cambridge: Cambridge UP.

Schivelbusch, Wolfgang. 1993. *Tastes of Paradise: A Social History of Spices, Stimulants, and Intoxicants.* Translated by David Jacobson. New York: Vintage Books.

Schneider, Stephen. 2008. "Good, Clean, Fair: The Rhetoric of the Slow Food Movement." *College English* 70 (4): 384-402.

Schoenberg, Thomas J. and Lawrence J. Trudeau, eds. 2006. "Food in Literature." *Twentieth-Century Literary Criticism* 170: n. pag. Farmington Hills: Gale Cengage. <http://www.enotes.com/food-literature-essays/food-literature>

Schofield, Mary Anne, ed. 1989. *Cooking by the Book: Food in Literature and Culture.* Bowling Green, Ohio: Bowling Green State U Popular P.

Schvaneveldt, Roger W. and Trevor A. Cohen. 2010. "Abductive Reasoning and Similarity: Some Computational Tools." In *Computer-Based Diagnostics and Systematic Analysis of Knowledge*, edited by Dirk Ifenthaler, Pablo Pirnay-Dummer and Norbert M. Seel, 189-212. New York: Springer. <http://interlinkinc.net/Roger/Papers/Schvaneveldt_Cohen_Ifenthaler_final.pdf>

Scrafford, Barbara. 2004. *Literary Feasts: Recipes from the Classics of Literature.* Lincoln: iUniverse, Inc.

Shapiro, Anna. 1996. *A Feast of Words: For Lovers of Food and Fiction.* New York: W. W. Norton and Company, Inc.

Skiadas, P. K., and J. G. Lascaratos. 2001. "Dietetics in Ancient Greek Philosophy: Plato's Concepts of Healthy Diet." *European Journal of Clinical Nutrition* 55 (7): 532-537.

Skubal, Susanne. 2002. *Word of Mouth: Food and Fiction After Freud.* New York: Routledge.

Slater, Nigel. 2006. "Food Memories." *The Observer*, July 23. <http://www.guardian.co.uk/lifeandstyle/2006/jul/23/foodanddrink.recipes1>

Spivey, Diane M. 1999. *The Peppers, Cracklings, and Knots of Wool Cookbook: The Global Migration of African Cuisine.* Albany: State U of New York P.

Sobal, Jeffery and Brian Wansink. 2007. "Kitchenscapes, Tablescapes, Platescapes, and Foodscapes: Influences of Microscale Built Environments on Food Intake." *Environment and Behavior* 39 (1): 124-142. <http://search.proquest.com/docview/200881152?accountid=16775.>

Stets, Jan E. and Peter J. Burke. 2000. "Identity Theory and Social Identity Theory." *Social Psychology Quarterly* 63 (3): 224-237.

Super, John C. 2002. "Food and History." *Journal of Social History* 36 (1): 165-178.

Sutton, David E. 2001. *Remembrance of Repasts: An Anthropology of Food and Memory.* Oxford and New York: Berg.

Sweeney, Kevin W. 2007. "Can a Soup Be Beautiful? The Rise of Gastronomy and the Aesthetics of Food." In *Food and Philosophy: Eat, Think and Be Merry*, edited by Fritz Allhoff and Dave Monroe, 117-132. Malden: Blackwell Publishing.

Symons, Michael. 2004. *A History of Cooks and Cooking.* Champaign: U of Illinois P.

—. 1991. *Eating into Thinking: Explorations in the Sociology of Cuisine.* PhD diss. Flinders U of South Australia.

—. 2007. "Epicurus, The Foodies' Philosopher." In *Food and Philosophy: Eat, Think and Be Merry*, edited by Fritz Allhoff and Dave Monroe, 13-30. Malden: Blackwell Publishing Ltd.

Taylor, Laura Elise. 2007. *A Taste for Paprika: A Memoir.* Toronto: Penguin Global.

Taylor, Timothy. "Food/Crime Fiction." n. pag. March 29, 2013. <http://www.timothytaylor.ca/10/08/20/foodcrime-fiction>

Theophano, Janet. 2002. *Eat My Words: Reading Women's Lives Through the Cookbooks They Wrote.* New York: Palgrave.

Thomson, Hendry Douglas. 1978. *Masters of Mystery: A Study of the Detective Story.* Philadelphia: R. West.

Todorov, Tzvetan. [1966] 2008. "The Typology of Detective Fiction." In *Modern Criticism and Theory: A Reader.* 3rd ed., edited by David Lodge and Nigel Wood, 225-232. Harlow: Pearson Education Limited.

Tolan, Stephanie S., M.A. 2006. "Imagination to Intuition: The Journey of a Rationalist into Realms of Magic and Spirit." *Advanced Development* 10: 45-57. <http://search.proquest.com/docview/197460168?accountid=16775>

Tomlinson, Mark, and Alan Warde. 1993. "Social Class and Change in Eating Habits." *British Food Journal* 95 (1): n. pag. < http://search.proquest.com/docview/225153316?accountid=16775>

Tönnies, Ferdinand. [1957] 2004. *Community and Society.* New Brunswick: Transaction Publishers.

Towell, Lavaughn C. 2009. "The Uncanny and Domesticity in the Stories of Arthur Conan Doyle, 1883—1903." PhD diss., The U of Tulsa, Oklahoma.

Verdaguer, Pierre. 2005. "Borrowed Settings: Frenchness in Anglo-American Detective Fiction." *Yale French Studies* 108: 146-159.

Walker, Alexander. 2001. "Food for Murder: The Colour of Lies." *Evening Standard*, July 12.

Wall, Wendy. 2002. *Staging Domesticity: Household Work and English Identity in Early Modern Drama.* Cambridge: Cambridge UP.

Watson, James L and Melissa L Caldwell, eds. 2005. *The Cultural Politics of Food and Eating: A Reader.* Malden: Blackwell Publishing.

Waxman, Barbara Frey. 2008. "Food Memoirs: What They Are, Why They Are Popular, and Why They Belong in the Literature Classroom." *College English* 70 (4): 363-83. <http://search.proquest.com/docview/236937249?accountid=16775>

Wells, Carolyn. [1913] 2007. *The Technique of the Mystery Story.* A Project Gutenberg of Australia eBook. Accessed April 20, 2015. <http://gutenberg.net.au/ebooks07/0701151h.html#ch19>

Welty, Eudora. [1955] 1998. "Place in Fiction." In *Stories, Essays and Memoir*, edited by Richard Ford and Michael Kreyling, 781-96. New York: Library of America.

Wheat, Carolyn. 2005. "The Real Queen(s) of Crime." *Clues: A Journal of Detection (Heldref Publications)* 23 (4): 87-90.

White, George W. 2004. *Nation, State, and Territory: Origins, Evolutions, and Relationships.* Vol. 1. Lanham, Maryland: Rowman and Littlefield Publishers.

Wigley, Mark. 1992. "Heidegger's House: The Violence of the Domestic." *D: Columbia Documents of Architecture and Theory* 1: 91-121.

Wild, John. 1927. "The Resurrection of Hedonism." *International Journal of Ethics* 38 (1): 11-26.

Wilkins, John, ed. 1996. *Food in European Literature.* Exeter: Intellect Books.

Winson, A. 2004. "Bringing political economy into the debate on the obesity epidemic." *Agriculture And Human Values* 21 (4): 299-312. *Agricola*, EBSCO*host.*

Woodward, Kath, ed. 2004. *Questioning Identity: Gender, Class, Ethnicity.* 2nd ed. London: Routledge.

Woolgar, C M, D Serjeantson and T Waldron, eds. 2006. *Food in Medieval England: Diet and Nutrition.* Oxford: Oxford UP.

Wright, Wynne and Elizabeth Ransom. 2005. "Stratification on the Menu: Using Restaurant Menus to Examine Social Class." *Teaching Sociology* 33 (3): 310-316.

Wrye, Jen. 2007. "Should I Eat Meat? Vegetarianism and Dietary Choice." In *Food and Philosophy: Eat, Think and Be Merry*, edited by Fritz Allhoff and Dave Monroe, 45-57. Malden: Blackwell Publishing.

Wu, Chia-ying. 2007. "The Importance of Being Cosy: Agatha Christie and Golden Age British Detective Fiction." PhD diss. State U of New York at Buffalo.

Xu, Wenying. 2008. *Eating Identities: Reading Food in Asian American Literature.* Honolulu: U of Hawai'i P.

Yasmeen, Gisèle. 2008. "Plastic Bag Housewives' and Postmodern Restaurants? Public and Private in Bangkok's Foodscape." In *Food and Culture: A Reader* 2nd ed., edited by Carole M. Counihan and Penny van Esterik, 17-27. New York: Routledge.

"Zabila som Poirota, vážení!" 2013. *TV MAX.* January 28.

Zepeda, Lydia. 2007. "Carving Values with a Spoon." In *Food and Philosophy: Eat, Think and Be Merry*, edited by Fritz Allhoff and Dave Monroe, 31-44. Malden: Blackwell Publishing.

INDEX